Busi

A Practice Book

Rose Buhlig

Alpha Editions

This edition published in 2022

ISBN : 9789356150423

Design and Setting By
Alpha Editions
www.alphaedis.com
Email - info@alphaedis.com

Contents

PREFACE

THE author of this book and the writer of this preface have never met. Their respective fields of labor are a thousand miles apart. Yet such is the force of ideas that many of their thoughts and sympathies are common.

Business English! The very name is an anomaly. From a literary point of view there is no such thing. English is English whether it be used to express the creations of our imagination, our aesthetic appreciations, or our daily wants. There is no magical combination of words, phrases, and sentences that is peculiar and distinctive to business transactions. Business English as used in these pages means effective communication, both oral and written. The author's aim throughout has been to teach the art of using words in such a way as to make people think and act. To do this she has applied the principles of literary composition to the highly complex and ever increasing problems of our business life. She realizes that business is vital, and that the problems of commerce are not to be met and handled with dead forms and stereotyped expressions of legal blanks.

To use our language effectively it is necessary to have an understanding of its elements. Thus the author has very wisely devoted much space to word-study and English grammar. This is a field commonly neglected in books on the subject. The people engaged in business are, on the whole, woefully weak in the grammar of our language. It is believed that the treatment herein will be a great aid in correcting this deficiency. If we have ideas, we must express them in words, and our words should be so chosen and arranged as not to offend, but to please and interest. This result can be secured by a systematic study of Part I.[iv]

Part II deals with oral and written composition. Here the author has arranged her subjects in such a way as to give the whole a cumulative effect. The method throughout is inductive, and sufficient examples are always given to warrant the conclusions drawn. Most textbooks on Business English neglect the subject of oral English. This book regards the spoken word as important as the written word.

If there be any one feature in this textbook more to be commended than another, it is the exposition in Part III. The situations arising in many different kinds of business are here analyzed. The author believes that the way to become a good business correspondent is, first, to learn what the situation demands and, second, to practice meeting the demands. We must know before we write. Given a knowledge of the subject, we must have much practice in expressing ourselves in such a way as to make our composition effective. The author meets this need by supplying many and varied exercises for practice. These exercises are live, practical, and up-to-date. The problems to be solved are real, not imaginary. Thus the power to be gained in meeting these situations and solving these problems will prove a real asset to those who contemplate a business career. It is confidently hoped that both teachers and pupils will find in this work material which will help them to prepare themselves to meet the many problems and demands of our growing commercial needs.

DANIEL B. DUNCAN

COLUMBIA UNIVERSITY
January, 1914.

CHAPTER I

INTERESTING WORDS

BUSINESS English is the expression of our commercial life in English. It is not synonymous with letter writing. To be sure, business letters are important, but they form only a part of one of the two large divisions into which the subject naturally falls.

First, there is *oral expression*, important because so many of our business transactions are conducted personally. Thousands of salesmen daily move from place to place over the entire country, earning their salaries by talking convincingly of the goods that they have to sell. A still greater number of clerks, salesmen, managers, and officials orally transact business in our shops, stores, offices, and banks. Complaints are adjusted; difficulties are disentangled; and affairs of magnitude are consummated in personal interviews, the matter under discussion often being thought too important to be entrusted to correspondence. In every business oral English is essential.

Second, there is *written expression*. This takes account of the writing of advertisements, circulars, booklets, and prospectuses, as well as of letters. And in the preparation of these oral English is fundamental. It precedes and practically includes the written expression. For example, we say colloquially that a good advertisement "talks." We mean that the writer has so fully realized the buyer's point of view that the words of the advertisement seem to speak directly to the reader, arousing his interest or perhaps answering his objection. Oral English is fundamental, too, in the writing of letters, for most letters are dictated and not written. The correspondent dictates them to his stenographer or to a recording machine in the same tone, probably, that he would use if the customer were sitting before him.

But in taking this point of view, we should not minimize the importance of written business English. In a way, it is more difficult to write well than it is to talk well. In talking we are not troubled with the problems of correct spelling, proper punctuation, and good paragraphing. We may even repeat somewhat, if only we are persuasive. But in writing we are confronted with the necessity of putting the best thoughts into the clearest, most concise language, at the same time obeying all the rules of spelling, punctuation, and grammar. The business man must be sure of these details in order to know that his letters and advertising matter are correct. The stenographer, especially, must be thoroughly familiar with them, so that she may correctly transcribe what has been dictated.

Business English is much the same as any other English. It consists in expression by means of words, sentences, and paragraphs. Moreover, they are much the same kind of words, sentences, and paragraphs that appear in any book that is written in what is commonly called the literary style. In a business letter the words are largely those of every day use, and but few are technical. It is the manner in which the words are put together, the idea back of the sentence, that makes the only difference.

We shall begin the study of business English with a study of words, for in all expression, whether oral or written, a knowledge of words, of their meaning and suggestive power, is fundamental. On the choice of words depends not only the correctness but also the effectiveness of expression—the courtesy of a letter, the appeal of an advertisement, the persuasiveness of a salesman's talk. A mastery of words cannot be gained at once. Every time one speaks, he must consider what words will best convey his idea. In this chapter only the barest beginning of such study can be made. The exercises show the value of the subject.

The study of words is interesting because words themselves are interesting. Sometimes the interest consists in the story of the derivation. As an example, consider the word *italic.* Many words in this book are written in italic to draw attention to them. Literally the word means "relating to Italy or its people." It is now applied to a kind of type in which the letters slope toward the right. The type was called italic because it was dedicated to the states of Italy by the inventor, Manutius, about the year 1500. An unabridged dictionary will tell all about the word.

The word *salary* tells a curious story. It is derived from a Latin word, *salarium*, meaning "salt money." It was the name of the money that was given to the Roman soldiers for salt, which was a part of their pay. Finally, instead of signifying only the salt money, it came to mean the total pay.

Practically all of this information a good dictionary gives. In other words, a dictionary is a story book containing not one, but hundreds of thousands of stories. Whenever possible it tells what language a word came from, how it got its different meanings, and how those meanings have changed in the course of time. For it is natural that words should change just as styles change, names of ancient things being lost and names for new things being made. As the objects themselves have gone out of use, their names have also gone. When a word has gone entirely out of use, it is marked *obsolete* in the dictionary. On the other hand, new inventions must be named. Thus new words are constantly being added to the language and the dictionary because they are needed.

There is a large class of words that we shall not have time to consider. They are called *technical.* Every profession, business, or trade has its distinctive words. The technical words that a printer would use are entirely different from those which a dentist, a bookkeeper, or a lawyer would use. You will learn the technical terms of your business most thoroughly after you enter it and see the use for such terms.

None of the words, therefore, that you will be asked to search out in the dictionary are, strictly speaking, technical. It is evident that it will do you no good to search out the words in the dictionary, unless you learn them—unless you use them correctly in speaking and writing. There is pleasure in thus employing new material, as everybody knows. Use your eyes and ears. When you hear a new word, or read one, focus the mind upon it for a moment until you can retain a mental picture of its spelling and of its pronunciation. Then as soon as possible look it up in the dictionary to fix its spelling, pronunciation, and definition. Do this regularly, and you will have reason to be proud of your vocabulary.

An excellent way to increase the number of words that you know is to read the right kind of books. The careful study of the words used in the speeches and addresses of noted men is good practice. The conditions that called forth the speech were probably important, and the speech itself interesting, or it would not be preserved. When a man has an interesting or important message to give, he usually gives it in clear, exact, simple language. Therefore the vocabulary that he uses is worth copying. As for stories, there is a kind that furnishes a wealth of material that modern authors are constantly using or referring to, and this is found in stories of the Bible, stories of Greek and Northern gods and goddesses, stories of the *Iliad*, the *Odyssey*, the *Æneid*, stories of chivalry—all old stories. Every one should know them well, because they are the basis of many allusions in which a single word oftentimes suggests a whole story. The meaning of the word *herculean*, for instance, is missed if you do not know the story of Hercules and know that he was famous for his strength.

Exercise 1

Atlas is an interesting word. Originally it was the name of a Greek god, who carried the world on his shoulders. Then it is supposed that in the sixteenth century the famous geographer Mercator prefixed his collection of maps with the picture of Atlas supporting the world. Thus a collection of maps in a volume came to be called an *atlas*. Consult an unabridged dictionary for the origin of each of the following:

rival	fortune	cereal	boycott
dollar	finance	china	derrick
bankrupt	milliner	java	mercury
cash	pullman	cashmere	colossal

mint	grocer	macadam	turbine

Exercise 2

The days of the week and the months of the year are interesting in their derivation. Monday, for example, represents the day sacred to the Moon as a deity. Explain the origin of each of the following:

Sunday	Saturday	May	October
Tuesday	January	June	November
Wednesday	February	July	December
Thursday	March	August	
Friday	April	September	

Exercise 3

Look up the derivation of the following:

cancel	bead	ambition	hospital
pecuniary	paper	influence	pavilion
cheat	book	virtue	mackintosh
speculation	bayonet	peevish	chapel
phaëton	tawdry	disaster	omnibus

Exercise 4

Explain the origin of each of the following:

curfew	tulip	turquoise	good-bye
pompadour	aster	amethyst	dismal
hyacinth	dunce	tantalize	titanic
dandelion	humor	umbrella	volcano
dahlia	villain	sandwich	tangle
begonia	echo	lunatic	babble

Exercise 5

Name the image that each of the following suggests to you:

howl	sputter	rasping	munch
skim	prance	clatter	trickle
squeal	click	wheeze	shuffle
moan	thud	trudge	bulge
squeak	patter	chuckle	gobble
squawk	spatter	toddling	swish

Exercise 6

Bring to class a list of words which, because they are the names of modern inventions, have come into the language in modern time.

Exercise 7

How many words can you name which might be called the technical terms of school life, words which always carry with them a suggestion of the school room? Bring in a list of twenty such words.

Exercise 8

How many words can you name which are used only in the business world? Bring in a list of twenty such words.

Exercise 9

How many words can you name which apply particularly to money and the payment or non-payment of money? Bring in a list of twenty or more such words.

CHAPTER II

PRONUNCIATION

WE are judged by our speech. If we clip syllables, run words together, or pronounce them incorrectly, we shall merit the criticism of being careless or even ignorant. Yet clear enunciation and correct pronunciation are sometimes difficult. We learn most words by hearing others say them, and, if we do not hear the true values given to the different syllables, we shall find it hard to distinguish the correct from the incorrect forms. Children whose parents speak a foreign language usually have to watch their speech with especial care; Germans, for example, find difficulty in saying *th* and Irish people in saying *oi* as in *oil.* The exercises in this chapter are given for the purpose of correcting such habits. The words in the exercises should be pronounced repeatedly, until the correct forms are instinctive.

Train the ear to hear the difference between sounds, as in *just* and in *jest.* Don't slide over the final consonant in such words as *going* and *reading.* Watch words containing *wh.* The dictionary tells us that *where* was originally written *hwar*, the *h* coming before the *w;* and we still pronounce it so, although we write the *w* before the *h.* The word *whether* is of the same kind. The dictionary tells us that it was first spelled *hweder.* Such words should be carefully noted and their pronunciation practiced.

Then there is the habit of slurring syllables. We may understand what is meant by the expression "C'm' on" or "Waja say?", but most of us would prefer not to be included in the class of people who use either. Correct speech cannot be mastered without an effort.

In the following exercises watch every vowel and every consonant so that you may give each one its full value.

Exercise 10—Diacritical Marks

Although an *a* is always written *a*, it is not always given the same quality or length of sound. When we discover a new word, it is important that we know exactly the quality to give each of the vowels in it. For this purpose *diacritical marks* have been invented. They are illustrated in the following list from Webster's *International Dictionary.*

Transcriber's Note: Due to the constraints of HTML, a letter with a tack above such as a̍ cannot be displayed. For this reason [+x] has been used to denote a letter with a tack above it.

ā as in āte, fāte, lāb´or

[+a] " " sen´[+a]te, del´ic[+a]te, [+a]e´rial

â " " câre, shâre, pâr´ent

ă " " ăm, ădd, răn´dom

ä " " ärm, fär, fä´ther

ȧ " " ȧsk, grȧss, pȧss, dȧnce

a̱ " " fi´na̱l, in´fa̱nt, guid´ānce

a̤ " " a̤ll, a̤we, swa̤rm, ta̤lk

ē " " ēve, mēte, serēne´

[+e] " " [+e]vent´, d[+e]pend´, soci´[+e]ty

ĕ " " ĕnd, mĕt, ĕxcuse´, ĕfface´

ẽ " " fẽrn, hẽr, ẽr´mine, ev´ẽr

e " " re´c*e*nt, de´c*e*ncy, pru´d*e*nce

ī " " īce, tīme, sīght, inspīre´

[+i] " " [+i]dea´, tr[+i]bu´nal, b[+i]ol´ogy

ĭ " " ĭll, pĭn, pĭt´y, admĭt´

ō " " ōld, nōte, ō´ver, prōpose´

[+o] " " [+o]bey´, t[+o]bac´co, sor´r[+o]w

ô " " ôrb, lôrd, ôr´der, abhôr´

ŏ " " ŏdd, nŏt, tŏr´rid, ŏccur´

ū " " ūse, pūre, dū´ty, assūme´

[+u] " " [+u]nite´, ac´t[+u]ate, ed[+u]ca´tion

ṳ " " rṳde, rṳ´mor, intrṳde´

ụ " " fụll, pụt, fụlfill´

ŭ " " ŭp, tŭb, stŭd´y

û " " ûrn, fûr, concûr´

y̆ " " pit´y̆, in´jury̆, divin´ity̆

o͞o " " fo͞ol, fo͞od, mo͞on

o͝o " " fo͝ot, wo͝ol, bo͝ok

ou " " out, thou, devour´

oi " " oil, noi´sy, avoid´

ā is called long *a*, and is marked with the *macron*

ă is called short *a*, and is marked with the *breve*

â is called caret *a*, and is marked with the *caret*

ä is called Italian *a*, and is marked with the *diaeresis*

ȧ is called short Italian *a*, and is marked with the *dot*

ẽ is called tilde *e*, and is marked with the *tilde* or *wave*

Exercise 11—Vowels

Of the twenty-six letters in the alphabet, how many are vowels? Name them. What are the other letters called?

Compare the *ă* in *hat* and the *ā* in *hate*. Which has more nearly the sound of *a* in the alphabet? This is called the natural or long sound of the vowel. The other is called the short sound.

Drop the *e* from *hate*. Explain the result.

Name other monosyllables ending in *e* and containing the long *a* sound.

Explain the difference in pronunciation between *Pete*, *pet*, *ripe*, *rip*, *hope*, *hop*, *cube*, *cub*.

Find other monosyllables ending in *e* and containing a long vowel that becomes short if the *e* is dropped.

Monosyllables ending in silent *e* usually contain a long vowel sound, which becomes short when the final *e* is dropped.

Exercise 12

Pronounce carefully the following words containing the short Italian *a:*

advȧnce	clȧss	lȧnce	plȧster
advȧntage	contrȧst	lȧst	pȧstor
ȧfter	enchȧnt	mȧsk	prȧnce
bȧsket	Frȧnce	mȧster	rȧfter
brȧnch	glȧnce	mȧstiff	shȧft
brȧss	glȧss	pȧss	surpȧss
chȧff	grȧss	pȧst	tȧsk

Exercise 13

Pronounce the following carefully, noting each *a* that is marked:

häl f	ideȧ	cälm	audācious
pȧth	cȧn't	āpricot	ȧghȧst
ȧsk	cătch	mȧdrăs	ălgebrȧ
fäther	v[+a]cātion	ăgile	forbăde
dȧnce	extrȧ	cȧst	trȧnce
lȧss	cȧsket	grȧnt	āviātion

Exercise 14

Pronounce the vowel *o* in the following very carefully. Don't give the sound *feller* or *fella* when you mean *fellow*.

fellow	swallow	theory	borrow
potato	follow	position	heroism
window	original	factory	donkey
pillow	evaporate	ivory	memory
chocolate	mosquito	licorice	oriental

Exercise 15

The vowel *u* needs particular attention. When it is long, it is sounded naturally, as it is in the alphabet. Do not say *redooce* for *reduce*.

reduce	picture	educate	figure

produce	stupid	judicial	duty
conducive	student	calculate	accumulate
endure	genuine	curiosity	Tuesday
duration	induce	regular	particular
singular	avenue	tune	institute
nutriment	constitution	culinary	January
revenue	introduce	opportunity	manufacture

Exercise 16

Using diacritical marks indicate the value of the vowels in the following. Try marking them without first consulting a dictionary. After you have marked them, compare your markings with those used in a dictionary.

pupil	different	diacritical	gigantic
alphabet	several	radiating	gymnasium
natural	letter	Wyoming	system
result	eraser	typical	merchant

Exercise 17

Pronounce carefully, noting that in each word at least one consonant is silent, and sometimes a vowel as well. Draw an oblique line through the silent letter or letters in each.

through	chasten	sword	island
although	often	fasten	daughter
wrong	soften	calf	might
yacht	subtle	hasten	bouquet
gnaw	almond	naughty	honest
psalm	glisten	thumb	palm
whistle	salve	should	knack
salmon	chestnut	knowledge	castle
answer	folks	listen	thigh

knot	right	debt	honor

Exercise 18

Pronounce the following, paying particular attention to the vowels. Distinguish between the meanings of the words in each group.

accept	bile	least	prevision
except	boil	lest	provision
affect	carol	eleven	poor
effect	coral	leaven	pure
addition	descent	neither	radish
edition	dissent	nether	reddish
assay	emerge	pasture	sentry
essay	immerge	pastor	century
baron	Francis	pillar	sit
barren	Frances	pillow	set
been	jest	point	wrench
bean	just	pint	rinse
	gist		

Exercise 19

Enunciate the consonant sounds carefully in the following. Distinguish between the meanings of the words in each group.

acts	close	treaties	rows
ax	clothes	treatise	rouse

advice	crossed	princes	rues
advise	across	princess	ruse
alms	formerly	prince	either
elms	formally	prints	ether
bodice	grays	price	running
bodies	grace	prize	ruin
cease	lose	recent	walking
seize	loose	resent	walk in
chance	plaintive	sects	weather
chants	plaintiff	sex	whether
does	pair	news	worst
dose	payer	noose	worsted (yarn)
doze			

Exercise 20

Pronounce the following, making sure that each syllable is correct. Guard against slurring the words in the last column.

been	such	barrel	Did you?
gone	put	faucet	Don't you?
to	with	suburb	Go on.
for	tiny	hearth	Our education
aunt	and	nothing	You are
far	poem	office	You're not
our	catch	peril	We're coming

kept	toward	forbade	They're coming
says	donkey	spirit	What did you say?
rid	again	semi	Where are you going?
since	against	scared	Where have you been?
sleek	honest	saucy	I want to go.
creek	savage	turnip	I'm going to go.
where	swept	roof	To-morrow morning
boil	velvet	proof	Next month
hoist	direct	hydrant	Last Saturday

Exercise 21

Enunciate carefully:

salary	gentleman	supple	gymnasium
because	library	subtle	perspiration
ideal	wrestle	italic	clapboards
suite	vessel	insect	cupboard
thirty	friendship	orchid	archangel
tomato	judgment	hovel	candelabra
grimy	cowardice	several	extraordinary
patron	miserable	pumpkin	civilization
omelet	guarantee	accurate	horseshoe
hundred	gelatine	guardian	laboratory
coupon	glycerine	delinquent	tenacious
awkward	paraffine	secretary	measure
hurrah	portrait	audacious	February
pigeon	mercantile	conquer	cellar
history	juvenile	conquest	perfect
diamond	thousand	congress	grandmother

asylum	overalls	licorice	generally

Exercise 22

Be especially careful of the sounds *th* and *wh*. Add no syllable to a word and omit none. Consult a dictionary for any word below about which you are not certain:

when	length	diphthong	generally
where	strength	diphtheria	forget
while	height	anesthetic	recognize
wharf	width	betrothal	hungry
which	depth	theory	geography
wheel	there	theme	instead
wheeze	them	arithmetic	isolated
why	eleventh	bathe	writing
whiff	twelfth	lathe	kettle
whence	thought	believe	language
whet	throat	bronchitis	leisure
what	wreaths	government	volume
whale	paths	courteous	column
wheat	months	different	always
wheedle	mouths	engine	once
whelp	myths	English	twice
whimper	breadths	surprise	arctic
whip	moths	deaf	Italian
whit	bath	children	picture
whither	earth	cruel	often

Exercise 23—Homonyms

A homonym is a word having the same sound as another but differing from it in meaning. Use each of the following in a sentence to show its meaning.

aloud	draft	fowl	principal
allowed	draught	foul	principle
ascent	faint	gate	peal
assent	feint	gait	peel
aught	canvas	great	quire
ought	canvass	grate	choir
bad	cereal	hew	seen
bade	serial	hue	scene
bale	cession	kernel	soul
bail	session	colonel	sole
berry	cite	leased	strait
bury	site	least	straight
boy	coarse	lesser	stair
buoy	course	lessor	stare
by	compliment	mite	sweet
buy	complement	might	suite
council	feign	miner	there
counsel	fain	minor	their
current	flour	need	wood
currant	flower	knead	would

Exercise 24

Do the same with the following:

aisle	clause	kill	sail
isle	claws	kiln	sale
awl	climb	key	ring
all	clime	quay	wring
base	draught	lie	serge
bass	draft	lye	surge
blew	dew	medal	sole
blue	due	meddle	soul
bough	done	peer	shone
bow	dun	pier	shown
bread	dual	pore	steel
bred	duel	pour	steal
bear	flue	profit	stationary
bare	flew	prophet	stationery
bridal	freeze	quarts	wade
bridle	frieze	quartz	weighed
capital	guilt	rest	wave
capitol	gilt	wrest	waive
ceiling	heard	root	wrap
sealing	herd	route	rap

Exercise 25—Syllabication

What is a syllable?

Choose a word and notice that every vowel sound in it makes a syllable. Therefore, you never have two vowels in one syllable unless the two are pronounced as one sound.

In pronouncing notice carefully to which syllable a consonant belongs; as in *dif-fer-ent*, *beau-ti-fy*, *dai-sy*.

Divide the following words into syllables. If you cannot decide with which syllable a consonant belongs, consult a dictionary.

paper	grocer	rotate	mystery
tomato	erect	repeat	regular
vinegar	polish	general	arithmetic

If a syllable, especially an accented syllable, ends in a vowel, what is usually the length of the vowel?

If the syllable ends in a consonant, what is usually the length of the vowel of the syllable?

When a consonant is doubled, the division is usually made between the two letters; as,

blot-ter	skip-ping	remit-tance
neces-sary	throt-tle	span-ning

As a rule, a prefix constitutes one syllable; as,

pro-long	pre-fer	con-stant	de-fect	ad-mit
re-ceive	se-lect	dis-trust	e-merge	im-merse

As a rule, a suffix constitutes one syllable; as,

labor-er	soft-ly	beauti-fy	selec-tion
mole-cule	revolution-ist	percent-age	fanat-ic

When two or more letters together give one sound, they must not be divided; as,

math-ematics	ex-change	paragraph-ing	abolish-ing
bow-ing	toil-ing	nation-al	gra-cious

Can a word of one syllable be divided?

Do not divide a syllable of one letter from the rest of the word. The division *ever-y* is wrong.

Exercise 26

Divide the following words into syllables, using the suggestions given in the preceding exercise:

accountant	dissatisfaction	manufacturer	reference
advertisement	economy	material	repeatedly

anecdote	employment	mechanical	salesman
annually	energetic	neighborhood	security
application	environment	occupation	separate
automobile	especially	opportunity	signature
beginning	establishment	organized	specification
collection	expenditure	permanent	stenography
comparison	factory	preparation	suburban
competent	furniture	president	superintend
confirmation	illustration	quotation	systematic
consequence	impression	realize	telephone
correspondence	improvement	receptacle	treasurer
counterfeit	judgment	recognition	unanimous
customer	machinist	recommend	unusual

Exercise 27—Accent

What is accent?

Divide into syllables, indicate the accent, and pronounce the following:

expand	volume	defect	interesting
mischievous	usually	incomparable	theatre
exquisite	tedious	hospitable	generally
column	inquiry	impious	

In the following words the meaning changes with the accent. Use each word in a sentence to show its meaning.

ob´ject	subject	contrast	desert
ob-ject´	insult	protest	extract
tor´ment	essay	conflict	compact
tor-ment´	transfer	compound	survey

minute (notice the vowel change)

refuse (notice the consonant change)

Bring to class a list of words that you have heard mispronounced in your classes. Be sure that you can pronounce them correctly.

Exercise 28

The following words are frequently mispronounced. Divide them into syllables, mark the accent, and pronounce carefully.

municipal	exquisite	champion	accurately
interesting	gondola	inquiry	Genoa
influence	finance	inexplicable	alias
illustrate	deficit	despicable	expert
inventory	pretense	mischievous	impious
alternate	dirigible	perfume	detail

CHAPTER III

SPELLING RULES

Exercise 29—Plurals of Nouns

(*a*)	(*b*)
dress, dresses	chair, chairs
splash, splashes	wave, waves
business, businesses	book, books
church, churches	pencil, pencils
fox, foxes	paper, papers

The usual way of forming the plural of English nouns is illustrated by the words in column (*b*) above. What is it?

If you add *s* to the singular form *dress*, could you distinguish the pronunciation of the plural from the pronunciation of the singular? Does this suggest a reason for adding *es* to form the plural?

How many syllables must you use to pronounce the plural of fox? Does this suggest another reason for adding *es* to form the plural?

Every word that ends in a sibilant or hissing sound (*ch*, *s*, *sh*, *ss*, *x*, *z*) forms its plural like *fox*. Give several illustrations.

Rule 1.—Nouns regularly form the plural by adding *s*, but those ending in a sibilant must add*es*.

Exercise 30

(*a*)	(*b*)
lady, ladies	valley, valleys
ally, allies	alley, alleys
soliloquy, soliloquies	journey, journeys

Name five words belonging to group (*a*) above. Does a vowel or a consonant precede the *y* in each case?

Name other words belonging to the group (*b*) above. Does a vowel or a consonant precede the *y* in each case?

Rule 2.—Nouns ending in *y* preceded by a consonant (and nouns ending in *quy*) form the plural by changing *y* to *i* and adding *es*.

Exercise 31—Words ending in o

(a)

potato, potatoes	hero, heroes	mulatto, mulattoes
tomato, tomatoes	buffalo, buffaloes	cargo, cargoes
negro, negroes	echo, echoes	motto, mottoes

(b)

solo, solos	piano, pianos	memento, mementos
halo, halos	lasso, lassos	canto, cantos
zero, zeros	quarto, quartos	soprano, sopranos
	stilletto, stillettos	

The older English words ending in *o* form the plural by adding *es*, as in potatoes; those more recently taken into the language form the plural by adding *s*, as in quartos.

Exercise 32—Nouns in f and fe

leaf, leaves	calf, calves	wife, wives
loaf, loaves	sheaf, sheaves	shelf, shelves
half, halves	wolf, wolves	elf, elves
life, lives	beef, beeves	wharf, wharves (or wharfs)
self, selves	knife, knives	

With the exception of the words given above, nouns ending in an *f* sound form the plural in the regular way; as,

hoof, hoofs	scarf, scarfs	beliefs, beliefs
chief, chiefs	reef, reefs	grief, griefs

Exercise 33—Irregular Plurals

Some nouns form their plural by a change of vowel; as,

man	men	foot	feet

woman	women	tooth	teeth
goose	geese	mouse	mice

A few words retain the old time plural *en;* as,

brother brethren

child children ox oxen

A few words are the same in both singular and plural; as,

sheep, trout, deer

Some nouns have two plurals which differ in meaning; as,

Singular	*Plural*	
brother	brothers	brethren
penny	pennies	pence
pea	peas	pease
die	dies	dice

Consult a dictionary for the difference in meaning between the two plurals of each word.

Exercise 34—Compound Nouns

Singular	*Plural*
brother-in-law	brothers-in-law
father-in-law	fathers-in-law
court-martial	courts-martial
commander-in-chief	commanders-in-chief
man-of-war	men-of-war
major general	major generals
goose quill	goose quills
bill of fare	bills of fare
spoonful	spoonfuls
cupful	cupfuls

Rule 3.—Compound nouns usually add the sign of the plural to the fundamental part of the word.

NOTE.—In *spoonfuls* the thought is of one spoon many times full.

Plural of Letters and Figures

Rule 4.—Letters and figures form the plural by adding the apostrophe (') and *s*; as,

a	a's	3	3's
w	w's	5	5's

The same rule applies to the plural of words which ordinarily have no plural; as,

Don't use so many *and's* and *if's*.

Exercise 35—Foreign Plurals

Some nouns derived from foreign languages retain their original plural. The following are in common use.

Consult a dictionary for their pronunciation and definition.

Singular	*Plural*	*Singular*	*Plural*
crisis	crises	stratum	strata
thesis	theses	radius	radii
hypothesis	hypotheses	parenthesis	parentheses
focus	foci	synopsis	synopses
datum	data	basis	bases
alumnus	alumni	automaton	automata
alumna	alumnae	analysis	analyses
oasis	oases	nucleus	nuclei
axis	axes	phenomenon	phenomena
genus	genera		

Some words admit of two plurals, one the foreign plural, and one the regular English plural; as,

Singular	*Plural*	
beau	beaux	beaus
formula	formulae	formulas
vertex	vertices	vertexes
index	indices	indexes
cherub	cherubim	cherubs
seraph	seraphim	seraphs
bandit	banditti	bandits

Consult a dictionary to see whether there is any difference of meaning between the two plurals of these words.

Exercise 36—The Formation of Participles

Rap, rapping, rapped   *Reap, reaping, reaped*

Rap is a monosyllable ending in a single consonant preceded by a single vowel. The final consonant in such words is doubled before a suffix beginning with a vowel is added.

In *reap* the final consonant is not doubled because it is preceded by two vowels.

Make the participles of the following verbs:

chat	lap	suit	step
cheat	leap	sit	steep
rot	train	sop	trot
root	trim	soap	treat

Trap, trapping, trapped   *Track, tracking, tracked*

Why is the final consonant in *trap* doubled before *ing* or *ed* is added?

The final consonant in *track* is not doubled because *track* ends with two consonants.

Pin, pinning   *Pine, pining*

Pine drops the silent *e* because the tendency in English is to drop endings that are not needed for pronunciation before adding a suffix beginning with a vowel.

Form the participles of the following verbs:

knot	rob	flop	
note	robe	elope	
deal	swim	quit	(*u* is not here a vowel)
clap	strike	crawl	(*w* is here a vowel)
stop	oil	wax	(*x* equals *cks*)
peal	rush	bow	(*w* is here a vowel)

Exercise 37

Exercise 36 applies also to words of more than one syllable accented on the last syllable, if they retain the accent on the same syllable after the suffix is added. Thus we have

Rule 5.—Monosyllables or words accented on the last syllable, ending in a single consonant preceded by a single vowel, double the final consonant before adding a suffix beginning with a vowel.

Form participles from the following words that are accented on the last syllable:

prefer	intervene	escape	expel
refer	reveal	acquire	contain
occur	repeal	secure	forbid
permit	pursue	conceal	incur
interfere	erase	arrange	forget
retain	control	acquit	repel

Form participles from the following words not accented on the last syllable:

benefit	travel	marvel	shelter
revel	answer	exhibit	render
quarrel	profit	shovel	limit

Words in which the accent changes do not double the final consonant before adding a suffix beginning with a vowel; as,

confer	conference	infer	inference
refer	reference	prefer	preferable

Explain why the final consonant is *not* doubled in each of the following words:

neglect	neglecting	lean	leaning
prefer	preference	select	selecting
creep	creeping	receipt	receipting
wonder	wondering	answer	answering

Exercise 38

Rule 6.—In forming the present participle of verbs ending in *y*, retain the *y* before adding *ing;* as,

study	studying	obey	obeying
carry	carrying	convey	conveying
pity	pitying		

In forming the perfect participle, if in the present tense the *y* is preceded by a consonant, the *y* is changed to *i* and *ed* added; if the *y* is preceded by a vowel, the *y* is retained; as,

study	studied	carry	carried	pity	pitied

but

obey	obeyed	convey	conveyed

Compare with Rule 2.

Exercise 39

Rule 7.—In words containing a long *e* sound spelled either *ie* or *ei*, *ei* follows *c; ie* follows one of the other consonants; as,

ei	*ie*

deceive	relieve	siege
perceive	believe	yield
receive	belief	grief
conceive	chief	field
conceit	priest	piece
receipt	niece	wield
	reprieve	lien

Exceptions.—Either, neither, weird, seize, leisure.

The following couplet may help in remembering when to write *ie* and when to write *ei:*

When the letter *c* you spy,
Put the *e* before the *i.*

Exercise 40—The Pronunciation of *c* and *g*

The letter *c* is pronounced sometimes like *s* and sometimes like *k*.

What sound does *c* have before *a?* Illustrate.

Before *e?* Illustrate.

Before *i?* Illustrate.

Before *o?* Illustrate.

Before *u?* Illustrate.

Before *y?* Illustrate.

If *c* is pronounced like *k*, it is called hard and is marked *[\c]*.

If *c* is pronounced like *s*, it is called soft and is marked *ç*. The mark used to indicate the soft *c* is called the *cedilla.*

Make a statement telling when *c* is hard and when it is soft.

What sound does *g* have before each of the vowels, as in *game*, *gone*, *gymnasium*, *Gunther*, *gentle?*

Rule 8.—*C* and *g* usually are soft before *e*, *i*, and *y*.

Exercise 41

Words ending in silent *e*, according to Rule 5, drop the *e* before a suffix beginning with a vowel. Exceptions occur when the *e* is needed to preserve the soft sound of *c* and *g*. Tell why *e* is dropped in *encouraging* and retained in *courageous*.

In words containing *dg*, as in *judge* and *lodge*, the *d* gives the *g* the soft sound, and there is no need to retain the *e* before adding a suffix, as in *judgment*.

Rule 9.—Words ending in silent *e* usually drop the *e* before adding a suffix beginning with a vowel, unless the *e* is needed to preserve the pronunciation; as after soft *c* and *g*, when the suffix begins with *a* or *o*.

Tell why the *e* is retained before the suffix in the following:

noticeable	damageable	pronounceable	outrageous
courageous	peaceable	serviceable	manageable

Tell why the *e* is dropped before adding the suffix in the following:

managing	curable	erasure
besieging	admirable	realization
receiving	obliging	precedence
	perseverance	

The fact that *c* has two different sounds causes a slight peculiarity in words ending in *c*. Final *c* has the sound of *k*. When words end in *c*, the letter *k* is usually added before a suffix beginning with either *e*, *i*, or *y*, to show that *c* is not pronounced like *s;* as,

frolic frolicked frolicking

If the *k* is not added, the *c* changes its pronunciation; as,

public publicity

Exercise 42

It follows by inference from Rule 9 that words ending in silent *e* retain the *e* before a suffix beginning with a consonant; as,

move	movement	disgrace	disgraceful
defense	defenseless	fate	fateful
arrange	arrangement	fierce	fiercely
noise	noiseless	manage	management

severe	severely	rude	rudeness

Exceptions.—Truly, duly, wisdom, awful, wholly.

Bring to class a list of twenty words that retain the final *e* before a suffix beginning with a consonant.

Exercise 43

What spelling rule does each of the following words illustrate?

advantageous	gigantic	boxes	admittance
mimicking	piece	libraries	occurrence
arrangement	receipt	keys	acquittal

Exercise 44—Abbreviations

Write abbreviations for the months of the year. Are there any that should not be abbreviated?

The abbreviations for the states and territories are:

Alabama, Ala.	Maryland, Md.
Arizona, Ariz.	Massachusetts, Mass.
Arkansas, Ark.	Michigan, Mich.
California, Cal.	Minnesota, Minn.
Colorado, Colo.	Mississippi, Miss.
Connecticut, Conn.	Missouri, Mo.
Delaware, Del.	Montana, Mont.
District of Columbia, D.C.	Nebraska, Nebr.
Florida, Fla.	Nevada, Nev.
Georgia, Ga.	New Hampshire, N.H.
Idaho, Idaho	New Mexico, N. Mex.
Illinois, Ill.	New York, N.Y.
Indiana, Ind.	New Jersey, N.J.
Iowa, Ia.	North Carolina, N.C.
Kansas, Kans.	North Dakota, N. Dak.

Kentucky, Ky.	Ohio, O.
Louisiana, La.	Oklahoma, Okla.
Maine, Me.	Oregon, Ore.
Pennsylvania, Pa.	Utah, Utah
Philippine Islands, P.I.	Vermont, Vt.
Porto Rico, P.R.	Virginia, Va.
South Carolina, S.C.	Washington, Wash.
South Dakota, S.D.	Wisconsin, Wis.
Tennessee, Tenn.	West Virginia, W. Va.
Texas, Tex.	Wyoming, Wyo.

NOTE.—It is much better to write the full name rather than the abbreviation whenever the former would make the address clearer, especially as regards similar abbreviations, such as Cal. and Colo.

Exercise 45—Abbreviations of Commercial Terms

A 1, first class	doz., dozen
@, at	E. & O.E., errors and omissions excepted
acct., account	ea., each
adv., advertisement	e.g., for example
agt., agent	etc., and so forth
a.m., forenoon	exch., exchange
amt., amount	ft., foot
app., appendix	f.o.b., free on board
atty., attorney	gal., gallon
av., average	i.e., that is
avoir., avoirdupois	imp., imported
bal., balance	in., inches
bbl., barrel	inst., this month (instant)
B/L, bill of lading	Jr., junior
bldg., building	kg., keg

B/S, bill of sale

bu., bushel

C.B., cash book

C., hundred

coll., collection, collector

Co., company

C.O.D., cash on delivery

cr., creditor

cwt., hundredweight

D., five hundred

dept., department

disc., discount

do., ditto

dr., debtor, debit

pkg., package

pp., pages

pr., pair

pc., piece

pk., peck

prox., next month

pt., pint

Sr., senior

lb., pound

ltd., limited

mdse., merchandise

mem., memorandum

mo., month

M.S. (MSS)., manuscript

mtg., mortgage

N.B., take notice

no., number

O.K., all right

per, by

p.m., afternoon

%, per cent

St., street

str., steamer

ult., last month

U.S.M., United States Mail

viz., namely

vol., volume

W/B, way bill

wt., weight

CHAPTER IV

WORD ANALYSIS

To learn English words thoroughly we must spend some thought on the way in which they are made up, on the language from which they have been derived, and on the changes in meaning made by adding prefixes and suffixes. Three important influences in building the English have been the Anglo-Saxon, the Greek, and the Latin languages. The simplest words in the language are Anglo-Saxon. The following exercises illustrate how words have been multiplied by Anglo-Saxon prefixes and suffixes.

Exercise 46

Name as many words as you can that make use of each of the following prefixes. Give only such as are recognizable English words without the prefix.

a—aboard *mis*—misjudge

be—becalm *un*—unknown

fore—foretell *up*—uproot

Give the meaning of each of the prefixes used above.

What part of speech does each prefix make?

Exercise 47

Using the following Teutonic suffixes, form English words. Be careful that the root taken alone is an English word.

dom—kingdom *ness*—goodness

hood—manhood *ship*—friendship

What does each suffix mean?

What part of speech does it make?

Exercise 48

As above, form words using the following suffixes:

en—darken *ful*—fearful

en—golden *ly*—smoothly

ish—sweetish	*like*—childlike
less—fearless	*some*—lonesome

Define each suffix.

What part of speech does it make?

Exercise 49—Greek Roots

Below is given a list of common Greek roots with the English meaning of each. Form words using one or more of the roots for each word, and define the words you make. For instance, give the meaning of *telephone*, *telegraph*, and *monarch*.

Greek English	*Greek English*
phon—hear	*chron*—time
tele—far	*cycl*—circle
graph—write	*geo*—earth
scop—see	*polit*—government
micro—small	*cra*—rule
mono—one	*demo*—people
arch—chief	*hydro*—water
metr—measure	*poly*—many
baro—pressure, weight	*pluto*—riches

How many names of modern inventions have you made?

Exercise 50

What words belonging to your vocabulary end in the following suffixes? Choose only such as have an English word for the root.

Adjective Suffixes

1. *able*, *ible*—able to be, fit to be
Readable, fit to be read.
2. *al*, *eal*, *ial*—relating to, having to do with
3. *ant*, *ent*—being, inclined to
4. *ate*—having the quality of, inclined to
5. *ic*—like, relating to
6. *ive*—relating to, of the nature of, belonging to

7. *ory, ary*—relating to
8. *ous*—full of, abounding in

Verb Suffixes

1. *ate*—to make
2. *fy, ify*—to make
3. *ise, ize*—to make

Noun Suffixes

1. *age*—condition, act, collection of
2. *ance, ancy, ence, ency*—state of being
3. *ary, ory*—one who, place where, that which
4. *ant, ent*—one who
5. *ist, ite*—one who
6. *ion, sion, tion*—act of, state of being
7. *ity, ty*—quality of being
8. *ment*—that which, act or state of being
9. *or, er, ar*—one who
10. *try*—state of
11. *tude, itude*—condition of being
12. *ure*—condition of being, that which

Exercise 51

The following is a list of the more commonly used Latin prefixes:

1. *a, ab*—away from
2. *ad*—toward
3. *ante*—before
4. *anti*—against
5. *bi*—two, twice
6. *circum*—around
7. *con*—together with, against
8. *contra*—against
9. *de*—from, apart from, down from
10. *dis*—apart, not
16. *intro*—toward the inside
17. *mono*—one
18. *non*—not
19. *ob*—in the way of, against
20. *per*—through
21. *pre*—before
22. *post*—after
23. *pro*—before
24. *re*—again, back
25. *semi*—half, partly

11. *dia*—through

12. *ex*—out of

13. *in, en*—into

en—to cause to be

14. *in, un*—not

15. *inter*—between

26. *se*—away from

27. *sub*—under, below

28. *super*—above, more than

29. *trans*—across

30. *uni*—one

Exercise 52

Analyze the following words, telling prefix, root, suffix, part of speech, and meaning:

business	package	truthfulness	unsuccessful
useless	anteroom	workmanlike	agreement
prefix	monotone	nervousness	uniformity
beautify	breakage	disrespectful	misguidance
semicircle	pleasant	perfection	crystallize
kingship	sameness	progressive	precaution
incase	subway	undeniable	imaginary
enrich	disown	displeasure	supernatural
pianist	readmit	endurance	melodious
bicycle	adjuster	reaction	interlineal

Exercise 53

When the prefixes *ad*, *con*, and *in* are used to form English words, the final consonant of each is often changed to the initial consonant of the root to which it is joined.

Ad assumes the forms *ab*, *ac*, *af*, *ag*, *al*, *an*, *ap*, *ar*, *as*, *at*, assimilating the *d* with the first letter of the word to which it is prefixed; as,

ab-breviate	al-literation	ar-rest
ac-cept	al-lot	as-sign
ac-cumulate	an-nex	as-sist
af-fect	an-nounce	at-tract

af-flict	ap-position	at-tribute
ag-gregate	ap-prove	at-tune

Con assumes the forms *col*, *cor*, *com*, by assimilation; it takes the form *com* before *p;* and it drops the *n* before a vowel; as,

col-lateral	com-mercial	com-pose
col-lect	cor-relate	co-operate
com-mission	cor-respond	co-ordinate

In assumes the forms *il*, *im*, *ir*, by assimilation and takes the form of *im* before *p*.

il-lusion im-migrate ir-ruption im-port

Exercise 54—Peculiar Adjective Endings

The suffixes *able* and *ible* are sometimes troublesome because it is difficult to know which ending to write. As a rule, if the new word was made from another English word, the ending is *able*, as *blamable*. The words ending in *ible* are derived from the Latin, and, as a rule, the ending cannot easily be separated from the root and still leave the latter an English word. Examples are:

divisible	intelligible	digestible	audible
visible	permissible	flexible	incredible
possible	terrible	horrible	indelible

The suffixes *ant* and *ent* must also be carefully noted. No rule can be given for using one rather than the other. Whenever in doubt, consult a dictionary. Note the following:

ant	*ent*
important	independent
pleasant	convalescent
triumphant	competent
luxuriant	convenient
stagnant	confident

The endings *eous* and *ious*, where *e* and *i* are often confused, are illustrated in the following:

eous	*ious*
hideous	delirious
miscellaneous	impious
courteous	studious

The endings *cious* and *tious* are shown in the following:

cious	*tious*
conscious	fictitious
precious	superstitious
delicious	cautious
gracious	ambitious
suspicious	nutritious

The endings *gious* and *geous* are illustrated in the following:

gious	*geous*
religious	courageous

Exercise 55—Peculiar Noun and Verb Endings

Nouns in *ance* and *ence:*

ance	*ence*
acceptance	intelligence
appearance	reference
annoyance	patience
acquaintance	negligence
remittance	diligence
ignorance	residence

Nouns in *sion*, *cion*, and *tion:*

sion	*cion*	*tion*
exclusion	coercion	acquisition
aversion	suspicion	precaution

Verbs in *ise*, *yze*, and *ize:*

ise	*yze*	*ize*
advise	analyze	baptize
supervise	paralyze	recognize

Verbs in *ceed*, *sede*, and *cede:*

ceed	*sede*	*cede*
exceed	supersede	concede
proceed		intercede
succeed		precede

Exercise 56

What other words can you form from the following? Explain what prefixes or suffixes you use in each case and what part of speech you form.

success	consider	real	change
please	doubt	publish	attend
occur	apply	regular	satisfy
emphasize	industry	operate	assess
second	busy	practice	resist
expense	distribute	organ	define
depend	locate	work	sense
attract	install	desire	preside
effect	vital	count	sign

Exercise 57

There are many words the meanings of which are easily confused. The spelling and the definitions of such must be mastered. Analysis in this exercise and in the one following does not require separation into prefix, root, and suffix, but it necessitates a careful study of the words, first, to note the difference in spelling; second, to consult a dictionary, if necessary, for the difference in meaning.

Define each word clearly.

Use each in a sentence to illustrate its meaning.

accept—except	common—mutual

add—annex

advice—advise

affect—effect

after—afterward

ascend—assent

assure—promise

attain—obtain

benefit—advantage

brief—concise

center—middle

claim—maintain

combine—combination

complementary—complimentary

continual—continuous

contraction—abbreviation

contradiction—denial

currant—current

defective—deficient

deprecate—depreciate

effective—efficient

eligible—illegible

eminent—prominent

expect—hope

intelligent—intelligible

Exercise 58

As above, define each word carefully and use it in a sentence to illustrate its meaning.

healthful—healthy

inventory—invoice

invite—invitation

last—latest

later—latter

liable—likely—apt

loose—lose

need—want

perspective—prospective

positive—definite

practicable—practical

precede—proceed

principal—principle

proficient—efficient

proscribe—prescribe

purpose—propose

quiet—quite

recommend—recommendation

refer—allude

repair—fix

requirement—requisite—requisition

respectfully—respectively

scarcely—hardly

stationary—stationery

therefore—accordingly

500 SPELLING WORDS

Lesson 1

business	losing	surprising	height
receive	loosely	Saturday	depth
believe	across	Wednesday	eighth
wholly	whether	excellent	daily
obliged	describe	exercise	earnest

Lesson 2

attached	decision	probable	seize
attacked	buying	usable	siege
gentlemen	studying	salable	friend
although	relying	desirable	Messrs.
thoroughly	occasion	honorable	nickel

Lesson 3

disappoint	knew	acquittal	stopped
disappear	design	occurrence	referred
disapprove	forty	compelling	planned
disagree	fourth	beginning	swimming
anxious	purpose	permitted	submitted

Lesson 4

all right	persuade	Norwegian	variety
already	pursued	possession	prairie
tongue	prepared	accumulate	neighbor
separate	repaired	dissatisfy	soldier
crystal	necessary	dissolve	shoulder

Lesson 5

their	awkward	opportunity	scheme
advise	mucilage	development	schedule
advice	familiar	statistics	accurately
laboratory	peculiar	accidental	efficient
until	similar	competent	Spaniard

Lesson 6

policy	patient	merchandise	conscious
rough	ancient	mercantile	precious
disease	partial	scarcity	suspicion
balance	facial	indebted	physician
decease	ambitious	estimate	caution

Lesson 7

ascend	noticeable	vengeance	emergency
assent	serviceable	address	compliance
minute	manageable	salary	reference
conceal	exchangeable	currency	apparel
immense	advantageous	withhold	typical

Lesson 8

edition	especially	appreciate	imitate
addition	pamphlet	essential	initial
identify	illustrate	eligible	official
illegal	February	legible	curtain
nuisance	punctual	illegible	adjacent

Lesson 9

later crystallize lieutenant lenient
latter neutralize anthracite naphtha
weighed conceit bituminous liquid
destroy catarrh rheumatism gauge
indelible colonel influential sieve

Lesson 10

duly interfered analyze attorneys
durable transferred analysis specialty
mutual reconcile paralyze sympathy
bargain accidental banana campaign
misspell irregular molasses mattress

Lesson 11

ached designate vicinity recognize
social available guardian technical
forfeit adequately celebrate hygiene
opposite subordinate porcelain angel
parallel sufficient poultice angle

Lesson 12

society associate rumored remittance
sirloin definitely courtesy remuneration
laborer spherical obstinacy restaurant
visitor commercial financial government
souvenir permissible sapphire acquaintance

Lesson 13

quite appropriate convenient knowledge

least	distinguish	exaggerate	principal, *a*
written	mysterious	confidential	stationary, *a*
among	appearance	endeavoring	judgment
psalm	conference	immediately	implement

Lesson 14

assure	greatly	embarrassment	auxiliary
expect	grateful	organization	conciliate
prompt	deserve	advertisement	principle, *n*
eliminate	bureau	assessment	stationery, *n*
illuminate	deficient	accommodate	parenthesis

Lesson 15

coupon	indispensable	measure	proprietor
length	innumerable	condemn	transient
vehicle	investigate	security	persistent
customer	incandescent	liniment	signature
costumer	effervescent	mosquito	mischievous

Lesson 16

canal	company's	repetition	sulphur
channel	real estate	abbreviated	benefited
liquid	equivalent	unabridged	unanimous
recent	assignment	assurance	itemize
trough	extravagant	pneumatic	calcimine

Lesson 17

precede	freight	authority	leisure
proceed	achieve	mortgage	neuralgia
procession	between	specimen	dyspepsia

precision	imagine	solicitor	substantial
extinguish	autumn	coöperates	passenger

Lesson 18

merely	mechanical	preliminary	omitted
cashier	permanent	miscellaneous	omission
urgent	prominent	subscription	committee
hesitate	precaution	incredible	commission
anchored	interval	anticipation	precisely

Lesson 19

specify	preparation	athletics	deceit
equity	coincidence	excursion	receipt
accrue	irresolute	suggestion	obstacle
concrete	vaccination	courageous	promissory
summary	glycerine	concession	compulsory

Lesson 20

deficit	sceptical	anniversary	rhythm
mansion	conscience	presumption	rhubarb
mention	interruption	guaranteed	fatigue
reckoned	approximately	prejudice	synopsis
license	avoirdupois	privilege	emphatic

Lesson 21

scholar	Elkhart	industrious	collision
scissors	Memphis	hideous	delusion
career	Niagara	artificial	oxygen
sincere	Raleigh	cantaloupe	martyr

chiffonier	Oregon	unscrupulous	apology

Lesson 22

receipt	Cincinnati	sovereign	chemical
welfare	Des Moines	committee	frontier
feigned	Decatur	ingredients	fulfilled
chord	Dubuque	counterfeit	facsimile
scythe	Alleghany	responsible	identical

Lesson 23

exceed	Paducah	foreign	Cheyenne
succeed	Eau Claire	solemnity	metallic
secede	Peoria	assassinate	nauseated
immigrant	Savannah	pneumonia	invariably
emigrant	Manila	diphtheria	injurious

Lesson 24

adoption	Minneapolis	fraudulent	mahogany
scientific	Indianapolis	negligence	corduroy
guidance	Syracuse	diligence	Schenectady
syllable	Milwaukee	ridiculous	duplicate
Fort Wayne	Valparaiso	comparative	reënforce

Lesson 25

Duluth	Massachusetts	preferable	periodical
Missouri	Connecticut	preferred	insertion
Wisconsin	enthusiastic	publicity	excursion
luxurious	acknowledgment	prevailing	plateau
twelfth	professional	damageable	tragedy

CHAPTER V

THE SENTENCE AND ITS ELEMENTS

In the preceding chapters we have seen words as they are used singly. We studied their pronunciation and the way in which they were formed to express a definite meaning. In this chapter we shall begin a review of grammar, a study of words not according to their pronunciation or their definition, but according to their use as they are arranged with other words to express complete ideas. The simplest group into which words are thus arranged is the sentence, consisting of two important parts, the subject and the predicate. The subject is the part about which something is told, and the predicate is the part that tells about the subject; as,

Subject	*Predicate*
The sun	shines brightly

There are several different kinds of sentences, named according to the meaning which they express. They are as follows:

The *declarative* sentence states a fact.
The *interrogative* sentence asks a question.
The *imperative* sentence commands or entreats.
The *exclamatory* sentence expresses deep feeling.

Illustrations

Declarative: John closed the door.
Interrogative: Did John close the door?
Imperative: Close the door.
Exclamatory: What a noise the door made!

Sentences are classified, also, according to their structure or form. If a sentence has one subject and one predicate, it is a *simple* sentence. If it is made up of two independent parts, it is a *compound* sentence. If it has one independent part and one or more dependent parts, each of which contains a subject and a predicate of its own, the sentence is *complex*. The independent part of the sentence is called a *principal clause*, and the dependent part is called a *subordinate clause*. A *phrase* is also a dependent part of a sentence, but it differs from a subordinate clause in that it contains no subject or predicate. Both phrases and subordinate clauses are used as parts of speech, as nouns, adjectives, or adverbs. Thus we have the following definitions:

A *simple* sentence contains one principal clause.

A *compound* sentence contains two or more principal clauses.

A *complex* sentence contains one principal clause and one or more subordinate clauses.

A *phrase* is a group of related words used as a part of speech. (See Exercises 68 and 69.)

A *clause* is a group of words containing a subject and a predicate. A subordinate clause is used as a part of speech. It usually has an introductory word to distinguish it from a principal clause. (See Exercise 71.)

Illustrations

Simple sentence: To-day most of the world's big questions are business questions.

Complex sentence: The view *that* business is only humdrum routine and sordid money-making needs revising, *since* most of the world's big questions are business questions.

Compound sentence: Many people still belittle business, calling it humdrum routine and sordid money-making, *but* this view needs revising.

Phrase: (*a*) *of* the world's big questions.
(*b*) *calling* it humdrum routine and sordid money-making.

Subordinate clause: (*a*) *that* business is only humdrum routine and sordid money-making.
(*b*) *since* most of the world's big questions are business questions.

Exercise 59

Write two of each of the following kinds of sentences: *a.* Declarative, *b.* Interrogative, *c.* Imperative, *d.* Exclamatory.

Examine each of the sentences below and tell

a. Whether it is simple, complex, or compound.

b. Its subject and its predicate.

c. Its phrases and its subordinate clause (if there are any).

1. Your subscription expires with this issue.

2. This special offer will continue until the tenth of November.

3. The last shipment of castings that you made to us is decidedly unsatisfactory.

4. Your imitation typewritten letters have greatly assisted us in the sale of our property, and we thank you for calling our attention to them.

5. The advertised poster was sent to you to-day in a special tube.

6. Without doubt you will be interested in the booklet which we enclose.

7. The machine which is standing there has just been repaired.

8. The wheel that holds the type may be changed in an instant by the operator.

9. Whenever he wishes, the operator may write in different sizes of type on the same sheet of paper.

10. Many of our styles have been copied exactly from the best designs that have recently been displayed in the Parisian exhibits.

11. Why are the department stores acquiring motor wagons?

12. One reason is the economy of the motor wagon.

13. Economy does not entirely explain the keenness which department stores are displaying in acquiring motor wagons.

14. In such establishments the quick delivery of merchandise is a necessity.

15. The best means of transportation must be employed, or a loss of trade will follow.

16. Any one can cite examples that prove that faults in delivery cause a loss of trade.

17. Machine service develops fewer errors than horse service (develops).

18. The area which department stores serve is being greatly increased from year to year, and not even the establishment of the parcel post has avoided the necessity for sending package merchandise too far distant for conveyance by horses.

19. Electric machines usually make the house-to-house package deliveries, and gasoline trucks, besides hauling furniture, transfer large loads from the store or warehouse to the distributing stations.

20. In one store each transfer truck is loaded twice daily with fifty trunks containing parcels.

Exercise 60—Sentence Errors

S. 1. THE BABY BLUNDER.—In writing, one of the most elementary forms of correctness is shown in the proper division into sentences. The ability instinctively to end a sentence at the right place is called the "sentence sense." Students who do not possess it or who have not learned the difference between sentences, subordinate clauses, and phrases frequently make the mistake of setting off too much or too little for one sentence. For example, they run two sentences together as one; as,

Wrong: Motor wagons are economical, department stores of all large cities are acquiring them.

The sentence, as written above, contains one form of the sentence error—one of the worst possible mistakes in writing. It is sometimes called the *comma fault* or the *baby blunder.* For brevity we shall call it *S 1* (sentence error number one). *Motor wagons are economical* is a principal clause. *Department stores of all large cities are acquiring them* is also a principal clause. Two such clauses may not stand in the same sentence separated only by a comma. To correct, divide into two sentences; as,

Right: Motor wagons are economical. Department stores of all large cities are acquiring them.

Sometimes the thought in the two principal clauses is closely connected. In that case they may be put into the same sentence, provided they are properly connected or separated. Use a comma *plus* a coördinate conjunction (as *and, or, but*) to connect them, or a semicolon (;) to separate them.

Be particularly careful of the conjunctive adverbs *so, then, therefore, thus, also, still, otherwise, however, hence, consequently, moreover, nevertheless.* When they are used to join the principal clauses of a compound sentence, a comma is not sufficient punctuation between the clauses. A semicolon or a comma and a coördinate conjunction must be used.

Wrong: He had been a good customer, so they were sorry to lose his trade.

Right: He had been a good customer; so they were sorry to lose his trade.

Right: He had been a good customer, and so they were sorry to lose his trade.

S. 2.—The first form of the sentence error (*S 1*) is made by using too much for one sentence. The second form (*S 2*) is made by using too little. It consists in writing a subordinate clause or a phrase as a sentence; as,

1. *Wrong:* I told her I would attend to the matter at my earliest convenience. *Probably on my way from work in the evening.*

2. *Wrong:* His doctor advised him to go to Arizona. *Which he decided to do.*

Exercise 61

Each sentence should express one complete thought. Some of the following are really two sentences (*S 1*), and some are only parts of sentences (*S 2*). Correct each, naming the mistake.

1. You will find the booklet interesting it is also instructive.

2. Up to last January he was a salesman for Colgate & Co. since then he has opened a business of his own.

3. I didn't know you had come, when did you arrive?

4. Did any one take the newspaper, I left it here only a moment ago.

5. I shall take my vacation in September have you had yours?

6. I must go now good-bye I'll see you on Saturday.

7. The opening sentence held the man's attention, he read it again and again.

8. I'll have to run to catch the train, otherwise I shall be late for work.

9. The advertisement is attractive, still it has not paid well.

10. We wished to reduce office drudgery therefore we installed adding and addressing machines.

11. These problems all require a knowledge of square root for example, take the fourth.

12. Do you expect to come home for Christmas or shall you stay in New York I don't remember now which you said.

13. First I read a statement that recommended the bonds then I read an article that condemned them without question the result was that I didn't know what to do.

14. One-half of the statements are here, the others are in the safe.

15. If your name is not correct on this envelope, please notify us we wish to insure your receiving our bulletin regularly.

16. The supply of fruit was greater than the demand, that is why fruit was cheap.

17. Flies are dangerous. Especially in a sick room from which they carry germs to others.

18. In the country the trees were loaded with fruit, their branches had to be propped so that they would not break.

19. When he was twenty-three years of age, Richard T. Crane, the late millionaire head of the immense Crane Manufacturing Company, came to Chicago, he started a brass foundry, which grew into the present giant establishment.

20. We spent last summer in the Bitter Root Valley we camped within view of Willoughby Falls.

21. I want to congratulate you on your appointment I heard of it only yesterday.

22. It surely was not I whom you saw I wonder who it could have been.

23. Not one of us has a salary of three thousand dollars so we do not worry over the income tax.

24. Please send me the booklet you offered in the Business Magazine, I'd also like particulars of your advertised discount sale of typewriters.

25. Sooner or later shingles are sure to warp and curl, thus they pull out the nails and allow the rain to beat in, furthermore, shaded shingles soon rot and allow the water to soak through.

26. This sealing and stamping machine is endorsed by business men in all our large cities nevertheless it is not expensive.

27. If you wish to prove the excellence of our paper, just tear off a corner of this sheet then tear off a corner of your present letterhead with a magnifying glass examine both torn edges.

28. The superior paper will show long, linen fibers the poorer, on the other hand, will have short, woody fibers.

29. When a German army is on the march, it stops every twenty minutes for a rest. Experiments having shown that a soldier can cover more ground when he is given this period of relaxation.

30. Two thousand convicts will be released according to a plan worked out by the governor; five hundred will be given their freedom at once, and, if the plan is a success one thousand five hundred others will be released. One-half their wages of fifty cents a day to go to their families and one-half to the penitentiary fund. If they leave the state or commit any crime while they are on parole, to serve the balance of their term and an extension of

time. They will be put to work on roads and bridges the counties need several thousand such laborers but cannot pay union prices.

Exercise 62

Rewrite the following, dividing into sentences:

1

Dear Sir:

There is no safer way to invest money than in a good first mortgage on city real estate by a good mortgage we mean one that is properly drawn and with such security as absolutely insures the holder against loss we have made a specialty of first mortgage loans, and we offer investors the benefit of our wide experience in such matters we investigate properties frequently and keep investors informed on their investment we look after all details and collections without extra charge you will find it to your interest to consult us.

Yours truly,

2

Stick to your legitimate business do not go out into outside operations few men have brains enough for more than one business to dabble in stocks, to put a few thousand dollars into a mine, a few more into a manufactory, and a few more into an invention is enough to ruin any man be content with fair returns do not become greedy do not think that men are happy in proportion as they are rich and therefore do not aim too high be content with moderate wealth make friends a time will come when all the money in the world will not be worth to you as much as one staunch friend.

3

Sacramento City is a great commercial center its wholesale and jobbing business extends hundreds of miles to the north, south, west, and east it is fast becoming a substantial manufacturing center large six and eight story buildings are rapidly taking the place of the old two story structures a new city hall has just been completed which cost $150,000 and a new court house $1,000,000 the city has recently issued bonds amounting to $800,000 for new schools scarcely a week passes without recording some new enterprise all the main highways are macadamized so that automobile travel is possible every day of the year and the farmer can haul his produce to market at a minimum cost market conditions are good and any class of produce finds ready sale at remunerative prices.—(From an advertisement.)

Classify the sentences that you have formed in the foregoing exercise:

1. According to meaning.

2. According to form.

Exercise 63—Parts of Speech

There are eight different kinds of words called parts of speech, which are used to make sentences. They are as follows:

Noun: The *horse* is brown.

Pronoun: He is the best horse of all.

Verb: He *galloped* to town.

Adjective: The *brown* horse is my favorite.

Adverb: He runs *swiftly*.

Preposition: We shall ride *to* town.

Conjunction: The night is clear *and* cold.

Interjection: Oh! My horse stumbled.

Thus a *noun* names something. A word that stands for a noun is a *pronoun*. Sometimes a different part of speech is used like a noun, and for the time being it becomes a noun. The *verb* is a very important part of speech, since without it there can be no sentence. The verb makes an assertion, asks a question, or gives a command. *Adjectives* are words that belong to or describe nouns or pronouns. Adverbs go with or modify verbs, adjectives, or other adverbs. *Prepositions* and *conjunctions* connect. Prepositions join their objects to other words in the sentence; conjunctions join words, phrases, or clauses. An *interjection*, such as the exclamation *oh*, is used without having grammatical relation to any other word in the sentence. A preposition always takes an object, the preposition and its object making a *phrase*. Grouping this information, we have:

PARTS OF SPEECH

Nouns are names of persons and things.

Pronouns are substitutes for nouns.

Verbs make assertions, ask questions, or give commands.

Adjectives modify nouns and pronouns.

Adverbs modify verbs, adjectives, and adverbs. They usually answer the questions *how? when? where? why? to what degree?*

Prepositions join object nouns or pronouns to other words in the sentence.

Conjunctions join words, phrases, and clauses.

Interjections are independent words used as exclamations.

A word is not always the same part of speech. We may say, "Did you *starch* the clothes?" in which case *starch* is a verb. A grocer may say, "The *starch* in these packages is always clean." In this sentence *starch* is a noun. The part of speech depends entirely on the way the word is used.

In the following, name the part of speech of each word in italic. Judge by the way the word is used in the sentence.

1. The desks have *green* pads.
2. *Green* is a restful color.
3. In the valley is a *mill*, which grinds *flour*. It is a *flour* mill.
4. I saw him *stretch* out his hand.
5. The *stretch* of *waste* land amazed him.
6. Europeans say that Americans *waste* more than they use.
7. One of our great problems is how to lessen *waste*.
8. After the stormy *night*, the *day* dawned bright and clear.
9. He has been working *night* and *day*.
10. The old man went *home* sad and weary.
11. *Home* is the best place in the world.
12. We must *fine* you for such an offense.

13. Your *fine* is five dollars.

14. We use *fine* sand in our concrete.

15. I can talk *better* than I can write.

16. John wrote the *better* circular.

17. Talking will not *better* the matter.

18. Young people should learn to respect their *betters.*

19. Suddenly there was a *pause* in the music.

20. Did you see those men *pause?*

21. He was our guide for he knew the *ins* and *outs* of the place.

22. Have you ever been *in* the house?

23. Where are you going—*in* or *out?*

24. *Good* apples are expensive.

25. The *good* of the people is our first consideration.

26. I shall not go *if* it rains.

27. What is the use of saying *if?*

28. I *like* to see her just *like* this, for in *like* mood I do not know her *like.*

29. *Little* drops of water make the mighty ocean.

30. I can do *little* of the work until the typewriter is repaired.

31. Do not *belittle* your work.

32. She studies too *little.*

Exercise 64

Each of the following may be used as different parts of speech. Write sentences illustrating as many uses as possible for each word.

sound	paper	dress	ring
light	shoe	box	dawn
ride	long	ink	curb
iron	warm	walk	use
hear	cold	rule	cement

Exercise 65

Tell which of the words in italic are adjectives and which are adverbs. Remember that an adjective goes with a noun or pronoun; an adverb with another adverb, an adjective, or a verb, and usually answers the question *how? when? where? why? how much?* or *how long?*

1. You are walking too *fast.*
2. Send perishable articles by *fast* freight.
3. He has been a *well* man since he has stopped working indoors.
4. He writes very *well.*
5. The fire is *bright.*
6. It burns *brightly.*
7. That is a *very poor* reason.
8. The berries look *good,* but they taste *sour.*
9. They are not *good* berries.
10. The sun shone *brilliant* above us. (Compare with *brilliantly.*)
11. The bookkeeper looks *angry.*
12. He looked at us *angrily.*
13. The flowers are *sweet.*
14. They smell *sweet.* (May we say, *The flowers smell sweetly?*)
15. Act *frankly*, speak *gently.*
16. Let your actions be *frank*, your speech *gentle.*
17. Laborers complain that they have to work *too hard.*

Exercise 66

Change the following adjectives to adverbs. In each case use both parts of speech in sentences.

cold	sure	polite	courteous
smooth	exact	precise	easy
bitter	bad	extreme	nice
loud	general	honest	glad

Exercise 67

Tell which of the Words in italic are prepositions and which are adverbs. Remember that a preposition begins a phrase. It must be followed by an object.

1. He is the best man *in* the office.

2. John was leaving as I came *in* this evening.

3. He did not have his coat *on.*

4. It was hanging *over* his arm.

5. He stood *on* the top step several minutes, wondering whether he should wear the coat.

6. The handle fell *off* as I took the cup *off* the shelf.

7. The aeroplane flies *over* the city.

8. I am going *over* to the factory.

Write sentences using *above*, *across*, *down*, *up*, *underneath* both as adverbs and as prepositions.

Exercise 68—Prepositional Phrases

Illustrations

Adjective: The opinions *of some people* must be taken with caution.

Adverb: We shall return *within a year.*

Noun: From New York to San Francisco is a long trip.

What part of speech is each of the italicized phrases below? Remember that an adjective modifies a noun; an adverb modifies a verb, an adjective, or an adverb.

1. The waves are rolling in, white *with foam.*

2. A million dollars was invested *in the business.*

3. I will abide *on thy right side* and keep the bridge *with thee.*

4. *In summer* milk soon turns sour.

5. I have come *for help.*

6. The people *on the bridge* cheered *for hours.*

7. He threw up his hat *for joy*.

8. *On the table before them* stood a deer roasted whole.

9. We shall stay here *until spring*.

10. We came *in sight of the king's palace*.

11. We drove *to the factory* today *with the superintendent*.

12. He works *from sunrise to sunset*.

Exercise 69

The phrase introduced by a preposition is the most common. A list of prepositions follows. They should be learned.

about	before	except	toward
above	behind	for	under
aboard	below	from	underneath
across	beneath	in	until
after	beside	into	up
against	between	of	upon
along	betwixt	on	with
amid	beyond	over	within
amidst	but (except)	past	without
among	by	through	to the extent of
around	concerning	throughout	from under
athwart	down	till	according to
at	during	to	except for

Write three sentences containing prepositional *adjective* phrases.

Prepositional *adverbial* phrases may express the following ideas:

Time, telling *when* something happened.
Place, telling *where* something happened.
Manner, telling *how* something happened.
Means, telling *how* something happened.
Cause or purpose, telling *why* something happened.
Degree, telling *how long* something lasted; *how far* it went; *how much* it cost, etc.

Agent, telling *by whom* it was done.
Accompaniment, telling *with whom* it was done.

Write a sentence containing a prepositional phrase telling:

1. when	6. how far
2. where	7. how much
3. why	8. by whom
4. in what way	9. with whom
5. how long	10. by what means

Exercise 70

Name all the prepositional phrases in Exercise 179, explaining whether they are adjective or adverbial.

Exercise 71—The Clause

A *subordinate clause*, like a phrase, is a group of words used as a part of speech, the chief difference being that a clause must have a subject and a predicate. Clauses are introduced

1. By *relative pronouns:*

who, whose, whom, which, what, that

2. By *subordinate conjunctions:*

when	because	than	unless
where	since	provided	till
while	if	whereas	until
as	as soon as	wherever	before
as if	as long as	whether	after
though	in order that	why	for
although	lest	that	whenever

Illustrations

ADJECTIVE: A lamp that *smokes* is a torture to a student.

A *smoking* lamp

ADVERB: *When she was good* / *Sometimes* — she was very, very good.
When she was bad / *Sometimes* — she was horrid.

Does the clause or the simple adverb give the more definite idea?

NOUN: I know *where he lives.* / *the house.*

Write three sentences illustrating adjective clauses, three illustrating adverbial clauses, and three illustrating noun clauses.

Exercise 72

Name all the clauses in Exercises 179, 185, and 186. Explain the use of each.

Exercise 73

Write sentences using each of the following words to introduce a phrase, and to introduce a clause.

1. after
2. before
3. for
4. since
5. until

Remember that just as a preposition must be followed by an *object* to form a phrase, a conjunction must be followed by a *subject* to form a clause.

Illustration

I have not seen him *since* *Christmas.*—OBJECT. / *he* went away.—SUBJECT.

Exercise 74

Name the complete subject in the following. Then name the simple subject, explaining by what elements—words, phrases, or clauses—it is modified.

Name the complete predicate. Then name the simple predicate, explaining by what elements the verb is modified.

1. Modern business cannot be carried on by old-fashioned methods.

2. When a man engages in business, he buys or sells.

3. The great routes of trade have changed from time to time.

4. Your order will be filled within a few days.

5. Both blanks were properly filled out at the time.

6. Means of travel have developed from the slowly moving caravan to the palatial railway coach.

7. Commerce originated when one human being demanded something which had to be supplied by some one else.

8. The latest American and European styles will be displayed in our new millinery department, which will be formally opened on the first of March.

9. The prosperity of nations rests very largely on the six inches of soil between the surface and the subsoil of the territory.

10. One of the greatest losses to the Ohio farm lands in the floods of 1913 came about because the water took off the top soil from the hillside and valleys and carried the vegetable material with it.

11. The conserving of the top soil is one of the greatest problems in national prosperity.

12. We trust that shipment about September 8 will be satisfactory to you, as it is the best that we can do under the circumstances.

CHAPTER VI

THE NOUN AND THE PRONOUN

FOR the plural of nouns see Chapter III.

The classes to which nouns belong are distinguished as follows:

A *common* noun is the name given to an object to denote the class to which it belongs; as, *book*, *man*.

A *proper* noun is the name given to a particular object to distinguish it from others of the same class; as, *Mary*, *Republicans*, *England*. Proper nouns should always be capitalized.

A *collective* noun is a name which in the singular denotes a collection. It is usually plural in idea but singular in use; as, *congregation*, *crowd*.

An *abstract* noun is the name denoting a quality of an object; as, *power*, *purity*, *strength*.

A *verbal* noun is the name of an action. As its name suggests, it is made from a verb; as, *Sweeping* is good exercise.

Exercise 75

In the following sentences supply necessary capital letters. Explain why the same word in one expression needs a capital and in another does not.

1. I have just taken out an endowment policy in the northwestern mutual life insurance company.

2. There are many mutual life insurance companies in the country.

3. His refusing the terms was practically a declaration of independence.

4. On the fourth of July we celebrate the signing of the declaration of independence, the first step in the revolutionary war.

5. Mexico has had many revolutionary wars.

6. And king Arthur said, "The king who fights his people fights himself."

7. When does the bank close?

8. I have an account with the first national bank.

9. This is the first national bank that was ever established in this country.

Explain to which class each noun in the foregoing sentences belongs. Be particularly careful to distinguish between common and proper nouns.

Exercise 76—Pronouns

The different classes of pronouns are distinguished as follows:

The *personal* pronoun is used in place of the name of a person or thing. The pronoun of the *first* person indicates the speaker, the pronoun of the *second* person indicates the person spoken to, and the pronoun of the *third* person indicates the person spoken of. They are declined as follows:

First person

	Singular	*Plural*
Nom.	I	we
Poss.	my, mine	our, ours
Obj.	me	us

Second person

Nom.	you (thou)	you (ye)
Poss.	your, yours (thy, thine)	your, yours
Obj.	you (thee)	you

In modern usage *you* is used for both the singular and the plural, but the verb that goes with *you* is always plural.

Third person

	Singular			*Plural*
	Masc.	*Fem.*	*Neut.*	
Nom.	he	she	it	they
Poss.	his	her, hers	its	their, theirs
Obj.	him	her	it	them

NOTE.—The forms *mine, thine, yours, hers, ours, theirs*, and sometimes *his* are possessive case in form, but nominative or objective case in use. That pencil is *mine* really means, That pencil is *my* pencil. *Mine* is used as a substitute for a possessive pronoun and the noun it modifies.

The personal pronouns compounded with *self* are of two kinds:

1. *Emphatic* pronouns; as,

The buyer *himself* told me.

2. *Reflexive* pronouns, referring back to the subject and at the same time being in the objective case; as,

John slipped and hurt *himself.*

The *relative* pronoun is so called because it relates or refers to another word, called its antecedent, to which it joins the clause that it introduces. The relative pronouns are *who, which, what, that;* and the compound relatives are *whoever, whosoever, whichever, whichsoever, whatever, whatsoever.*

They are declined as follows:

Singular and Plural

Nom.	who	which	whoever	whosoever
Poss.	whose	of which	whosever	whosesoever
Obj.	whom	which	whomever	whomsoever

That, what, whichever, whichsoever, whatever, and *whatsoever* are not declined. They have the same form in the nominative and objective cases, and are not used in the possessive case.

What is peculiar in that it never has an antecedent expressed, but itself stands for both antecedent and relative. It is called the *double relative.* Compare the following:

I did not hear *the words that* he said.

I did not hear *that which* he said.

I did not hear *what* he said.

That is called the restrictive relative, because it limits or restricts its antecedent to the meaning expressed in the clause introduced by *that.* A restrictive clause is one, therefore, that is needed to make the meaning of the sentence clear. Compare the following:

Non-restrictive: John Brown, *who* has no disease, needs no physician.

Restrictive: He *that* hath no disease needs no physician.

Notice that a restrictive, or necessary, clause is not separated from the rest of the sentence by commas.

Who and *which* are sometimes used with restrictive force; as,

1. Those *who* have finished their work may leave. (Not everybody.)

2. Have you read the book *which* he recommended? (He recommended but one.)

Interrogative pronouns are used in asking questions. They are *who*, *which*, *what*. *Who* refers to persons; *which* refers to persons or things, and is used to distinguish one object from another; *what* refers to things. They are declined as follows:

Singular and Plural

Nom.	who	which	what
Poss.	whose	(of which)	(of what)
Obj.	whom	which	what

The interrogative pronouns *which* and *what* are frequently used as adjectives. In this case they are called *pronominal adjectives*. Compare:

Pronoun: *Which* of these hats do you prefer?

Adjective: *Which* hat do you prefer?

The *demonstrative* pronouns are *this* and *that* with their plurals *these* and *those*. They are always used to point out, or demonstrate, the noun to which they refer. *This* and *these* are used for objects near at hand, or recently named; *that* and *those* are used for objects far away, or not recently named.

The demonstrative pronouns are frequently used as adjectives; as,

Pronoun: *That* is my book.

Adjective: *That* book is mine.

Indefinite pronouns refer to objects or persons, but do not define or limit them. The indefinite pronouns are *each*, *every*, *either*, *neither*, *one*, *none*, *other*, *another*, *few*, *all*, *many*, *several*, *some*, *each other*, *one another*, and the compounds *any one*, *some one*, *every one*, *something*, *nothing*. Indefinite pronouns are frequently used as adjectives. *Each*, *every*, *either*, *one*, *another*, *any one*, *some one*, *every one*, whether they are used as pronouns or as adjectives, are singular in number. If another pronoun is used to refer to one of them, it must be in the singular number.

Exercise 77—Classes of Pronouns

In the following sentences, explain which pronouns represent the person speaking, which represent the person spoken to, and which represent the person spoken of. Tell which pronouns ask questions; which are used as adjectives; which are used to connect subordinate clauses to the word for which they stand. If the antecedent is expressed, point it out.

1. Who is talking?

2. The man who is speaking is the head of the credit department.

3. If you are going, get ready.

4. Which is the better piece of cloth?

5. This is the better piece of cloth.

6. The one who wishes to succeed must exercise great care in his work.

7. He that would succeed must work.

8. Many men fail because of laziness.

9. What did you say?

10. Can you guess whom I saw?

11. He himself told us.

12. A cousin of ours is coming to town.

13. The man whose life is above criticism need fear no one.

14. Whoever lives the truth need fear no criticism.

15. I wish you would remove those files.

16. Ink that is thick makes illegible writing.

17. What paper should I destroy?

18. I cannot understand what any one is saying.

19. This is not my umbrella. It is yours.

20. No friend of his would talk in that way.

21. This is no book of theirs; it belongs to us.

22. Whatsoever he saith unto you, do it.

23. I shall ask whomever I see.

24. Each of us has his work assigned.

25. Every boy has his work assigned.

Exercise 78

In the following sentences *he*, *his*, *they*, *their*, *them*, *it*, or *its* should be inserted. Give the reason for your choice.

1. No man is allowed to leave —— desk untidy.

2. Every one must put —— tools away before leaving the shop.

3. Every office worker is required to be in —— place at eight-thirty every morning.

4. In my business a person must learn to make up —— mind quickly.

5. It was cold this morning. Every one wore —— wraps.

6. Every clerk must do —— own work.

7. If an employee has ideas for the improvement of the business, —— is requested to report —— suggestions to the superintendent.

8. The superintendent is anxious to have every workman feel that —— (has, have) a definite place in the organization, and that if —— (does not, don't) do —— work, the business will suffer.

9. No goods will be accepted unless —— (are, is) in good condition.

10. Every newspaper is anxious to increase —— classified advertising.

11. No one cares to see —— friends frown.

12. Every one must agree that —— (has, have) —— faults.

13. Not one of the banks had —— deposits decreased.

14. Will any one let me take —— umbrella?

15. Every one says that —— had a delightful evening.

16. Who was it said I had —— book?

17. Does each state pay over a part of —— taxes to the federal government?

18. Every one will find in the current publications a wealth of information applicable to —— specific needs, much of which —— will wish to file for easy reference, no matter in what department of the world's work —— interest centers.

19. If any one could tell beforehand when —— opportunities would arrive, —— might be ready to grasp each as —— came.

20. If every one here would follow the directions that —— (has, have) received, —— would make fewer mistakes in shipments.

21. Any one who wishes may give —— opinion.

22. No one need expect to leave before —— work is finished.

23. Every one in the office took —— vacation early this year except me.

24. Each of the twenty banks sent —— representative to the meeting.

25. On applying for a position, each man is given a blank that —— must fill out carefully, making —— answers as definite as possible.

Some of the following are right, and some are wrong. Correct those that are wrong, explaining why they are wrong.

1. Neither one of them know what they are expected to do.

2. Applicant after applicant handed in their names.

3. If any one has a complaint to make, he should report it in writing to the superintendent.

4. Have either of the stenographers finished their letters?

5. I wish everybody would do their own work and let me do mine.

6. Each man did his work faithfully.

7. Has neither the carpenter nor the plumber yet brought his tools?

8. Every one of the clerks must hand their report to the head bookkeeper before five o'clock.

9. One of them must have neglected to hand in his report.

10. Man after man yesterday promised me that they'd be on hand to work this morning, and not one of them showed themselves.

Exercise 79

In the following exercise, tell which of the italicized pronouns introduce restrictive, and which introduce non-restrictive clauses:

1. This is the best bargain *that* we have ever offered.

2. This is Mr. Burton, *whose* work I recommended to you.

3. The city *that* I enjoyed most was Quebec.

4. I enjoyed walking on the old wall *that* still surrounds the town.

5. The club to *which* I belong will hold a meeting next week.

6. The club *that* I belong to will hold a meeting next Monday.

7. All those *whose* daily work showed an improvement were given an increase in salary.

8. The horse *that* ran away belonged to my partner.

9. The greatest man is he *who* feels himself the least.

10. An old story tells us that when Caesar, *who* was a great Roman emperor, returned from a conquest *which* has ever since been famous, he brought back to Rome a formula *that* has revolutionized the world. It was a formula for making soap, and was considered one of the greatest treasures *that* was captured during the campaign. Caesar immediately saw the value *that* it would have in the eyes of the world, and he forced the soap-makers to reveal their secret.

11. The garrison is a handful of invalid soldiers, *whose* principal duty is to guard some of the outer towers.

12. This is the gentleman *whom* we met in Boston.

13. Mr. Carter, *who* was a member of our Boston firm, will take charge of our city sales.

14. We honestly believe that our latest Style Book, *which* goes with this letter, offers you more for every dollar *that* you spend than you can get elsewhere.

Exercise 80—Case

Case is that modification of a noun or a pronoun which denotes its relation to other words in the sentence. There are three cases: the *nominative*, the *objective*, and the *possessive*. Although nouns are used in all three cases, no change of form occurs except in the possessive case.

The *nominative* case is used in the following ways:

1. The principal use of the nominative case is as *subject* of the sentence; as,

Noun: The *business* is prosperous.

Pronoun: *It* has been established for five years.

2. Sometimes a noun or pronoun is used to complete the meaning of such verbs as *be*, *become*, *seem*, *appear*, *taste*, *feel*. Such a noun is in the nominative case, and is called a *predicate nominative*, or a *subjective complement;* as,

Noun: Mr. Brown is the *manager*.

He seems a *gentleman*.

Pronoun: I think it is *she*.

3. A noun in *apposition* with another noun in the nominative case is also in the nominative case; as,

Mr. Brown, *the manager*, is very capable.

The man to whom you should apply is Mr. Brown, *the manager.*

4. Sometimes a noun or a pronoun is used in direct address or in an exclamation, without having any grammatical relation to the rest of the sentence. It is then said to be *nominative independent;* as,

Mr. Brown, a gentleman wishes to speak to you.

A *strike!* Why are they declaring a strike?

You! I thought you were in South America.

5. Sometimes a noun or pronoun is used with a participle to express an adverbial relation. Such a noun is in the nominative case, and is called *nominative absolute*, because it has no grammatical relation to any other part of the sentence; as,

Mr. Brown having gone, we told the gentleman to see Mr. Jones.

He being the guide, we asked no questions.

It is much better to use a clause to express such an idea; as,

As Mr. Brown had gone, we told the gentleman to see Mr. Jones.

Write a sentence containing a noun and one containing a pronoun in each of the following uses of the nominative case:

1. Subject.
2. Predicate Nominative.

Write a sentence containing a noun used

1. In direct address.
2. In exclamation.
3. In apposition with another noun in the nominative case.

Exercise 81—The Objective Case

A noun or a pronoun may be used in the objective case in the following ways:

1. Direct object of a transitive verb; as,

I have a good *position.*
Do you know *him?*

2. Object of a preposition; as,

I have just returned from the *library*.
Bring the book to *me*.

3. Indirect object of such verbs as *ask*, *give*, *teach*, showing the person for whom or to whom the action is done; as,

She brought *her mother* some flowers.
I gave *her* singing lessons.

4. A noun as *second object* after verbs of *making*, *choosing*, *calling*, *electing;* as,

They chose John *secretary*.

5. A noun in *apposition* with another objective; as,

Send your report to the secretary, *John Wilson*.

6. Adverbial modifier; as,

We are going *home*.

Write a sentence containing a noun and one containing a pronoun in each of the following uses of the objective case:

1. Direct object of a transitive verb.
2. Indirect object.
3. Object of a preposition.

Write a sentence containing a noun used as

1. Adverbial objective.
2. Second object.
3. Appositive of another noun in the objective case.

Exercise 82—The Possessive Case

To form the possessive case of nouns add an *apostrophe* and *s* to all singular nouns, and to all plural nouns that do not end in *s;* if a plural *noun* ends in *s* add only an apostrophe; as, *child's*, *children's*, *boys'*.

Exception.—When, in long words, the additional *s* in the singular would cause a disagreeable sound, some writers use only the apostrophe; as,

We awaited the *princess's* decision.
We awaited the *princess'* decision.

It is often better in such cases to use a phrase; as,

We awaited the decision *of the princess*.

Thus, an *of* phrase may be used instead of the possessive case. In speaking of an inanimate object one should use it instead of the apostrophe and *s;* as, *the top of the mountain*. However, we use such expressions as *last year's prices*.

When, as in the name of a firm, two or more nouns are taken together with the idea of common possession, the sign of the possessive is added to the last noun only. If separate possession is implied, the sign of the possessive is added to each noun; as,

Have you seen *Wilson & King's* new building?
This is *Mary and Helen's* room.
Is this *Mary's or Helen's* coat?

A noun or pronoun is in the possessive case before a verbal noun; as,

I prefer to have *John's* studying done before dinner.
I prefer to have *his* studying done before dinner.

Write sentences expressing relation between the words in the following pairs. Use one of them in the possessive case or use an *of* phrase, whichever seems better.

the manager, desk	city, harbor
desk, top drawer	proprietor, private office
book, cover	typewriter, keys
city, mayor	ledger, first page

Bring to class five incorrect possessive phrases taken from advertisements. Explain and correct the mistakes.

Exercise 83

Which of the italicized words would you use? Why?

1. Have you heard of *Mr. Bennett, Mr. Bennett's* being appointed chairman of the meeting?

2. It will probably delay *him, his* coming here.

3. I don't understand *him, his* refusing to accept the position.

4. We have heard a great deal of *him, his* making a success of photography.

5. The man's industry has resulted in *him, his* gaining fame.

6. Will you sign this permit for *us, our* visiting the factory?

7. What do you say to *us, our* making some candy?

8. I am very sorry that *me*, *my* interrupting you yesterday delayed your work.

9. The machine is in excellent condition. There is no reason for *it*, *its* needing any repair.

10. *Everybody*, *everybody's* being on time is absolutely necessary.

Exercise 84

Each of the following sentences is incorrect because the sign of the possessive case has been omitted. Insert the apostrophe or the apostrophe and *s*, wherever either is needed.

1. There is a new boys school in our town.

2. James brother John is our new bookkeeper.

3. For entrance to this course three years work in mathematics and one years work in German are required.

4. This new building will be occupied by J. M. Hopkins mail order department.

5. The superintendents inspection was thorough.

6. The trouble will be in John agreeing to the proposition.

7. All applications for help should be made to the Womens Committees.

8. The employees rest rooms are on the sunny side of the building.

9. Our fifteen years experience in selling bonds has convinced us that investments paying a low rate of interest are the safest.

10. In to-days mail I received a very large order from Graham & Moore's successors.

11. Jones Brothers new store is on the corner of Madison Street.

12. Last month sales show an increase of two thousand dollars.

13. Everybodys business is nobodys business.

14. It is when to-morrows burden is added to the burden of to-day that the weight is more than a man can bear.

15. The present governor was the peoples choice.

16. I prefer Tennysons poems to Longfellows.

17. I have read both Longfellow and Tennysons poems.

18. I bought the book at Barlow and Companys new store.

19. We are going to insist on Mary taking a long vacation this year.

20. I have had the pleasure of staying at both your friends houses.

Exercise 85—The Apostrophe

Some of the following sentences are right, and some are wrong. Correct those that are wrong, explaining why they are wrong.

1. The man who's coming this way is Mr. Burton.

2. Whose coat is that?

3. The man who's place you are taking has been with this firm for twenty years.

4. The next one whose to give a report is the treasurer.

5. The next one whose report we must hear is the treasurer.

6. Don't you think it's too early to start?

7. He is a ladies tailor.

8. Remember your to let us know at once who's elected.

9. Its too late now to change its wording.

10. Mr. Jones' house is being repaired.

11. The Joneses' house is being repaired.

12. There coming as fast as their horse will bring them.

13. I think you're typewriter needs cleaning.

14. Your coming too, are'nt you?

15. Every business has it's problems.

16. The Bon Ton has a big sale in mens' and womens' coat's.

17. Why, it's March! No wonder their having a sale.

18. We shall give you a special discount if you will send your dealer's name.

19. Most of the dealer's advertise very little.

20. It's just a year ago since we received your last order.

21. Its not willingness we lack; it's time.

22. If you use our safety device, you may leave you're window open with security, and you will arise refreshed, ready for a big days work.

23. Lets take our vacation when they take their's.

24. I think we shall have to take our's in August. Two of us must stay during July, for the work will not do it's self, you know.

25. In any explanation it should be the writers purpose to so describe his good's that the reader will desire them. A good salesman never shows a necktie in a box. He takes it out and with a deft twist forms it's length into a four-in-hand over his finger. The customer then sees not only the scarf, it's color and its weave, but he sees it in it's relation to himself, as it will look when it's tied.

Exercise 86

Supply *who* or *whom:*

1. —— did you take me for?

2. The shipping clerk, —— I consider responsible for the mistake, must go.

3. The shipping clerk, —— I feel certain is responsible for the mistake, must go.

4. —— is it?

5. —— shall I say called?

6. —— do you wish to see?

7. —— did you say was elected?

8. He is the one —— every one thought should be elected.

9. Choose the one —— you think will give the best service.

10. Choose the one —— you think you can trust.

11. She asked me —— did it.

12. —— do you think is the best salesman in the firm?

13. —— do you regard as the best salesman in the firm?

14. —— was that —— you were talking to?

15. He is the one —— I was speaking about.

16. —— do we play next week?

17. He is a workman —— can be trusted.

18. He is a workman upon —— you can depend.

19. This letter comes from Robert, —— we all know very well.

20. This letter comes from Robert, —— we all know writes good letters.

21. —— do you consider to be most capable? [The subject of the infinitive *to be* must be in the objective case.]

22. This booklet was written by the man —— Mr. Bardon considers [to be] the best correspondent in our office.

23. He is the one —— every one believes to be worthy of the highest honors.

24. The critic —— every one thought gave the most truthful account of the performance is a man of great culture.

Supply *whoever* or *whomever*:

1. Give the book to —— needs it.

2. Give it to —— you think best.

3. —— I send can be trusted.

4. Send me —— is there.

5. Send me —— you find there.

6. —— reaches the line first will receive the cup.

7. The cup will be given to —— reaches the lines first.

8. In the country lane he spoke to —— he met.

9. —— you choose may compete for the prize.

10. —— you bring is welcome.

Exercise 87

Read the following sentences, using one of the forms in italic. Be able to give a reason for your choice.

1. *He—him* and *I—me* are going camping next summer.

2. It is a question that refers to you and *I—me.*

3. It is a question between you and *I—me.*

4. I am sure that it was *she—her.*

5. I am sure that we saw you and *he—him.*

6. *We—us* boys are going camping.

7. Will you go camping with *we—us* boys?

8. *They—them* and their cousins are going camping.

9. We bought a large piece of ground so that my brother and *I—me* could have a garden.

10. It was bought for *he—him* and *I—me.*

11. Is that *he—him* entering the gate? Yes, that is *he—him.*

12. *Who—whom* should I meet at the station but old Mr. McGregor, *who—whom* I had not seen for several years.

13. If I were *he—him*, I should start at once.

14. There is no need of *him—his* staying any longer.

15. He does not work so rapidly as *I—me.*

16. Mary and *she—her* work in the same office.

17. There is no danger of *me—my* failing.

18. Please let *she—her* and *I—me* do the work together.

19. There is no use of *us—our* trying any more.

20. *Us—our* giving up now will spoil everything.

21. My mother objected to *me—my* going.

22. Why did you insist upon *us—our* coming to-day?

23. I hardly think it is *he—him who—whom* is to blame.

24. I should like to be *she—her.*

25. *They—them* that do wrong shall be punished.

26. *They—them* that do wrong I shall punish.

27. *He—him* that is your friend you can call upon in your hour of need.

28. *He—him* that is your friend will respond to your call.

29. The manager praised both the bookkeepers and *we—us* girls.

30. Was it you who called? Yes, it was *I—me.*

31. It surely was not *I—me* whom you saw.

32. He reproved us both but *I—me* more than *she—her.*

33. Are you sure it's *I—me* whom he appointed?

34. If it's really *I—me* who was appointed, I'm sure I should have been notified.

35. I'm sure it can't be *I—me.*

Exercise 88—*Same* as a Pronoun

One of the worst constructions found in business letters of today is the use of *same* as a pronoun. The word may be an adjective or a noun but never a pronoun.

Wrong: Will you please fill out the enclosed blank and return *same* as soon as possible?

Right: Will you please fill out the enclosed blank and return *it* as soon as possible?

In each of the following sentences substitute a noun or a pronoun for *same:*

1. Will you not send us a check by Friday so that we may use same for our pay roll on Saturday?

2. Do you wish to bid for our cinder output this year? We have a sample car that we shall be glad to have you inspect if you think you will have any use for same.

3. We have no use for the material this year, but we thank you for giving us an opportunity to bid for same.

4. If you are dissatisfied with the machine, return same at our expense.

5. You state that you sent us an order on June 10, but we cannot find any trace of same.

6. We are in the market for two dozen Standard clothes wringers, and we should be glad to receive your lowest price on same.

7. We have given you credit for this amount and desire to thank you for your promptness in sending same.

8. We have your letter of November 6 and thank you for same.

9. If you think you can use this type of machine, we shall be glad to send you same on ten days' trial.

10. We have decided to use your machine if you will give us a satisfactory guarantee as to strength, efficiency, and freedom from leaks. As soon as possible let us hear from you in regard to same.

Exercise 89—Nouns and Pronouns Incorrectly Used

Wrong	*Right*
1. We saw *lots* of curious things.	We saw *a number* of curious things.

2. Do you know that *party?*	Do you know that *man?*
3. I stayed at home the *balance* of the day.	I stayed at home the *rest* of the day.
4. What *business* have you to go?	What *right* have you to go?
5. The dress will be done in a *couple* of days.	The dress will be done in a *few* days.
6. I'll walk a *piece* with you.	I'll walk a *short distance* with you.
7. Did you get a *raise* in pay?	Did you get an *increase* in pay?
8. I'll send you a *postal.*	I'll send you a *postal card.*
9. Christmas is still a long *ways* off.	Christmas is still a long *way* off.
10. What *line* of business are you in now?	What *kind* of business are you in now?
11. If you expect to open a grocery, let me give you a little advice *along that line.*	If you expect to open a grocery, let me give you a little advice *on the subject.*
12. Have you anything new in the neckwear *line?*	Have you any new neckwear?
13. I have a *date* with the dentist.	I have an *appointment* with the dentist.
14. Have you a *date* for this evening?	Have you an *engagement* for this evening?
15. He always does his work in good *shape.*	He always does his work *well.*
16. That is a good *write-up* on the tariff.	That is a good *article* on the tariff.
17. *Yourself* and friends are invited.	*You* and your friends are invited.
18. Don't *they* have street cars in your town?	Are there no street cars in your town?
19. *It* said in this morning's paper that the traffic men would strike.	This morning's paper said that the traffic men would strike.
20. The book *what* he advised is not fiction.	The book *that* he advised is not fiction.

CHAPTER VII

THE ADJECTIVE AND THE ADVERB

AS a rule, adverbs present more difficulty than do adjectives. Careless pupils frequently use an adjective when an adverb is necessary; as,

Wrong: He solved the problem very *quick*.

Right: He solved the problem very *quickly*.

Wrong: This is *real* good candy.

Right: This is *really* (or *very*) good candy.

Until the habit of correct usage is formed, every sentence must be watched. When a word modifies a verb, an adjective, or an adverb, another adverb must be used, and an adjective may not correctly be substituted. As a rule, adverbs express the following ideas:

Time: We arrived *early*.

Place: We have been *here* since January.

Manner: He walked *steadily* onward.

Cause: *Why* did you refuse the offer?

Degree: I am *very much* surprised.

Number: I did it *once* not *twice*.

Assertion: }
Denial: } I do *not* agree.

Adverb modifying a verb: See how *slowly* the man walks!

Adverb modifying an adjective: The weather has been *extremely* warm.

Adverb modifying an adverb: He dictates *very* rapidly.

It must be remembered, however, that verbs of the senses—*taste*, *feel*, *look*, *smell*, *sound*, and the like—are sometimes almost equal in meaning to the verb *be*. In that case, they are followed by adjectives and not by adverbs; as,

Adjective: He looked *angry*.

Adverb: He looked *angrily* at us.

Exercise 90

Name the adjectives in the following selection, explaining with what noun each belongs.

Name the adverbs, explaining what part of speech each modifies.

Since 1904 the number of live cattle exported from this country has been steadily growing smaller. Exports of dressed beef have also shrunk to such insignificant proportions that the United States is no longer an important factor in the foreign markets for beef. Often has it been said that the competition of cheap Argentine beef has deprived us of foreign markets. It would be more nearly true to say that foreigners buy the inferior article only because we cannot supply them with all they want of the best grade. Take, for instance, the Englishman's willingness to pay considerably more for American corn-fed beef than for Argentine.

The raising of cattle is important, also, from the standpoint of the leather business. Obviously, with a 21 per cent increase in population in each decade, many more shoes are necessary. Automobile and other industries are making constantly increasing demands for leather. Shoes cannot become cheaper in the face of increased demand and diminished supply. Too much depends upon the cattle industry for us to allow it to wane.

Exercise 91

Which of the italicized words should you use in the following, and why?

1. Why do you walk so *slow—slowly?*

2. Speak *louder—more loudly.*

3. I cannot explain why he spoke so *gentle—gently.*

4. The automobile was going very *swift—swiftly.*

5. The well has been dug very *deep—deeply.*

6. He is not *near—nearly* so tall as you are.

7. Are you cutting that *even—evenly?*

8. She does pen and ink sketches *beautiful—beautifully.*

9. Why can't I grow *quicker—more quickly?*

10. I feel *bad—badly* this morning.

11. Can you do all I have asked? *Easy—easily.*

12. She does her work *good—well.*

13. She does her work *fine—finely.*

14. I am *real—very much* surprised to see you.

15. He became *real—very* angry.

16. I'm afraid it's not *near—nearly* big enough.

17. She works twice as *quick—quickly* as you do.

18. He *sure—surely* is a good speaker. He seems *sure—surely* of himself.

19. Are you going? *Sure—surely?*

20. He says he is *near—nearly* starved.

21. He worked *steady—steadily* all morning. The others did not work *near—nearly* so hard.

22. I am speaking as *serious—seriously* as I can.

23. The orange tastes *bitter—bitterly.*

24. Don't you think he has been acting *queer—queerly?*

25. The coat is finished *nice—nicely.*

Exercise 92

Explain the proper position of the italicized adverbs in the following sentences. Remember that an adverb must stand as closely as possible to the word that it modifies, but remember also that an infinitive, although made up of two parts, is *one* word and should not be split by an adverb.

1. I *merely* want the Milwaukee list of customers.

2. You *almost* write like her.

3. Your writing is like hers *almost.*

4. I can *not* find one of the papers I had on the desk.

5. He told me to *carefully* add the figures in the column.

6. I expect to *quickly* finish my dictation.

7. I don't *even* understand the first problem in the lesson.

8. Don't say you don't *ever* expect to go to school again.

9. All the statements are *not* on my desk.

10. He promised to *quickly* settle the matter.

11. I wish you to *clearly* understand the situation.

12. I *only* have two more items to enter.

13. I *only* expect to take a short vacation this year.

14. He *only* spoke of two causes of the loss in trade.

15. I *only* decided to take the Western instead of the Eastern trip at the last moment.

Exercise 93—Comparison

Adjectives are compared so as to express different degrees of quality. There are three degrees of comparison, the *positive*, the *comparative*, and the *superlative*. When the object modified or described by the adjective is not compared with another, the first or *positive* degree is used. When two objects are compared, the second or *comparative* degree is used to denote more or less of the quality expressed by the adjective. When several objects are compared, the *superlative* degree of the adjective is used to express the highest or the lowest possible degree of the adjective.

The usual method of comparing an adjective is to add *er* to the positive to form the comparative, and *est* to form the superlative. Frequently, however, especially for an adjective of two or more syllables, the comparative is formed by prefixing *more* or *less* to the positive, and the superlative by prefixing *most* or *least*. Besides the adjectives in these two classes there are some which do not follow any regular method and must, therefore, be watched a little more closely.

The following table illustrates the different methods of comparison:

Positive	*Comparative*	*Superlative*
bright	brighter	brightest
dangerous	more dangerous	most dangerous
beautiful	more beautiful	most beautiful
good	better	best
bad	worse	worst
ill	worse	worst

Be careful to avoid using a double sign for the comparative degree; as,

Wrong: This writing is *more neater* than yours.

Some adverbs are also compared; as,

Positive	*Comparative*	*Superlative*
well	better	best
quickly	more quickly	most quickly

Some adjectives and adverbs cannot be compared because the positive degree in itself expresses a complete or *absolute* meaning; as,

absolute,-ly	eternal	perfect	sufficient
circular	extreme	perpendicular	supreme
continual	faultless	perpetual	unanimous
dead	full	right	unique
decisive	impossible	round	universal
empty	incurable	square	white

Compare those of the following adjectives that may be compared. Explain why some do not admit of comparison.

great	spotless	expensive	wise
tall	dear	parallel	high
desirable	east	old	new
honorable	early	exclusive	blank

Exercise 94

In the following exercise, select the correct one of the two italicized forms. Remember that the comparative degree is used in comparing two objects, the superlative in comparing three or more.

1. I had three pens. I have lost the *better—best* one.

2. I have two clerks. John is the *older—oldest.*

3. Of the two colors, I think the tan is the *more—most* becoming to you.

4. You are the *taller—tallest* of all the boys.

5. Of two professions, choose the *more—most* honorable.

6. He is the *faster—fastest* workman in the shop.

7. Which of your hands is the *cleaner—cleanest?*

8. Which do you like *better—best*, skating or sleighing?

9. Which of your eyes has the *better—best* vision?

10. Of all the shops, she likes Leslie's *better—best.*

11. Which is *more—most* durable, serge or broadcloth?

12. Which tree lives *longer—longest*, the poplar or the elm?

13. Which is the *best—better* policy, honesty or dishonesty?

14. He is the *wittier—wittiest* one in the class.

15. He is the *wittier—wittiest* boy in the class. There is only one boy in the class besides him.

16. Of our twenty salesmen, he is considered *better—best* because he is *quicker—quickest* witted than any other.

17. You should not mention the two men in one breath. The *former—first* is famous and the *latter—last* infamous.

18. Which of you two do you think deserves *more—most* praise?

19. Which of you two deserves *less—least* praise?

20. Which of you two can run the *faster—fastest?*

Exercise 95

Remember that the double negative is wrong; as,

Wrong: I haven't no paper.
Right: I have no paper.

Correct any of the following sentences that contain this mistake:

1. None of them didn't come.

2. I couldn't do the problem neither.

3. This paper isn't very good, I don't think.

4. Couldn't you find no better pen?

5. I didn't choose none of them.

6. I don't see nothing to complain of.

7. He couldn't hardly see across the street.

8. We didn't find the paper nowhere.

9. They can't scarcely believe the report.

10. She couldn't stay with us only a few minutes.

Exercise 96—Fewer, Less

Fewer refers to a smaller number by counting, *less* refers to a smaller quantity by measuring. Insert the correct word:

1. You are making —— mistakes each day.

2. I am having —— difficulty in writing shorthand.

3. There are —— houses on this street than I had thought.

4. The farther inland we went the —— signs of habitation we saw.

5. Each year there is —— opportunity for an uneducated man to rise.

6. Each year there are —— opportunities for the uneducated man to rise.

Most, Almost

Most refers to quantity or number; *almost* means *not quite*. Insert the correct word:

7. —— people enjoy their work.

8. I have —— finished the course in stenography.

9. —— European cities are beautiful.

10. —— all European cities are beautiful.

Real, Very

Real is an adjective meaning *actual; very* is an adverb of degree. Insert the correct word:

11. I'm —— glad to see you.

12. Is your comb —— amber?

13. The men of the Titanic were —— heroes.

14. He is a —— good soloist.

15. She is —— entertaining in conversation; it was a —— pleasure to meet her.

Exercise 97—Adjectives and Adverbs Incorrectly Used

Wrong	*Right*

1. I don't like *those* kind of pens.	I don't like *that* kind of pens.
2. What sort of *a* course are you taking?	What sort of course are you taking?
3. His statements made me *mad.*	His statements made me *angry*.
4. Yours *respectively*.	Yours *respectfully*.

(Consult a dictionary for the correct use of *respectively*)

5. Do you want *in?*	Do you want *to come in?*
6. Go *some place* with me.	Go *somewhere* with me.
7. My father is *some* better.	My father is *somewhat* better.
8. He comes *every once in a while.*	He comes *occasionally*.
9. Did you recognize the girl who drove *past?*	Did you recognize the girl who drove *by?*
10. The two are *both* alike.	The two are alike.
11. He is *liable* to come any minute.	He is *likely* to come at any minute.
12. That ring has a *funny* design.	That ring has an *odd* design.
13. I'd *sooner* stay at home.	I'd *rather* stay at home.
14. Are you *most* ready?	Are you *almost* ready?
15. I'm *kind of* sleepy.	I'm *rather* sleepy.
16. What *size* hat do you wear?	What *sized* hat do you wear?
17. *This here* book is the one I wish.	*This* book is the one I wish.
18. He spoke *angry like.*	He spoke *angrily.*
19. His ideas are *no* good.	His ideas are *worthless* (or *not good*).

20. He *seldom ever* makes a mistake.	He *seldom* (*hardly ever*) makes a mistake.
21. I didn't work *any* last night.	I didn't work *at all* last night.
22. I walked *this* far yesterday.	I walked *as far as this* yesterday.
23. I want to see you *badly*.	I want to see you *very much*.
24. He sells insurance *on the side*.	*In addition to his other business* he sells insurance.
25. Don't talk *out loud*.	Don't talk *aloud*.
26. She is *very* disappointed.	She is *very much* disappointed.

(Before a perfect participle *too* or *very* may not be used without the addition of the adverb *much*)

27. She is a *cute* (or *cunning*) child.	She is a *pretty* child.

(Look up the words *cute* and *cunning* in a dictionary)

28. He was lying face *down* on the grass.	He was lying face *downward* on the grass.

CHAPTER VIII

THE VERB

VERBS may be *transitive* or *intransitive.*

A verb is transitive when it needs an object to complete its meaning; that is, when the action passes over (Latin, *transire*, to pass over) from the subject or doer to the object or receiver; as,

He *hit* the ball.

A verb is intransitive when it needs no object to complete its meaning; as,

The crowd *cheered.*

Some intransitive verbs require a predicate noun or pronoun in the nominative case, or an adjective, to complete their meaning. They are the verbs *be*, *become*, *appear*, *seem*, *feel*, *taste*, *look*, *smell;* as,

Adjective: The berries taste *sour.*

Noun: John is my *brother.*

Pronoun: It is *I.*

Such verbs are sometimes called *copulatives.*

Exercise 98

Tell whether each verb in the following sentences is transitive or intransitive and whether it is followed by a noun or a pronoun in the nominative or the objective case or by a complementary adjective.

1. Primitive people have left traces of very early commercial relations.

2. Explorers visited the Ohio valley and found articles of remote manufacture.

3. Checks and drafts are great conveniences to the business man.

4. The United States Supreme Court made a decision that labor unions are punishable under trust penalties.

5. A labor union is different from a trust.

6. This is the opinion of the labor leader.

7. What is your opinion?

8. The total value of merchandise sent to Latin-America from the United States exceeds that supplied by any other single country.

Write three sentences illustrating transitive verbs.

Write three sentences illustrating intransitive verbs.

Write three sentences illustrating copulative verbs.

Exercise 99—Voice

Voice is that property of the verb that shows whether the subject acts or is acted upon. If the subject acts, the verb is in the *active voice.* If the subject is acted upon, the verb is in the *passive voice.* Every sentence containing a transitive verb must have the following parts:

Agent(doer)	*Action*	*Receiver*
The runaway horse	injured	John.

When the sentence is in the order shown above, the subject is the agent, and the verb expresses the action of the agent. When the sentence is written in this order, the verb is said to be in the *active voice.*

However, without changing the meaning of the sentence, we may change the order of the ideas; thus,

Receiver	*Action*	*Agent*
John	was injured	by the runaway horse.

The receiver of the action has become the subject, and the agent has become part of the predicate, being expressed in the phrase *by the runaway horse.* When the sentence is expressed in this order, the subject receiving or "suffering" the action, the verb is said to be in the *passive voice.* Only transitive verbs, therefore, may be changed to the passive voice.

NOTE.—There are certain intransitive verbs that sometimes have a preposition so closely connected with them that the two are treated almost like a transitive verb, and may be made passive; as,

Active: The audience laughed *at* the speaker.
Passive: The speaker was laughed *at* by the audience.

Write five sentences in the active voice.

Change them to the passive voice.

In the sentences that you have written, is the active form of the verb or the passive form better? Which is more direct in its wording? Which, then, is the better form to use regularly?

Exercise 100—Number and Person

The number of the verb is decided by the number of the subject. If the subject is a singular noun, or a pronoun that stands for a singular noun, it requires a singular verb; if the subject is plural, it requires a plural verb. As a rule, there is no difference between the singular and the plural forms of the verb except in the form for the third person singular; as,

I say	We say
You say	You say
He says	They say

But as the third person of the verb is the one most often used, it must be carefully noted.

The following subjects of verbs are singular and require a singular verb to accompany them:

1. A collective noun that denotes a group of objects acting as one thing; as,

The crowd *is* scattering.

2. A group of words which, like a collective noun, is plural in form but singular in meaning; as,

Thirty dollars *is* what I paid for the ring.

3. A singular noun modified by *every*, *each*, *one*, *no*, *many a;* or the pronouns *each*, *everybody*, *either*, *neither*, and *none* when it means *not one;* as,

Each of us *has* his lesson.
Many an opportunity *has* been wasted.
Everybody *is* here now.

4. Singular[1] nouns or pronouns joined by *or*, *either—or*, *neither—nor;* as,

Either John or his father *is* coming.

5. Two nouns joined by *and*, denoting one person or thing; as,

The bookkeeper and stenographer *is* an expert.

NOTE.—If two persons are meant, the article should be repeated before the second noun.

The following subjects of verbs are plural and require plural verbs:

1. A collective noun denoting plurality; that is, referring to the individuals that compose the group; as,

The class *are* all studious.

2. A compound subject joined by *and*, when the objects joined are different; as,

The door and the window *are* both open.

3. The pronoun *you*, though it may denote only one person; as,

Right: You *were* right.
Wrong: You *was* right.

Exercise 101

In the following sentences, decide which of the italicized forms is correct. Give the reason for your choice.

1. Two dollars *is—are* too much for you to pay.

2. Bread and butter *is—are* what I prefer to eat.

3. Bread and butter *is—are* both sold here.

4. His opinion and mine *is—are* different.

5. The majority of the class *is—are* present.

6. The class *is—are* dismissed.

7. The congregation *is—are* asked to remain a few minutes after the close of the service.

8. The community *is—are* rapidly changing.

9. A few of the books *was—were* given to me.

10. There *was—were* forty people present.

11. The secretary and treasurer *was—were* asked to read *his—their* report.

12. One-third of the office *was—were* late this morning because the cars were not running.

13. He *don't—doesn't* understand what I mean.

14. If the quality and the price *is—are* right, buy.

15. There *come—comes* a crowd of people.

16. The library with its thousands of books *was—were* destroyed by fire.

17. There *don't—doesn't* seem to be much difference between the two.

18. The whole system of filing and indexing *is—are* wrong.

19. Safety as well as success *is—are* at stake.

20. The state of public affairs *calls—call* for quick action.

21. Many a man *has—have* neglected golden opportunities.

22. Many men *has—have* neglected golden opportunities.

23. The committee *has—have* given *its—their* report.

24. Our team *was—were* beaten.

25. One of us surely *is—are* mistaken.

26. Every one *was—were* happy when Tom was elected president.

27. Tom and James *is—are* going skating.

28. Tom with his brother James *is—are* going skating.

29. The only thing I have not prepared for dinner *is—are* the potatoes.

30. Fifty feet of sidewalk *was—were* laid to-day.

31. None of the boys *is—are* studying stenography.

32. Neither Tom nor his brother *is—are* studying stenography.

33. Both Tom and his brother *is—are* stenographers.

34. Every one *is—are* interested in the cost of living.

In the last sentence above substitute one of the following for *every one*, using the correct form of the verb with each:

each of us; everybody; all of us; several people; both of the men; neither of the men; neither Mary nor John; Mary and John; our club; our class; the nation; not only Europe but America; Europe as well as America; the nation as well as several of the larger cities

Exercise 102—Tense

The tense of the verb indicates the time of the action. There are three primary tenses, indicating action in the *present*, the *past*, and the *future*. Each of these tenses has also a *perfect* tense, which, represents the action as being perfect or complete in the present, the past, and the future.

The *present* tense is the simplest form. It denotes that the action takes place now; as,

I write	We write
You write	You write
He writes	They write

To be more exact, we may indicate that the action is continuing in the present time, and then we say,

I am writing	We are writing
You are writing	You are writing
He is writing	They are writing

This is called the *present progressive* tense.

It may be that you wish to be emphatic, and you say,

I do write	We do write
You do write	You do write
He does write	They do write

This is called the *emphatic present* tense.

The *past* tense indicates that the action took place in past time; as,

I wrote	We wrote
You wrote	You wrote
He wrote	They wrote

or, the *past progressive;* as,

I was writing	We were writing

You were writing	You were writing
He was writing	They were writing

or, the *past emphatic;* as,

I did write	We did write
You did write	You did write
He did write	They did write

The emphatic form is used only in the present and the past tenses.

The *future* tense denotes that the action will take place at some future time. It is formed by using *shall* or *will* with the simplest form of the verb; as,

I shall write	We shall write
You will write	You will write
He will write	They will write

The progressive form is not common. It is

I shall be writing	We shall be writing
You will be writing	You will be writing
He will be writing	They will be writing

The three perfect tenses are formed by using the verb *have* with the perfect participle of the verb.

The *present perfect* tense denotes that the action is complete at the present time. It is formed by the present tense of *have* and the perfect participle of the verb; as,

I have written	We have written
You have written	You have written
He has written	They have written

The progressive form is,

I have been writing	We have been writing
You have been writing	You have been writing
He has been writing	They have been writing

The *past perfect* denotes that the action was completed in past time. It is formed by using the past tense of *have* and the perfect participle of the verb; as,

I had written	We had written
You had written	You had written
He had written	They had written

The progressive form is,

I had been writing	We had been writing
You had been writing	You had been writing
He had been writing	They had been writing

The *future perfect* tense denotes that the action will be completed at some future time. It is formed by the future of *have* and the perfect participle of the verb; as,

I shall have written	We shall have written
You will have written	You will have written
He will have written	They will have written

The progressive form is rarely used. It is

I shall have been writing	We shall have been writing
You will have been writing	You will have been writing
He will have been writing	They will have been writing

Giving all forms singular and plural, first, second, and third persons of each tense constitutes the *conjugation* of a verb. Giving one person in each tense constitutes the *synopsis* of the conjugation.

The following is a synopsis of all the tenses of the active voice in the first person singular number of the verb *write:*

ACTIVE VOICE

- TENSE
  - *Primary*
    - *Present*
      - I write (simple form)
      - I am writing (progressive form)
      - I do write (emphatic form)
    - *Past*
      - I wrote (simple)
      - I was writing (progressive)
      - I did write (emphatic)
    - *Future*
      - I shall write (simple)
      - I shall be writing (progressive)
  - *Perfect or Secondary*
    - *Present Perfect*
      - I have written (simple)
      - I have been writing (progressive)
    - *Past Perfect*
      - I had written (simple)
      - I had been writing (progressive)
    - *Future Perfect*
      - I shall have written (simple)
      - I shall have been writing (progressive)

Exercise 103

Conjugate the following in the active voice:

1. Simple past tense of *walk*.
2. Present progressive tense of *walk*.
3. Present perfect of *drive*. (See Exercise 108 for the principal parts.)

4. Present perfect progressive of *drive.*

5. Future progressive of *ride.*

6. Past of *ride.*

7. Present progressive of *ride.*

8. Past emphatic of *ride.*

9. Past perfect of *ride.*

10. Present perfect progressive of *ride.*

Give a synopsis of the progressive tenses of *begin*, using *he* as the subject.

Exercise 104—Shall and Will

The auxiliary verbs used to form the future tenses are *shall* and *will.* The two must be carefully distinguished because they denote different ideas, according to the person with which they are used. The rule is, to express simple future time, use *shall* in the first person, *will* in the second and third persons.

The future tense of the verb *walk* is conjugated as follows:

I shall walk	We shall walk
You will walk	You will walk
He will walk	They will walk

This is the form to use when you expect the action to take place naturally.

On the other hand, instead of letting things take their natural course as they do in the simple future, you may force them to take place. You may, for example, be determined to walk, or determined to make some one else walk. In that case the use is reversed; as,

I will walk	We will walk
You shall walk	You shall walk
He shall walk	They shall walk

This form is used whenever the speaker has authority to bring about the action indicated by the verb.

In questions of the first person always use *shall.* In questions of the second and third persons use the same form that you expect in the answer; as,

Shall you be at home to-morrow? I *shall.*

In the following sentences insert *shall* or *will*, giving the reason for your choice:

1. I —— finish the work by three o'clock, I think.

2. To-morrow he —— feel sorry for this; I vow it.

3. I am sorry, but I —— not be able to finish the work before next week.

4. —— you finish your business course in February or in June? I —— finish in June, I think.

5. —— he finish in February? No, he —— finish in June.

6. The foreman declares he —— not have another chance.

7. He —— see his mistake when it is too late.

8. They —— surely be at the station to meet me.

9. I'm afraid you —— be kicked if you go near that horse.

10. If he doesn't take the examination, he —— fail.

11. I am determined that I —— win.

12. I —— sail probably on the fifteenth.

13. He —— be twenty-one to-morrow.

14. I —— go in spite of him.

15. —— you go by train, do you think?

16. I —— be greatly obliged if you —— send the book at once.

17. I promise you John —— know his lesson to-morrow.

18. —— you be at home this evening?

19. —— the train be on time?

20. —— the store be open this evening?

Conjugate the future and future perfect tenses of the following verbs:

drive	see	go	run	sweep
ride	choose	sing	eat	sell

Exercise 105—Should and Would

Should and *would* are the past tenses of *shall* and *will* and, in general, express the same ideas as do *shall* and *will*, except that *should* sometimes means *ought;* as,

You *should* not speak in that way.

Would, also, sometimes indicates an action that occurs frequently; as,

She *would* often sit at the window all the morning.

The use of *should* and *would* in indirect statements and questions is sometimes puzzling. First of all, decide whether *shall* or *will* would be used in the direct form of the sentence. If the direct form uses *shall*, use *should* in the indirect; if the direct uses *will*, use *would* in the indirect; as,

Direct: The market *will* improve.

Indirect: He said that the market *would* improve.

In conditional clauses (*if*), use *should* for all persons.

Insert *should* or *would.*

1. If I knew his address, I —— send him a telegram.

2. He promised that he —— not make the mistake again. (The direct form would read, I will not ——)

3. I promised that I —— not make the mistake again.

4. You promised that you —— not make the mistake again.

5. Do you think that I —— go?

6. I —— if I were you.

7. I —— think he —— know better than to apply for that position.

8. John said that, no matter what we thought, he —— not go.

9. If you —— decide to accept the offer, let me know at once.

10. I am sorry he did that. He —— not, of course.

11. If I —— see him, I'd let him know.

12. If he —— come during my absence, ask him to wait.

13. I —— think you would be more careful.

14. Let me know if you —— not be able to come.

Exercise 106

Change the italicized verbs to past tense, future, present perfect, past perfect, future perfect. Wherever necessary, add sufficient to make the meaning of the tense clear; as,

Present: The manager *is now* in his office.

Past: The manager *was* in his office *a few minutes ago.*

Future: The manager *will be* in his office *to-morrow at ten o'clock.*

Present Perfect: The manager *has been* in his office *all the morning.* (It is still morning.)

Past Perfect: The manager *had been* in his office *only a few moments when the president arrived.*

Future Perfect: In about five minutes the manager *will have been* in the president's office *exactly three hours.*

1. The cashier *opens* the safe in the morning.

2. The mechanic *earns* good wages.

3. The buyer *leaves* to-night.

4. The bookkeeper *makes* out the statements.

5. The correspondent *writes* the booklets.

6. The advertising manager *approves* the copy.

7. The adding machine *is broken.*

8. The chief clerk *attends* to the incoming mail.

9. The superintendent *visits* the factory every day.

10. The salesman *is selling* five thousand dollars' worth of goods a week.

Exercise 107

The present tense is used to indicate general truths—things true in past time and still true. Omit the incorrect form in the following sentences:

1. What did you say *is—was* the meaning of the term *bona fide?*

2. What *was—is* the name of that book that you enjoyed so much?

3. Didn't you know that the lion *is—was* called the king of beasts?

4. They told me that the legal rate of interest at present *is-was* six per cent.

5. Have you ever heard him try to prove that black *is—was* white?

6. What *is—was* the name of the banker who lectured to us yesterday?

7. I never could remember what the important products of my county *are—were.*

8. The advocate of Equal Suffrage argued that mothers *need—needed* the ballot to protect their children.

9. She said that a democracy *is—was* a government of the people, by the people, and for the people, and that women *are-were* people as well as men.

10. The speaker asserted that this country *needs—needed* a tariff to protect home industries.

Exercise 108—Principal Parts

No one can be certain of using the correct form of a verb unless he knows the principal parts. Some verbs are regular; that is, they form their past tense and their perfect participle by adding *ed* to the present tense; as,

Present	*Past*	*Perfect Participle*
walk	walked	walked

Some verbs, however, are very irregular, having a different form for each of the principal parts. A list of such verbs follows:

Present	*Past*	*Perfect Participle*
arise	arose	arisen
awake	awoke or awaked	awaked
be	was	been
bear (carry)	bore	borne
beat	beat	beaten
become	became	become
begin	began	begun
bid	bade	bidden
bite	bit	bitten
blow	blew	blown
break	broke	broken
choose	chose	chosen
come	came	come
do	did	done

draw	drew	drawn
drink	drank	drunk
drive	drove	driven
eat	ate	eaten
fall	fell	fallen
fly	flew	flown
forbid	forbade	forbidden
forsake	forsook	forsaken
freeze	froze	frozen
give	gave	given
go	went	gone
grow	grew	grown
hide	hid	hidden
know	knew	known
lie (to rest)	lay	lain
ride	rode	ridden
ring	rang	rung
rise	rose	risen
run	ran	run
see	saw	seen
shake	shook	shaken
show	showed	shown
shrink	shrank	shrunk
sing	sang	sung
slay	slew	slain
slide	slid	slidden
sow	sowed	sown
speak	spoke	spoken
spring	sprang	sprung

steal	stole	stolen
strive	strove	striven
swear	swore	sworn
swell	swelled	swelled, swollen
swim	swam	swum
take	took	taken
tear	tore	torn
throw	threw	thrown
wear	wore	worn
weave	wove	woven
write	wrote	written

Exercise 109

Some verbs, though irregularly formed, have the past tense and perfect participle alike. A list of such verbs follows:

Present	*Past*	*Perfect Participle*
bend	bent	bent
behold	beheld	beheld
beseech	besought	besought
bind	bound	bound
bleed	bled	bled
bless	blessed, blest	blessed, blest
bring	brought	brought
build	built	built
burn	burned, burnt	burned, burnt
buy	bought	bought
catch	caught	caught
cling	clung	clung
clothe	clothed, clad	clothed, clad
creep	crept	crept

deal	dealt	dealt
dig	dug	dug
dream	dreamed, dreamt	dreamed, dreamt
dwell	dwelt	dwelt
flee	fled	fled
grind	ground	ground
hang	hung, hanged	hung, hanged
have	had	had
hear	heard	heard
hold	held	held
kneel	knelt	knelt
lay	laid	laid
lead	led	led
leap	leapt	leapt
lend	lent	lent
pay	paid	paid
say	said	said
shine	shone	shone
sit	sat	sat
sleep	slept	slept
sling	slung	slung
speed	sped	sped
spin	spun	spun
stand	stood	stood
sting	stung	stung
strike	struck	struck
string	strung	strung
sweep	swept	swept
swing	swung	swung

teach	taught	taught
think	thought	thought
weep	wept	wept
win	won	won
wind	wound	wound
wring	wrung	wrung

Exercise 110

Some verbs have all three forms alike. A list of such follows:

Present	*Past*	*Perfect Participle*
bet	bet	bet
burst	burst	burst
cast	cast	cast
cost	cost	cost
cut	cut	cut
hit	hit	hit
hurt	hurt	hurt
knit	knit	knit
let	let	let
put	put	put
rid	rid	rid
set	set	set
shed	shed	shed
spread	spread	spread
sweat	sweat	sweat
wet	wet	wet

Exercise 111

Choose the correct form of the italicized words below, and give the reason for your choice.

1. If it *don't—doesn't* fit you, we shall alter it.

2. I *knew—knowed* I was right.

3. *Aren't—ain't* you glad we came?

4. *Ain't—isn't* he well?

5. We *done—did* the right thing.

6. *Let—leave* the book on the table.

7. *Let—leave* me do as I planned.

8. Mary has *broke—broken* her arm.

9. My mother has *gone—went* to Boston.

10. Where *was—were* you yesterday?

11. When the dinner bell *rang—rung*, we all *come—came* running in.

12. He *don't—doesn't* know what you said.

13. To what hospital have they *taken—took* him?

14. I *saw—seen* him a few minutes ago.

15. I *saw—seen* him yesterday.

16. I should *have—of* brought my book.

17. My winter coat is *wore—worn* out.

18. Have you ever *rode—ridden* in an aeroplane?

19. I have *shown—showed* you all the styles I have.

20. *Don't—doesn't* it seem odd that he *don't—doesn't* come?

21. She *don't—doesn't* remember you.

22. We *began—begun* the work yesterday.

23. I'm afraid my foot is *froze—frozen.*

24. We *ran—run* all the way.

25. I've *shook—shaken* him three times, but he *don't—doesn't* awake.

26. The bell *rang—rung* just before you entered.

27. She *sang—sung* very well.

28. He *swam—swum* all yesterday morning.

29. Why *don't—doesn't* some one tell John that his coat is *tore—torn?*

30. *Don't—doesn't* mother know that the vase is *broke—broken?*

Exercise 112—Troublesome Verbs

Lie, Lay

Lie is intransitive; *lay* is transitive. *Lie* signifies *to rest; lay, to place.* Insert the correct form in the following:

1. He told me to —— the book on the table. It —— there now.

2. I —— all day waiting for help to arrive.

3. Where did you —— the purse?

4. I —— it on your desk.

5. I have —— the letters on your desk.

6. They told me to —— down. I —— down for about two hours.

7. As I wished to bleach the clothes, I —— them on the grass.

8. —— the bundle down and listen to me.

9. You will probably find your cap ——ing where it has —— since you dropped it.

10. They let the field —— fallow.

11. How long has it —— fallow?

12. Yesterday he —— on the grass almost all day.

13. The hunter —— still and watched.

14. He —— his gun beside him and waited.

15. It will —— undisturbed till morning.

16. —— down awhile before dinner.

17. I don't know how long he has —— here.

18. He let his tools —— in the rain.

Exercise 113—Troublesome Verbs

Sit, Set

Sit is intransitive and signifies *to rest. Set* is transitive and means *to place.* Insert the correct form:

1. I have —— the ferns in the rain.

2. —— down for a few minutes.

3. She drew up a chair and —— down, while we were ——ting down the probable expenses of the new house.

4. Why don't you —— us a good example?

5. ——ting the table is not strenuous enough for one who has been ——ting all day.

6. The hen is ——ting on her eggs.

7. The man is ——ting out trees.

8. —— still; I'll go.

Fly, Flow, Flee

Remember that birds *fly;* rivers *flow;* hunted creatures *flee.*

9. Still the river —— on its accustomed course.

10. Every autumn the birds —— south.

11. The birds have not yet —— away.

12. The deer —— before the dogs.

Rise, Raise

Rise is intransitive; *raise* is transitive.

13. I have been trying all morning to —— this window.

14. I set the bread to ——.

15. He will surely —— in his profession.

Teach, Learn

16. Will you —— me how to play tennis?

17. I thought you had —— how to play tennis.

18. I —— (past tense) her the new system of filing.

May, Can

May signifies permission; *can* denotes possibility.

19. —— I use your book?

20. —— you write shorthand?

21. —— I go with you?

22. My mother says that I —— go with you.

Might, Could

Might is the past tense of *may*, and *could* is the past tense of *can.*

23. He said that I —— go.

24. He —— do the work if he wished.

25. Did you say I —— use your typewriter?

Exercise 114—Accept, Except

Accept means *to receive. Except* as a verb means *to exclude;* as a preposition it means *with the exception of.* Insert the correct form in the following:

1. Did you —— the position? Yes, no one applied for it —— me.

2. I have no other reason for not ——ing your invitation —— that I shall not be in the city.

3. —— Mary all ——ed the invitation.

4. He would not —— the money —— on one condition.

5. Why do you —— him from the general offer that you are making?

6. I agree with you —— on one point.

7. He ——ed the rebuke in silence.

8. We were forced to —— their conditions.

9. He said he would not —— the money —— that he knew he could return it.

10. You have answered everything —— what I asked you.

Exercise 115—Affect, Effect

Affect means *to influence.* It is always a verb. *Effect* as a verb means *to bring to pass;* as a noun it means *result.* Insert the correct form in the following sentences:

1. His opinion does not —— the case.

2. How does war —— trade?

3. His walking has had a good —— upon his health.

4. The ruling did not —— the wholesale dealers, but it had a big —— upon us.

5. What —— did the loss have upon him?

6. The failure of the bank ——ed the small depositors but had no —— upon the big business men.

7. The —— of the law has been startling because of the number of people ——ed by it.

8. They ——ed the consolidation, but thereby produced a bad —— upon the price of their stock.

9. The accident seriously ——ed his nervous system. In fact, the —— of the fall is only gradually disappearing.

10. Did the celebrated physician really —— a cure?

Exercise 116—Lose, Loose

Lose is a verb, while *loose* is usually an adjective. The two should be carefully distinguished. Insert the correct form:

1. I have a note book with —— leaves.

2. Aren't you afraid you will —— some of the —— leaves of that book?

3. Be careful that you don't —— that —— bolt.

4. Do you remember that you had warned me that I'd —— the —— button on my coat? I did —— it not five minutes afterward.

5. One of the hinges of the door has become ——.

6. Do not —— the —— change in that pocket.

7. He will —— the parcel as the cord is ——.

8. Did you —— the —— leaf journal?

9. She may —— the money, as the clasp of her purse is ——.

10. I keep my —— journal paper together by a rubber band so that there will be no chance of ——ing it.

Exercise 117—Had ought

Wrong: We had ought to go.
Right: We ought to go.
Wrong: We had ought to have gone.
Right: We ought to have gone.

Correct the following sentences:

1. I had ought to have studied harder.

2. You ought to do it, hadn't you?

3. Hadn't you ought to have gone?

4. Yes, I had ought to have gone yesterday.

5. Do you think I had ought to have accepted?

6. He had ought to come to-morrow.

7. The tickets had ought to have come from the printer's yesterday.

8. We had not ought to stay out so late.

9. You had ought to wear your coat.

10. He had ought to have become naturalized.

11. You had ought to have washed the dishes before you went out.

12. You had ought to take an umbrella.

13. You had ought to have heard what she said.

14. We hadn't ought to disagree.

15. You ought to have invested, hadn't you?

Exercise 118

Conjugation of the verb *be* in the

INDICATIVE MODE

Present Tense

Singular	*Plural*
I am	We are
You are	You are
He is	They are

Past Tense

I was	We were
You were	You were
He was	They were

Future Tense

I shall be	We shall be
You will be	You will be
He will be	They will be

Present Perfect Tense

I have been	We have been
You have been	You have been
He has been	They have been

Past Perfect Tense

I had been	We had been
You had been	You had been
He had been	They had been

Future Perfect Tense

I shall have been	We shall have been
You will have been	You will have been
He will have been	They will have been

The verb *be* is used to form the progressive tenses of the active voice (See Exercise 102) and the simple tenses of the passive voice; as,

PASSIVE VOICE

Present Tense

Singular	*Plural*
I am followed	We are followed
You are followed	You are followed
He is followed	They are followed

Past Tense

I was followed	We were followed
You were followed	You were followed
He was followed	They were followed

Future Tense

I shall be followed	We shall be followed
You will be followed	You will be followed
He will be followed	They will be followed

Present Perfect Tense

I have been followed	We have been followed
You have been followed	You have been followed
He has been followed	They have been followed

Past Perfect Tense

I had been followed	We had been followed
You had been followed	You had been followed
He had been followed	They had been followed

Future Perfect Tense

I shall have been followed	We shall have been followed
You will have been followed	You will have been followed
He will have been followed	They will have been followed

If we add the progressive form wherever it may be used, we have the following synopsis of the indicative mood:

PASSIVE VOICE

TENSES	*Primary*	*Present*	I am followed (simple) I am being followed (progressive)
		Past	I was followed (simple) I was being followed (progressive)
		Future	I shall be followed
	Perfect	*Present Perfect*	I have been followed
		Past Perfect	I had been followed
		Future Perfect	I shall have been followed

Exercise 119

Conjugate the following in the passive voice:

1. Simple present of *pay.*
2. Progressive past of *pay.*
3. Present perfect of *throw.*
4. Future of *praise.*
5. Past perfect of *forget.*
6. Progressive present of *choose.*
7. Past progressive of *choose.*
8. Future of *choose.*

9. Future perfect of *choose*.

10. Past perfect of *choose*.

Exercise 120

Supply the verb forms indicated. Use the active unless the passive is definitely called for.

1. The vegetables (present perfect of *lie*) in water all the morning.

2. Rumors (past progressive passive of *spread*) far and wide that Germany would fight England.

3. I thought the gingham (past perfect passive of *shrink*) before the dress (past passive of *made*).

4. I am afraid my ear (present progressive of *freeze*).

5. Is it true that your ring (present perfect passive of *steal*)?

6. A sudden storm (past of *arise*) yesterday afternoon, and a little boy (past passive of *drown*) in the river where he and several of his companions (past perfect progressive of *swim*) since noon.

7. I (present perfect of *speak*) of the matter to no one.

8. I suppose that it (present perfect passive of *break*).

9. I must (present perfect of *show*) him twenty different styles, but he (past of *choose*) none of them, for as soon as I (past of *show*) him one, he (past of *shake*) his head.

10. She (past progressive of *wring*) out the clothes when the door bell (past of *ring*).

11. I am afraid my purse (present passive of *lose*).

12. The knight (past of *say*) that he (past perfect of *decide*) (infinitive of *follow*) the quest.

13. I thought I (past perfect of *bring*) you the morning paper.

14. He (past of *swim*) the river twice yesterday.

15. There he stood (present participle of *ring*) the dinner bell.

16. His coat (present perfect passive of *wet*) through more than once.

17. The trip (past of *cost*) him a hundred dollars.

18. I (past of *see*) the superintendent yesterday, but he said that there (present of *be*) no vacancies at present.

19. They (past of *lay*) the clippings on the desk, and then they (past of *sit*) down.

20. As he (past of *speak*), he (past progressive of *shake*) from head to foot.

21. The clouds (past of *lie*) low on the horizon.

22. The building in which I work (present perfect passive of *burn*).

23. Your employer (present perfect *deal*) fairly with you.

24. I (present perfect of *have*) the same position for three years.

25. I (future of *lend*) him no money.

26. The floor (past passive of *lay*) by an expert workman.

27. The beads (past passive of *string*) on a waxed thread.

28. He (present perfect of *throw*) the whole office into confusion.

29. Before he came forward, he (past of *set*) the child down.

30. After the storm, leaves and twigs (past progressive of *lie*) thick upon the roads.

31. He (past of *drive*) to town yesterday. He (future of *go*) again to-morrow.

32. The dictionary (present progressive of *lie*) on the table where you (past of *lay*) it.

33. The dog (past of *lay*) the bone down, and then he (past of *lie*) down.

34. He (past of *set*) the chair by the window and then (past of *sit*) down.

35. I think we (future of *see*) him as we pass, for he usually (present of *lie*) on a couch by the window.

36. The snow (past perfect progressive of *fall*) for several hours and now (past of *lie*) deep on every path.

37. Everything (present perfect passive of *lay*) in readiness.

38. (Present participle of *lie*) in the hammock, he soon fell asleep.

39. I saw the man (present participle of *lie*) on the ground.

40. After he (past perfect of *lie*) there a few minutes, he suddenly (past of *sit*) up.

41. The biplane, which (past perfect progressive of *lie*) in the hangar since it (past perfect passive of *raise*) from the water in which it (past perfect of *lie*) for two weeks, (past of *rise*) up over the city.

42. Large crowds (past progressive of *sit*) on the fields, (present participle of *wait*) for the aeroplane (infinitive of rise).

43. Many people (past perfect of *set*) tents on the field during the night and now (past progressive of *get*) a good view of the flight.

44. All eyes (past progressive of *turn*) toward the aeroplane, which (past progressive of *rise*) steadily.

45. The biplane (past of *rise*) until it (past perfect of *rise*) about five hundred feet above the tallest building; then it (past passive of *raise*) about fifty feet more to get it out of an air current that (past progressive of *raise*) one end of it.

Exercise 121—Infinitives and Participles

Infinitives are verb forms that are used as nouns, as adjectives, or as adverbs. *Participles* are verb forms that are used as adjectives. Thus at the same time each acts as two parts of speech. As verbs both have the meaning of the verbs from which they are made; both have tense and voice; both may be modified by adverbial expressions; and, if they are made from transitive verbs, both may take objects.

The Participle

The tenses and voices of the participle are as follows:

ACTIVE VOICE

Present

Simple	*Progressive*
selling	——

Perfect

having sold	having been selling

PASSIVE VOICE

Present

being sold ——

Perfect

having been sold ——

The participle frequently introduces a phrase. Usually the phrase is used like an adjective; occasionally it is used like a noun (sometimes called the *gerund* phrase).

Adjective: Seeing your perplexity, I'll offer a suggestion. (Notice the punctuation.)

Noun(Gerund): *Playing tennis* is good exercise.

The Infinitive

The infinitive is distinguished by the word *to*, either expressed or understood. The tenses and voices of the infinitive are as follows:

ACTIVE VOICE

Present

Simple	*Progressive*
to sell	to be selling

Perfect

to have sold	to have been selling

PASSIVE VOICE

Present

to be sold ——

Perfect

to have been sold ——

The infinitive is often used to introduce a phrase; as,

Noun: To get to the top of the hill was a difficult matter.
Adverb: I went *to buy the sugar.*
Adjective: It's a drawing *to be proud of.*

Grouping all the facts that we have thus far learned about phrases, and expressing them in diagram form, we have the following:

Phrases may be classified:

According to Form	*According to Use*
Prepositional	Adverbial
Participial (Gerund)	Adjective
Infinitive	Noun

The prepositional and infinitive phrases may have all three uses; the participial phrase has two—adjective and noun (gerund).

Variety of Expression[2]

Phrases are important because, like clauses, they help us to vary the form of our sentences. They help us, above all, to avoid the childish *so* habit. Thus, instead of *They wished to make the ice smooth so they flooded the pond*, we may use, for example:

Subordinate clause: Because (as, since) they wished to make the ice smooth, they flooded the pond.

Participial phrase: Wishing to make the ice smooth, they flooded the pond.

Infinitive phrase: To make the ice smooth, they flooded the pond.

Gerund phrase: Flooding the pond made the ice smooth.

Prepositional phrase modifying noun subject: The flooding of the pond made the ice smooth.

Recast each of the following sentences in at least two of the ways shown above:

1. They wished to finish the work so they stayed till six o'clock.

2. John hoped to arrive before the others so he started early.

3. He saw that the cars were not running so he walked so he would be on time.

4. They needed some gasoline so they had to stop at a garage.

5. He wished to make a tool chest so he bought some lumber.

6. They saw that he liked to read so they gave him several books.

7. She wished to make a good appearance at the party so she bought a new dress.

8. He was in a hurry so he walked fast.

9. We were afraid that we'd be late so we ran.

10. The campers thought they'd like a fire so they gathered a quantity of dry leaves and wood.

11. I was very tired when I reached home so I couldn't go to the lecture.

12. The work was difficult so it took three hours to finish it.

13. The clock needed repairing so he took it to a jeweler's.

14. The coat did not fit so she sent it back.

15. She didn't know where to take the train so she asked a policeman.

Exercise 122—Mode

Mode is the form of the verb that indicates the manner of expressing the thought. The *modes*, or *moods*, that every one should be able to distinguish are the *indicative* and the *subjunctive*. If the verb indicates a fact, we say it is in the indicative mode; if it expresses a supposition, a doubt, a statement contrary to fact, or a wish, we say it is in the subjunctive mode.

You *are* good.	(A fact—indicative.)
I wish I *were* good.	(Contrary to fact, a wish—subjunctive.)

In form the indicative and the subjunctive differ in the present and the past tenses of the verb *to be*, as follows:

Indicative of *be*

Present		*Past*	
I am	We are	I was	We were
You are	You are	You were	You were
He is	They are	He was	They were

Subjunctive of *be*

Present		*Past*	
If I be	If we be	If I were	If we were
If you be	If you be	If you were	If you were
If he be	If they be	If he were	If they were

Other verbs in the subjunctive mode do not end in *s* in the third person singular number, but use the same form as the other persons in the singular number; as, *if he go*, *if she walk*.

If, *though*, *although*, or *lest* usually introduce the subjunctive form.

In modern English, the use of the subjunctive is becoming rare except in the past and past perfect tenses in statements contrary to fact, and in wishes, which are really statements contrary to fact; as,

1. If I were a king (but I'm not), I'd see that my laws were obeyed.

2. I wish I were a king! (but I'm not).

3. If I had been careful, my work would be good. (I was not careful.)

4. I wish I had been careful! (I was not.)

Notice that the verb is in the past or in the past perfect tense.

There are some careful writers who still use the present subjunctive to show a *possibility;* as,

Lest he start too late, remind him again that he must meet the 4:15 train.

In the following sentences, which form is better? May any of the sentences use either form?

1. I wish I *was—were* rich.

2. If I *was—were* you, I should go at once.

3. If his work *was—were* exact, he would have no trouble in holding a position.

4. If it *was—were* true, why didn't you say so?

5. If he *was—were* a millionaire, he could not have been more lavish.

6. If such a thing *was—were* possible, our government would be no government.

7. If the election *was—were* postponed, we should have been informed.

Exercise 123

Insert *was* or *were* in each of the following sentences, in each case giving a reason for your choice. Remember that the indicative *was* is used to denote a statement of fact in the past time, and the subjunctive *were* (singular and plural) is used to denote a possibility, something that is supposed to be true, or a statement entirely contrary to fact, as in a wish.

1. I wish I —— going with you.

2. As he —— not well, he could not go.

3. If he —— well, he could go.

4. If he —— attentive in class, he would not fail.

5. They treated me as if I —— one of the family.

6. When I —— in the South I visited New Orleans.

7. Suppose she —— your guest, how would you entertain her?

8. He would appear very tall —— it not for the breadth of his shoulders.

9. We decided that if it —— still raining by seven o'clock, we should not go.

10. If our strawberries —— ripe, I'd give you some.

11. If the package —— left yesterday, as you say, it must have been while I —— not at home.

12. If he —— late yesterday, he must start earlier to-day.

13. If every man —— honest, business life would be very pleasant.

14. I saw that he —— not interested.

15. If he —— not interested, he surely looked as if he ——.

16. —— I certain that the bonds —— safe, I should invest in them.

17. As the tablecloth —— stained, we laid it on the grass to bleach it.

18. If that stained tablecloth —— mine, I'd try bleaching it.

19. If I —— as interested in farming as you are, I'd buy a farm.

20. If her work —— best, why didn't she get the higher salary?

Exercise 124—Verbs Incorrectly Used

Wrong	*Right*
1. *Let* the book on the table.	*Leave* the book on the table.
2. *Leave* me go with you.	*Let* me go with you.
3. Don't *blame it on* me.	Don't *accuse* me.
4. Do you *carry* stationery?	Do you *sell* stationery?
5. The child *aggravates* me.	The child *irritates* me.
6. Please *except* my invitation.	Please *accept* my invitation.
7. Where have you *located?*	Where have you *settled?*

(*Locate* is a transitive verb.)

8. I *expect* you are very busy.	I *suppose* you are very busy.
9. I *disremember* seeing him.	I *don't remember* seeing him.
10. Do you *mind* where you saw it?	Do you *remember* where you saw it?
11. Where are you *stopping?*	Where are you *staying?*
12. Did you *extend an invitation* to him?	Did you *invite* him?
13. This clock needs *fixing.*	This clock needs *repairing.*
14. I should *admire* to go.	I should *like* to go.
15. I'd *love* to go.	I'd *like* to go.
16. He didn't *show up* on time.	He didn't *appear* on time.
17. I *had* a strange thing *happen* to me yesterday.	A strange thing *happened* to me yesterday.
18. I didn't *get to go.*	I *was unable to go.*
19. *Loan* me your pencil.	*Lend* me your pencil.

(*May I borrow your pencil?* is correct. *Loan* is a noun.)[3]

20. I *can't seem* to understand that problem.	I *seem unable* to understand that problem.
21. I don't *take any stock* in such schemes.	I *have no confidence* in such schemes.
22. How do you *size up* the situation?	What *do you think* of the situation?

23. I *beg to state. . . .*	Omit.

(This expression has been so overdone in business letters that it should be avoided)

24. He *dove* off the pier.	He *dived* off the pier.
25. He *claims* that he was deceived.	He *asserts* (maintains) that he was deceived.
26. *Can* I take your pencil?	*May* I take your pencil?
27. We expect to *get up* a club.	We expect to *organize* a club.
28. Did you notice how that show window was *got up?*	Did you notice how that show window was *decorated?*
29. It is *going on* ten o'clock.	It is *almost* ten o'clock.
30. He said *to go* at once.	He said *that we should go* at once.

NOTE.—The secretary's daily report will be found an excellent means of securing variety of expression in pupils' writing. A different pupil is elected each Monday to act as the secretary of the class for the ensuing week, his duty being to report each day the doings of the class on the preceding day. The conditions are that not more than one *and* be used in each report and not more than one sentence begin with the subject.

CHAPTER IX

THE PREPOSITION AND THE CONJUNCTION

Prepositions

IT is important in the study of prepositions to observe that there are certain words that are followed by certain prepositions. To change the preposition is to convey a different meaning from the one that the speaker intended, or to convey no meaning at all. A partial list of such words with their appropriate prepositions follows:

accompanied	with	anything having no life
accompanied	by	anything having life
acquit	of	
accuse	of	
adapted	to	a thing
adapted	for	a course, because of one's nature
adapted	from	an author
agree	to	a plan or proposition
agree	with	a person
agree	upon	something that must be decided
angry	at	a thing
angry	with	a person
compare	with	to bring out similar qualities
compare	to	without analyzing
comply	with	
confer	on	meaning to give to
confer	with	meaning to talk to
confide	in	meaning to put faith in
confide	to	meaning to commit to one's keeping
conform	to	
correspond	to, with	a thing, denoting similarity

correspond	with	meaning to write to
different	from	
dependent	on	a person
dependent	for	a thing
independent	of	
disappointed	in	
employed	at	a certain place or salary
employed	in	a certain kind of business
employed	by	a certain person or company
enter	upon	duties
enter	at	a door
followed	by	
influence	over, upon	
expect	of	
participate	in	
profit	by	
remonstrate	against	a thing
remonstrate	with	a person

Exercise 125

Insert the correct preposition in the following:

1. I shall comply —— your request.
2. The chairman came upon the platform accompanied —— the speaker.
3. He took a walk accompanied —— his dog.
4. The lecture will be accompanied —— stereopticon views.
5. Strikes are usually accompanied —— riots.
6. The years of prosperity were followed —— years of famine.
7. He was accused —— theft, but was acquitted —— the accusation.
8. She is well adapted —— the position that is open.
9. An electric iron is especially adapted —— summer use.

10. The selection was adapted —— Irving.

11. This cloth is well adapted —— summer clothing because it is very light in weight.

12. I agree —— you that the plan is impracticable.

13. Let us agree now —— a place to spend our summer vacation.

14. That is not a proposition —— which I shall agree.

15. It is silly to be angry —— an inanimate object.

16. Don't be angry —— a person because he tells you your faults.

17. His report corresponds in all respects — yours.

18. Mr. Giles suggested that you would be glad to have us correspond —— you concerning our new bond issues.

19. I shall confer —— my lawyer.

20. The public has conferred a great honor —— him.

21. One should always profit —— his experiences.

22. The new device is entirely different —— the old.

23. I am employed —— a fairly large salary —— a business that is growing daily.

24. All employees must conform —— the rules.

25. I am confiding —— you because I know that I can trust you.

26. She confided her child —— the care of her brother.

27. She is dependent —— her brother —— support.

28. You can have an influence for good —— him.

29. I have remonstrated —— the change several times.

30. Perhaps he will change his plans if we remonstrate —— him at once.

Exercise 126—Prepositions Incorrectly Used

Each of the incorrect sentences given below contains an unnecessary preposition. When the meaning of "Where are you going?" is entirely clear, there is nothing gained by saying "Where are you going *to?*" Omit such superfluous prepositions.

Wrong *Right*

1. I took it off *of* the shelf.	I took it off the shelf.
2. I shall accept *of* your hospitality.	I shall accept your hospitality.
3. Where are you *at?*	Where are you?
4. Where are you going *to?*	Where are you going?
5. It is a building *of from* twenty to thirty stories in height.	It is a building twenty to thirty stories in height.
6. Look out *of* the window.	Look out the window.
7. John copies *after* his father in everything.	John copies his father in everything.
8. I am wondering *about* what I should do.	I am wondering what I should do.
9. I shall consult *with* my lawyer.	I shall consult my lawyer.
10. He sat opposite *to* me.	He sat opposite me.
11. I shall leave later *on.*	I shall leave later.

and **for** ***to***

12. I shall try *and* go.	I shall try *to* go.

of **for** ***have***

13. I might *of* gone.	I might *have* gone.

The wrong preposition

14. He fell *in* the water.	He fell *into* the water.
15. She died *with* diphtheria.	She died *of* diphtheria.
16. Divide the work *between* the four of us.	Divide the work *among* the four of us.

(*Between* may be used in speaking of only two persons or things)

17. It will be done *inside* of an hour.	It will be done *within* an hour.
18. Are you angry *at* me?	Are you angry *with* me?

Preposition must be used

19. It's no use to try.	It's *of* no use to try.
20. My sister stayed home.	My sister stayed *at* home.
21. Why do you act that way?	Why do you act *in* that way?
22. We left the third of June.	We left *on* the third of June.

Exercise 127

The object of a preposition is always in the objective case. Some people have great difficulty in recognizing that in such expressions as *for you and me*, the pronoun *me* is as much the object of the preposition *for* as the pronoun *you*. Both words must be in the objective case. It is incorrect to say *for you and I*.

In the following sentences omit the incorrect italicized form:

1. The invitation is for father and *I—me.*

2. Every one has finished his work except *he—him* and *I—me.*

3. It's a question that you and *I—me* must decide; it refers to you and *I—me* alone.

4. Girls like you and *she—her* should have a good influence over the others.

5. All but you and *I—me* have left.

6. He did it for you and *I—me.*

7. No one objected but *they—them* and *we—us.*

8. She sat opposite you and *I—me.*

9. They were sitting near you and *I—me.*

10. We expect you to return with mother and *I—me.*

11. He wanted my brother and *I—me* to go into business with his brother and *he—him.*

12. Neither *she—her* nor her sister have I seen for several months.

13. My companion and *I—me* took up the trail of the bear at once. For some distance it led *he—him* and *I—me* over the soft, yielding carpet of moss and pine needles, and the footprints were quite easily made out.

14. *He—him* and *I—me* had, of course, to keep a sharp lookout ahead and around for the grizzly.

15. All are going on the excursion except *he—him* and *I—me.*

16. *He—him* and *I—me* went fishing.

17. The rule applies to *we—us* all—the manager, *they—them* who keep books, you, and *I—me.*

18. She beckoned to my companion and *I—me.*

19. The letter was to be read by the president or *I—me.*

20. He did it for the sake of my father and *I—me.*

21. We study Shakespeare with her sister and *she—her.*

22. *She—her* and her sister went to the lecture with my sister and *I—me.*

23. They sent for *she—her* and *I—me*, not you and *he—him.*

24. The program was arranged by the president and *I—me.*

25. They found that his father and *he—him* had already left.

26. Mother is going to buy a birthday present to-day for *she—her* and *I—me.*

27. The play is interesting not only to you older people but to *we—us* younger ones also.

28. They expected the work to be done by *she—her* and *I—me.*

29. The dispute between his neighbor and *he—him* over their lot line was settled by the surveyors this morning.

30. He wants to speak to you and *I—me.*

Exercise 128—Than, as

Than and *as* are not prepositions but conjunctions. They are used to introduce subordinate clauses. Usually the clause is incomplete, but the omitted part is easily understood from the preceding clause and must be supplied to show the case of the noun or the pronoun that is expressed; as,

Right: She is as tall as I [am].
Right: She is taller than he [is].
Right: I should invite you rather than her [than I should invite her].

Use the correct one of the italicized pronouns in the following sentences:

1. I'll agree that he is richer than *I—me*, but riches are not everything.

2. I shall send her rather than *he—him.*

3. No one felt sorrier than *she—her.*

4. No one knows more about an automobile than *he—him.*

5. You are more capable of doing the work than *he—him.*

6. We were nearer the goal than you or *he—him.*

7. You finished the work almost as quickly as *she—her.*

8. She writes fully as well as *he—him.*

9. The manager said he would rather send me than *he—him.*

10. I secured a position sooner than *she—her.*

11. It seems to me that they ought to go rather than *we—us.*

12. I am surprised that you arrived sooner than *they—them.*

13. They should have elected him rather than *I—me.*

14. I am not so well-fitted as *he—him* to hold the position.

15. You are more popular than *he—him.*

Exercise 129—Correlatives

There are certain conjunctions, called *correlatives*, that are used in pairs. They are

both—and	as—as, so—as
either—or	not only—but also
neither—nor	whether—or
so—that	such—as

Illustrations

Both—and	He has both skill and energy.
Either—or	I shall leave either Monday or Tuesday.
Neither—nor	I can neither sing nor play.
So—that	It rained so hard that we stayed at home.
As—as	We shall come as early as we can.
So—as	She is not so tall as you are. (Used in negative expressions.)

Not only—but also	We saw not only Mr. Brown but his wife also.
Whether—or	Whether I return to work or stay at home depends on my mother's health.
Such—as	We shall buy only such goods as we think we can sell.

Be very careful not to use the correlative *so as* incorrectly for *so that. So as* is used in negative expressions of comparison; *so that* is used to express result.

Wrong: We went early *so as* we could get good seats.
Right: We went early *so that* we could get good seats.

In the illustrations given above, notice that the correlatives always join two similar or *coördinate* expressions. It is important that they be placed each immediately before one of the two coördinate expressions.

Wrong: I *neither* can sing nor play.
Right: I can *neither* sing nor play.

Recast the following sentences, placing the correlative conjunctions before coördinate expressions:

1. Either you ordered it late or not at all.

2. He said he neither had money nor time.

3. We not only bought the books you wished but the games also.

4. We like the place in which we live both on account of its quietness and its pleasant surroundings.

5. I shall either go to Quebec or Montreal.

6. Either he must spray his trees or expect no fruit.

7. I neither like the appearance of the shop nor the attitude of the clerks.

8. They did it both for the sake of your brother and you.

9. This sample not only is much darker but heavier also.

10. They are barred who neither can read nor write.

Exercise 130—Either—or, Neither—nor

These conjunctions are correctly used in speaking of two things only. Care must be taken to use *or* with *either* and *nor* with *neither.* In comparing three or more things use *any of them*, *none of them*, or *no.*

In the following sentences use only the correct italicized forms:

1. Neither effort *nor—or* money was spared in the undertaking.

2. I have considered planting maple, oak, and elm trees, but *neither—none* of them seems to grow well in this climate.

3. We do not believe in *either* enduring oppression *nor—or* killing the oppressor. We believe in arbitration.

4. He has *no—neither* time, patience, *nor—or* energy.

5. If you ask me which of the three I prefer, I'll be frank and tell you I like *neither—none* of them.

6. Three courses will be given in the subject this year; you may take *either—any* one of them.

7. I had already passed three branch roads, but *neither—none* of them had looked familiar to me.

8. I hardly think he accepted *any—either* of the two offers he received.

9. Neither the doctor *or—nor* his wife was at home.

10. Both the books look shop-worn. I'll take *neither—none.*

Exercise 131—Except, Without, Unless

Except and *without* are prepositions, and are used, therefore, to introduce phrases; *unless* is a conjunction, and is used to introduce a clause.

In the following sentences insert the correct form, giving a reason for your choice:

1. —— you leave at once, you will miss your train.

2. I cannot learn to swim, —— some one teaches me.

3. I cannot learn to swim —— a teacher.

4. No one could do the work —— me.

5. John expects to learn —— studying.

6. John will discover that he cannot win promotion —— he works hard.

7. No one can learn how to spell —— first learning how to observe.

8. No one will learn to spell —— he learns to observe.

9. No one will succeed —— he has energy and patience.

10. No one will succeed —— energy and patience.

11. You cannot succeed in any way —— by seizing each opportunity as it comes.

12. It is impossible to grow beautiful flowers —— the soil is good.

Exercise 132—Like, as

Like is followed by a noun or pronoun in the objective case. *As* is a conjunction and introduces a clause, and is therefore followed by a verb. *Like* is not a conjunction and therefore may not be substituted for *as* or *as if*.

Wrong: I wish I could play *like* you can.
Right: I wish I could play *as* you can.

Insert the correct word in the following sentences:

1. The picture looks just —— you.

2. I haven't a voice —— my brother's.

3. I cannot sing —— my brother can.

4. He walks just —— you do.

5. I hope you will all enjoy the trip —— I did.

6. For pleasure and exercise I think there is no game —— tennis.

7. He said that the town looked just —— it had when he was a boy.

8. I cut the paper just —— you said I should.

9. He talks —— his father.

10. He has the same sort of drawl —— his father [has].

11. She was there —— you said she would be.

12. They worked —— beavers.

13. He looked —— a tramp.

14. To give the stitch the proper twist throw the thread over the needle —— I do.

15. He walks —— he were lame.

Exercise 133—As—as, So—as

Use *as—as* in stating equality; use *so—as* in negative comparisons.

1. You will find the new clerks fully —— courteous as were the old.

2. You will not find the new clerks —— courteous as were the old.

3. Elms do not grow —— well in this climate as do poplars.

4. We did not carry —— much advertising this year as we did last year, and we find that our receipts are smaller.

5. Under our system of individual instruction a student may advance —— rapidly as his ability permits.

6. You are not —— tall as your sister.

7. I do not seem to learn languages —— easily as mathematics.

8. This house is not —— large as the other.

9. He is —— active as he was twenty years ago.

10. He is not —— active as he was twenty years ago.

Exercise 134—Miscellaneous Blunders

To, Too, Two

To is a preposition; *too* is an adverb, and means *excessively* or *also; two* is a numeral adjective. Insert the correct form in each of the following sentences:

1. The —— sisters discovered that it was —— late for the 4:15 train.

2. It is —— dark in that corner; come —— the light.

3. He spends —— much time in dreaming, —— little in working.

4. He would have done better if he had not given —— little heed —— the advice of his —— older brothers.

5. —— more hours were passed in the all —— weary task of waiting.

6. It was —— cold —— stay out more than —— hours.

7. You may go ——, but don't stay —— long.

8. —— stay there for —— weeks would be —— tiresome.

9. The doctor said that the —— men were —— sick —— go home alone, and I thought so ——.

10. About —— hours ago I met Mary who said that she was going —— the country ——.

There, Their

11. —— are seven brothers in —— family.

12. —— books are —— on the table.

13. —— is no doubt that —— knowledge of mathematics is greater than —— knowledge of English.

Were, Where

14. —— have you been?

15. —— you ever on a farm —— alfalfa is grown?

16. —— —— you when the report was read?

17. I was just —— you ——.

Of, Have

18. You should —— read more distinctly.

19. I could —— done the work if I had had more —— the necessary tools.

20. If I had tried harder, I might —— done the work better.

PART II—COMPOSITION: ORAL AND WRITTEN

CHAPTER X

ORAL ENGLISH

Exercise 135

RETELL a story that you know or one that the instructor has read to you. See if you can tell the whole story in fairly long sentences without using a single *and*. You will be allowed to use three *and's*. As soon as you say the third, you must take your seat. Let the class keep count.

The story may be an anecdote, a fable, or any other short incident that can easily be told in one or two minutes. You probably have read many such or have heard your father and your mother tell them. A joke that can be told in two or three sentences will not be long enough.

The excessive use of *and* spoils the telling of many stories. It is a mistake to think that the gap between the end of one sentence and the beginning of the next appears as great to the listener as it does to us as we are deliberating what to say next. To avoid the gap we bridge the two sentences with *and*. Its use in this way is hardly ever necessary if we think out a sentence to the end before we begin to speak it. When we have finished the thought, we should finish the sentence without trying to bind it artificially to the next one. The sentences will be bound together if the thought of one grows out of the thought of the preceding one.

If the unfolding of the idea does not seem sufficient to tie the parts, there are better expressions to use than *and*. There are short expressions like *in this way*, *likewise*, *moreover*, *thus*, *therefore*, *besides*, *as might be expected*, and *too*. Another way to avoid *and* is to change the form of the sentence: (1) better than the form, "I opened the window *and saw*," is, "*Opening* the window, I saw;" (2) better than "I am going to the store *and buy* some sugar," is, "I am going to the store *to buy* some sugar;" (3) better than "There was a boy *and his name* was John," is, "There was a boy *whose* name was John;" (4) better than "I reached home *and found* that my cousin had arrived," is, "*When* I reached home, I found that my cousin had arrived." In place of *and*, therefore, we may use (1) participles, (2) infinitives, (3) relative pronouns, and (4) subordinate conjunctions.

Above all, avoid *and everything*, as in, "I washed the dishes and swept the floor and everything." To try thus to complete an idea that is already complete shows childishness.

Exercise 136

Very likely in telling the story as suggested above you found yourself frequently using the word *so* to connect two sentences. Perhaps, too, you used *why* to begin sentences.

Now tell one of your own experiences, being careful not to use *and*, *so*, or *why*. Introduce as much conversation as possible. What, if any, is the advantage of telling a story in the first person? Why is it good to introduce conversation?

In your conversation make use of several of the following words:

replied	whispered	spoke	inquired
answered	agreed	cried	explained
asked	exclaimed	shouted	remarked
questioned	repeated	continued	suggested
promised	maintained	objected	rejoined
interrupted	quoted	returned	added

Exercise 137

Far too many boys and girls pay but little regard to the matter of choosing the word that will give the exact meaning that they wish to convey. In order to lend force to their words they have formed the habit of speaking in superlatives; like the girl who said, "We had a perfectly grand time, but I'm so beastly tired now that I'm nearly dead," and yet she showed no evidence of suffering.

Isn't it a pity that our beautiful English language should be so degraded in common usage that it loses all its force and meaning? Instead of convincing people that she really was tired, the girl quoted above made herself ridiculous by her exaggeration. Yet isn't the quotation a fair example of the speech of many boys and girls? Surely everything about us is not either grand or beastly. The habit thus formed is difficult to break, but it must be broken if we wish to speak our language correctly.

Make a list of the slang phrases that you have acquired. For each one substitute a good English expression.

The reason we must watch our oral English closely is that it is in our conversation that our habits of speech are formed. The expressions we use then we unconsciously employ when we are writing or talking to the class. If we are accustomed to use considerable slang when we speak, we shall have difficulty in eliminating it from our writing or in finding a good word to express the idea for which we usually use slang. As a rule, slang and extravagant expressions of all kinds are used to serve such a variety of meanings that the use of them tends to limit the vocabulary to these expressions. Consider slang something undesirable and stop using it.

Exercise 138

Look up the words in each of the following groups. You will notice that there is a resemblance of meaning between all the words of each group, but that there is also a shade of difference in meaning that distinguishes each word from its companions. Discover that shade of difference. Use each word in a sentence.

1. Lovely, beautiful, pretty, handsome.
2. Awful, terrible, horrible, dreadful, fearful.
3. Nice, pleasant, delightful, dainty, fine, agreeable.
4. Grand, imposing, splendid, impressive.
5. Love, like, adore, admire, revere.
6. Smart, clever, bright, quick-witted.
7. Fierce, ferocious, wild.
8. Guess, think, suppose, imagine.
9. Hate, dislike, despise, abhor, detest.
10. Scholar, student, pupil.

Exercise 139

Carelessness in speaking frequently results in wordiness, since the speaker in an effort to be clear or forceful repeats the idea two or three times. Such speech is tiresome. In each of the following sentences there are too many words to express the idea. See how many you can omit and yet preserve the meaning. Sometimes the sentence needs revision.

1. I haven't got any time.
2. Where does he live at?

3. Don't stand up; there's a chair.

4. The woman she had an accident.

5. You had ought to take more exercise.

6. I was just going to go.

7. I excuse you because you are a new beginner.

8. I can finish the work in three days' time.

9. The offices are both alike in all respects.

10. He engaged the both of us.

11. We applied to Mr. Abbot, he being the manager.

12. My mind often reverts back to the time when I began in business.

13. That high building that is going up on Twelfth Street is going to be twenty stories high when it is finished.

14. From his appearance he looked to be in very poor circumstances.

15. He is afraid of the results that will ensue if he follows the course that he has planned.

16. The present state of affairs that is now confronting the public has become what it now is because the citizens are not public spirited.

17. The reason why I was not at work yesterday was because I was not feeling as well as I might.

18. I shall never forget the terrible sights that I saw the time that I witnessed the street car collision.

19. I have been debating in my mind whether I ought to accept the offer.

20. He was a mere little child when he first began to work in the mine.

21. Mix together both the butter and the sugar, and rub the two of them to a cream.

22. The two pieces of cloth are just exactly the same in every way.

23. You will find this chair equally as comfortable as the other.

24. He said that when he started in his business that he had almost no capital at all.

25. It was the office of Morgan & Son where I got my experience.

26. China is undergoing a vast change at the present time.

27. At about the age of fourteen years he left his home town.

28. They did it gladly and willingly.

29. He always shows great deference and respect when he speaks to those who are in authority.

30. He is the proprietor and owner of the News.

31. You can easily get the training that will make you a competent and efficient high-salaried trained man.

32. For sale, a large, commodious house, arranged with every convenience to make it comfortable.

33. We are making all the necessary improvements that are needed.

34. I went to high school to take up stenography.

Exercise 140—Making a Speech

One of the most profitable exercises to cultivate clear thinking and consequent clear expression is the making of speeches, usually spoken of as oral themes. In this exercise a pupil stands before the class to talk upon a subject about which he has thought, but upon which he has written nothing. He has two objects in view. First, he must choose those facts that will make his subject clear and interesting to his audience. Second, he must deliver them well; that is, he must stand in a good position before the class, use good grammar, no slang, and enunciate so that every one in the room can understand him. If his speech is to be longer than one paragraph, he should have an outline prepared, in which each division is clearly indicated, as well as the important details within each division.

In making a speech, the best way is to start with a clear statement of the subject. Suppose you take (9) below. You might begin, "I am going to talk of a street car transfer. First, I shall tell you how it looks; and second, how it is used. Then first, a street car transfer—(describe it fully). In the second place, it is used—(give details)." After you have explained fully, to show that you have said all you intend to say, finish with a sentence of conclusion. *Therefore, consequently, for these reasons, thus we may see*, are instances of words which may be used to begin a sentence of conclusion.

Use each of the following questions as the subject for a speech. Answer each question clearly and completely. Use illustrations to show exactly what you mean.

1. What does it mean to be a hero?

2. What does it mean to be successful?

3. What does it mean to be unfortunate?

4. What does it mean to be generous?

5. What does it mean to be lenient?

6. What does it mean to be mercenary?

7. What does it mean to be diffident?

8. What does it mean to be penurious?

9. What is a street car transfer? How does it look and how is it used?

10. What occupation do you wish to follow, and why? What preparations are you making?

11. Why do we have a smoke ordinance?

12. Why must buildings have fire escapes?

13. Why do the farmers of Kansas insure their barns against cyclones?

14. What is fire insurance?

15. Why is ventilation important?

16. Why do so many immigrants come to this country?

17. Why do cities grow?

18. Why was the steam engine an important invention?

19. Why was the telephone an important invention?

20. What is the principle of vaccination?

21. What is the principle of anti-toxin?

22. Of what good is the trade union to the laborer?

23. Why does the employer object to the union?

24. What is a monopoly?

25. What is meant by a corner in wheat?

Exercise 141

In your neighborhood you have frequently noticed a lawn and a garden that are very poorly kept, the garden needing weeding and the lawn both weeding and mowing. Imagine that you go to the owner to make him a proposition. You know the man slightly, and you have heard that he has a quick temper. Know exactly what work you will offer to do and how often you will do it. Be careful of your first sentences. Let them be especially courteous, so that you may not offend the gentleman by suggesting that he does not take care of his property. Tell him frankly that you would like to earn some money.

In this exercise the class will represent the owner. Moreover, they will watch carefully so that they may point out to the speaker wherein his speech was not quite courteous or not quite clear.

Exercise 142

From one of the newspapers cut an advertisement of a position for which you think you can apply. Bring the advertisement with you and convince the class that you are fitted for the position.

In this exercise you must be exact. Choose an advertisement for a kind of work about which you know something. If you have ever had any experience that would fit you for the position, do not fail to tell of it, since experience counts for much in the employer's estimate of an applicant.

Let the class judge whether the speaker has been convincing and whether he has shown the properly courteous attitude toward an employer. Let them ask themselves such questions as: Is he alert in his manner? Does he make one feel that he is capable? Does he stand and talk as if he has confidence in himself? Is he too meek? Does he seem over-confident? Let each be able to offer suggestions for improvement.

Exercise 143

Imagine that you are an agent. Choose an article that is especially useful to housekeepers. Try to sell it to the class, or choose an individual member to whom you wish to sell it. Bring a sample with you for the purpose of demonstrating its usefulness.

As in the preceding exercise the speaker must strive to be convincing. He must know all there is to be known about the article that he is demonstrating. If it is at all possible, he should have used it in order that he may explain exactly how it is operated and why it is better than a similar article that the housekeeper probably is at present using.

Exercise 144

You wish to start a business and need a certain amount of money. Try to convince the instructor or a selected pupil that you need it.

Be sure that you are able to tell definitely the kind of business for which you wish the money, where you will start the business, why you think that this particular location is good, when you will be able to return the money, and what security you can give.

Don't make the mistake of choosing something too big for a boy or a girl to carry through. Perhaps the following will be suggestive:

1. A newspaper stand.

2. A miniature truck farm in the empty lot next door.

3. A pop corn wagon.

4. A fruit cart or stand.

5. A shoe shining stand.

6. Raising ferns or flowers for sale.

7. Buying vegetables from a farmer and selling them to housewives.

8. Printing business cards and blotters on a small press.

9. Making place cards.

10. Making valentines.

11. Painting holiday postal cards or fancy cards for Christmas, Easter, Thanksgiving, and the like.

12. Printing on postal cards pretty scenes that you have photographed perhaps in your town or at a summer resort.

13. Making and selling cakes, doughnuts, and the like.

14. Selling crocheted or embroidered articles.

Exercise 145—Elements of Success

Prepare a short speech on each of the following. Wherever possible make your statements clear and forceful by using illustrations or examples.

1. Cheerfulness helps to bring success.

2. The habit of neatness is an asset.

3. The habit of punctuality is a necessity.

4. He was not promoted because he watched the clock.

5. He was not promoted because his excuse was always, "I forgot."

6. He was not promoted because he learned nothing from his mistakes.

7. He was not promoted because he was always grumbling.

8. He was not promoted because he was content to be a second-rate man.

9. He was not promoted because he ruined his ability by half-doing things.

10. He was not promoted because he did not learn to act on his own judgment.

11. One to-day is worth two to-morrows.

12. Experience is an expensive teacher.

13. Be not simply good—be good for something.

14. Not failure, but low aim, is crime.

15. To be successful one must have confidence in himself.

Exercise 146

As in the preceding exercise prepare a speech on each of the following:

1. A dishonest person cannot succeed.

2. There is no excuse for discouragement.

3. You may secure a position through another's influence, but you keep it through your own merit.

4. There is always room at the top.

5. There is no such thing as luck.

6. The proper attitude toward an employer is one of deference.

7. A business woman should dress simply.

8. Perseverance is the key to success.

9. To accomplish much one must work systematically.

10. It is possible to cultivate a good memory.

11. The ability to converse is a business asset.

12. The habit of exaggeration is dangerous.

Exercise 147—Successful Men and Women

How can one measure the success of men or women? Is it by the money they make? the land they acquire? the fame they win? the good they do? By what means have they won success? Was it through favorable circumstances? strength of character? favoritism? physical strength? mental energy? daring?

doing what they thought was right in spite of opposition? or simply doing nothing and waiting for success to come?

Study the life and character of one or more of the following. Have they gained what you consider success? What qualities of character do you recognize in them? Would you care to be like any of them?

Make a list of the habits that you recognize in their life and in the way they worked.

Make a list of the characteristics of the ones that you study.

Florence Nightingale	Frances Willard	Bismarck
David Maydole	Ella Flagg Young	Gladstone
R. L. Stevenson	Helen Gould Shepard	Marshall Field
Booker T. Washington	Jane Addams	Carnegie
Captain Scott	Napoleon	J. Pierpont Morgan
Mary Antin	Franklin	Edison
Daniel Boone	Lincoln	Roosevelt
Mary Lyon	Nathan Hale	Goethals

Exercise 148—Debating

A very great asset in business is the ability to see the truth or the falsity of a statement, and to advance proofs for or against it. This ability we shall try to acquire through the practice of debating; that is, through the making of speeches in which students take opposite sides of the same subject, trying by the presentation of facts and illustrations to prove that the side which they represent is the correct one. The statement that is thus argued is called a *proposition.*

Debating is excellent practice because it teaches not only clear-cut reasoning, but also forceful expression. If a debater fails to make any of his several arguments convincing, if he introduces irrelevant matter, or, though he has prepared strong proofs, if he expresses them in incorrect English, the result will be poor. In working out a debate, therefore, observe the following carefully:

1. Know your subject thoroughly. If you have insufficient knowledge, you cannot be convincing.

2. Understand your point of view exactly and explain it clearly. If you and your opponent have different ideas of the word *trust*, for example, you can never argue on a subject that concerns the trusts. Define your position first of all.

3. After you have gathered your facts, study them as a whole. What three arguments, let us say, stand out clearly in your mind as being irrefutable because of the strong proofs you have to back them? These are the ones that you should use; the rest will probably be of little value. Plan to give the weakest of the three first, so that your argument will gain force as you advance.

4. Work out the details of each argument. A mere statement of each is not enough. It must be supported by many facts and illustrations.

5. Prepare an outline. It will show you whether your arguments follow each other clearly, whether you have so arranged them as to secure climax. (See Exercise 152.)

6. In talking, follow the plan explained in Exercise 140, being especially careful in conclusion to summarize the proofs that you have presented.

The conclusions that you reach in your arguments must be based upon statements that are true. In the following, some of the statements are false, and therefore the conclusions based upon them are false. Point out wherein the falsity consists. In others of the following, irrelevant matter has been introduced. Point it out, explaining why it is irrelevant.

1. We shall forget a great many facts that we learn at school. Therefore it is useless to learn them.

2. Oil should be used instead of water in sprinkling our streets, because oil does not evaporate so quickly as water, and so does not allow the dust to rise. Moreover, as the street must be cleaned before the oil is laid, there is less dust to rise. When the oil lies on the streets, it is very sticky, and clings to everyone's shoes. In this way it is tracked into the houses and stores, making everything dirty. Therefore I think the streets should be oiled instead of being watered.

3. Half of the keys would not work on the typewriter that I used yesterday. This machine will work no better, as it is made by the same company.

4. Last year September was very warm, and the winter was extreme. This year September has been very warm, and therefore the winter will be extreme.

5. My cousin never went to high school, and when he went to work he earned eight dollars a week. I have gone to high school for one year. Therefore I shall receive more than eight dollars a week when I go to work.

6. When you are working, your employer will never ask you the definition of a noun. Therefore it is unnecessary to know any grammar.

7. Every one should be punctual in doing his work. If he is punctual, he will be promoted and earn a larger salary. Money is a very important item in this world, but it is not everything. A person must be satisfied with his work so that he can do it cheerfully; otherwise he will not succeed. Therefore I think every one ought to be on time.

8. The day is either sunny or it is not sunny. To-day is not sunny; therefore it is sunny.

9. It always rains when I wear new shoes. I am wearing new shoes; therefore it will rain to-day.

Exercise 149

Find three reasons for each of the following propositions. State them concisely, reserving the strongest for the last.

As above, find three reasons against each of the following.

Expand one of the reasons that you advanced for one of the propositions given below. Using your statement as the opening sentence, develop it into a paragraph by explanations and illustrations.

1. The high school should have the same session as the grades.

2. The high school session should begin at eight o'clock and close at one, with no recess for luncheon.

3. Final examinations shall be abolished.

4. Every high school should teach manual training.

5. Every high school should offer business courses.

6. Every high school pupil should receive a business training.

7. Stenography (or bookkeeping) is a more important study than wood-working.

8. If a pupil fails in the first semester of a subject, he should be allowed to try the second without repeating the first.

9. A pupil should not be expected to learn a lesson that he does not enjoy.

10. Moving picture shows do more harm than good.

Exercise 150

Let three or four pupils write upon the blackboard three arguments in support of the same one of the following propositions. Then let the class choose from all the arguments given those three or four that they think are best, giving in each case reasons for their choice.

In the same way let them work out the negative of the same proposition.

1. Every city should have a public park in the business district.

2. The large department stores should be abolished and smaller stores, selling only one kind of commodity, established.

3. The mail order house should be abolished.

4. It is bad business policy to conduct cut-price sales.

5. The newspapers are the greatest educators of the time.

6. Billboard advertisements destroy the beauty of a city.

7. Women should be allowed to vote.

8. Labor unions are a benefit to the public.

9. All government should be conducted on the civil service plan.

10. Underselling a competitor ruins trade.

Exercise 151

One or two weeks in advance let the class choose three members for each side of one of the following propositions. On the day of the debate let the rest of the class act as judges to decide which side has presented the most convincing arguments in the best English.

1. It is better to be a farm hand than a factory employee.

2. Every girl should prepare herself to earn her own living.

3. Trusts should be regulated, not abolished.

4. Strikes should be considered illegal.

5. Advertising has increased the cost of living. (See Exercise 152.)

6. Communism would lower the cost of living.

7. The business of a city should not be centralized.

8. Labor troubles are brought about because the poor ape the rich.

9. Contentment is better than wealth.

10. Tariff increases the cost of living.

Exercise 152—Outline for a Debate

Choose two or four members of the class to develop each side of the following debate. Wherever possible, definite figures should be used.

Resolved, THAT ADVERTISING HAS INCREASED THE COST OF LIVING.

Affirmative

I. Modern advertising is world-wide in extent.
(*a*) Practically all classes of articles are now extensively advertised.
(1) Food stuffs; e.g., breakfast foods.
(2) Clothing; e.g., men's suits.
(3) Luxuries; e.g., automobiles.
(4) Investments; e.g., real estate.
(*b*) Every possible medium is used.
(1) Newspapers.
(2) Magazines.
(3) Billboards and street cars.
(4) Circulars and booklets.
II. An enormous amount of money is spent in advertising.
(*a*) The use of advertising agencies is growing more widespread.
(1) One agency has made the statement that it has nine men whose salaries amount to $227,000 annually.
(*b*) More and more companies are engaging advertising managers.
(1) They draw large salaries.
(*x*) In many cases, $10,000 annually.
(*c*) Advertising rates are very high; for example,
(1) The rate for a certain magazine is $1000 a page per issue.
(2) Metropolitan newspapers charge as high a rate as $500 a page per issue.
(*d*) Many advertisers use each issue of a number of mediums, making the cost run to an enormous total; for example,
(1) *Cream of Wheat* is advertised in every issue of almost every magazine.
III. The consumer pays for the advertising.
(*a*) The price that the consumer pays for an article must cover the cost of production and the expense of distribution, leaving
fair margins of profit, since
(1) The manufacturer will no longer produce if his profit ceases.
(2) He is not willing to take the cost of advertising from his profit in manufacturing.

(3) The dealer will not take the advertising cost from his own profit.
IV. Advertising increases prices.
(*a*) The cost of manufacture and the expense of distribution have been steadily lowered, and yet prices of articles have steadily
advanced; therefore
(1) The rise is not due to the cost of manufacture.
(2) Nor to the expense of distribution.
(*b*) Competition necessitates an increased amount of advertising.
(1) If one firm begins to advertise, its competitors, for self-protection, must follow suit.
(*c*) Competitive advertising raises expenses above the point where there is a fair profit at the old price.
(1) For a given kind of goods there is usually a certain volume of business, which grows with population.
(2) If all the firms competing in those goods increase their expenses by advertising, they must raise prices to make the same
profit as previously.
(*d*) Advertised articles cost more than the unadvertised.
(1) Bulk rolled oats vs. package rolled oats.
(2) Bulk pickles and relishes vs. advertised brands.
(3) Bulk macaroni vs. package goods.

Negative

I. The present increased advertising is the result of normal growth.
(*a*) Multiplied manufactures necessarily multiply advertisements.
(1) Every day new products are being put on the market.
(2) No product has the chance of a sale until it is known.
(3) In the present scope of community life the advertisement is the most convenient means of acquainting consumers with
new products.
(*b*) Any unusual increase in advertising has a reasonable explanation.
(1) Automobile advertising has increased as the automobile has replaced the wagon and carriage, because of
(*x*) Greater convenience.
(*y*) Lower operating cost.
(2) Prepared breakfast food advertising has increased as these foods have replaced cooked foods, because of
(*x*) Greater convenience.
II. Increased advertising is done on the scale of old prices.
(*a*) Merchants dare not raise prices to make the consumer pay for the advertising, since

(1) They must compete with manufacturers who do not advertise and who have no overhead advertising expense.
(*b*) The most widely advertised articles are the inexpensive necessary accessories.
(1) Food products.
(2) Soaps and soap powders.
(3) Toilet articles.
(*c*) They have not advanced in price.
(1) Quaker Oats.
(2) Ivory Soap; Sapolio.
(3) Mennen's Talcum Powder.
III. Widespread advertising works to the advantage, not the disadvantage, of the consumer.
(*a*) It gives new opportunities
(1) To compare values.
(2) To buy to the best advantage; for example,
(*x*) In advertised bargain sales.
(*b*) It reduces the cost of production and the selling expense, thu tending to lower the price.
(1) By increasing sales, it reduces the cost per article.
(*x*) Maximum purchasing power means minimum cost to the manufacturer.
(2) In taking the place of salesmen, it reduces expenses, thus lowering the price; for example,
(*x*) In mail order firms.
(3) Therefore the advertising expense is unimportant in influencing a higher price.
IV. The most marked price advances have been in the unadvertised necessaries of life.
(*a*) In breadstuffs.
(1) Less in quantity for higher prices than formerly.
(*b*) In meats and poultry.
(1) An advance of from 25 per cent to 100 per cent and more.
(*c*) In butter and eggs.
(1) An advance similar to that shown in meats and poultry.

Exercise 153—Additional Subjects for Debates

1. The wages of women should be the same as those of men in the same occupation.

2. The government should grant old age pensions.

3. Employers should be liable for the life and health of employees.

4. The boycott is a legitimate method of obtaining employees' demands.

5. National expositions do not benefit the cities in which they are held.

6. Railroad combination lowers rates.

7. Piece-work should be prohibited by law.

8. National party lines should be discarded in municipal elections.

9. City governments should be allowed to decide their problems without intervention of the state legislature.

10. Municipal offices should be appointive and not elective.

11. The commission form of government is best for large cities.

12. Immigration is the cause of municipal evils.

13. A personal property tax cannot be levied with fairness.

14. The United States should not further extend its colonial dependencies.

15. The President should be elected by a direct vote of the people.

16. Ex-presidents of the United States should become life members of the Senate.

17. The President and the Vice-President should be prohibited from taking part in political campaigns.

18. The United States should subsidize a merchant marine.

19. Foreign-built ships, owned by Americans, should be granted the privilege of American register.

20. The governors of states should not have the power to pardon.

21. A three-fourths vote of a jury should be sufficient to render a verdict in criminal cases.

22. The coast defenses of the United States should be increased.

23. The farmer is to blame for the high prices.

24. The results of Arctic explorations have not justified the cost.

CHAPTER XI

CHOOSING SUBJECTS

IN Chapter X definite subjects were assigned for talks. Getting a subject for yourself sometimes seems difficult; you are likely to think that there is no topic upon which you can say more than a few sentences. Isn't it true that when you are talking to your friends you seldom are at a loss for something to say? Of course, what your companion says often suggests an idea on which you give your opinion. You speak about things that interest you, and the words come fairly easily. Why not apply the same principle to more formal composition, whether oral or written? Unless a subject interests you, do not use it. But be careful that you do not reject it as uninteresting until you have thought about it carefully, considering it from all sides. Often one subject will suggest another akin to it, but more interesting to you because you know more about it. For this reason choose very simple subjects, and become thoroughly familiar with them by thinking or reading about them, before you attempt to explain them.

Sometimes, again, you will find that the subject you have chosen is not good because it is not definite enough. You hardly know where or how to begin to explain it, because it suggests no definite ideas. Perhaps, for instance, you have decided to write on the automobile and can think of nothing to say until you remember that you once saw an automobile race about which you can tell several interesting details; or you have seen an automobile accident and can write on the topic *A Runaway Electric.* If you can speak or write on a topic taken from your own observation, your composition will probably be good. You know the facts, you have an interest in the subject, and you will very likely say something of interest to others. Subjects taken from school life or neighborhood happenings, especially such things as you yourself have seen, are excellent. Perhaps on your way to school you noticed that several old houses are being torn down. You remember that you heard that a candy factory is to be erected. At once several suggestions for themes will come to you; as, *Why the Factory is Being Erected in this Neighborhood*, *How Neighborhoods Change in a Large City*, *The Work the Wrecking Company Carries on.* Perhaps your father owns property in the neighborhood, and you could write on *How Real Estate Values have Changed in this Neighborhood.*

Next to your own experience, the best source from which to draw subjects is your reading. This may be divided into (1) books, (2) magazines and newspapers. Recall one of the books that you read in the grammar grades, perhaps *The Courtship of Miles Standish.* Drawing your material from this source, you can write *A Picture of Early Plymouth Days*, or a sketch of Miles

Standish's character, using the title *Practice What You Preach.* But to try to tell the whole story to any one in two or three minutes would result in failure, for it would be a subject entirely too big to treat in so short a time. All the interesting details would have to be omitted, and, if the details are omitted, the story loses its vitality.

It is the newspaper or the magazine, however, that offers us the most available source of subjects. Practically all that we know of the modern world and of the wonderful progress being made in invention and discovery, as well as of the accidents and disasters that take place, we have learned first from the newspaper and have verified later by the articles in magazines. Every issue of a newspaper or of a magazine contains suggestions for many subjects. Such magazines as *The World's Work*, *System*, *The Outlook*, *The Technical World*, and other magazines that deal with technical subjects in a popular way are excellent for this work.

A third important source of subjects is the studies that you are now pursuing. Every new study affords a new point of view, which should suggest many topics for oral and written themes. Sometimes a good subject is the comparison of two of your studies by which you try to show, perhaps, how the one depends on the other.

The subject, of course, is but the beginning of the composition. Developing the subject is fully as important as having a subject to develop. The ability to develop a subject clearly is very important in the business world. A business man sells his goods either by talking or by writing; by the salesman or by the letter and the advertisement. Unless the salesman talks in a convincing way, he probably will sell few goods. He must know not only what to say, but how to say it.

Exercise 154—The Subject as a Whole

First, you must see your subject in its entirety, as one thing. Ask yourself, "Just what does my title mean?" and if you have not as yet selected a title, study your subject from all sides until you can see how to narrow it to certain definite dimensions. Now you have set a sort of fence around your subject. Nothing outside must enter, but nothing inside must escape. The length of the composition you are to write usually helps you decide on the limits of your subject. If you are writing a book on Africa, you might include all that the title suggests to you of exploration, colonization, civilization, and Christianization. But if you are writing a very short theme—not over three pages—it is evident that the subject must be narrowed. Would *The Transvaal* be good? *The Jungles of Africa? Roosevelt in Africa? African Mission Stations? When I think of Africa I think of Stanley?*

Which of the following subjects would be good for short compositions, either oral or written? The oral theme should occupy two or three minutes, the written perhaps three pages. What is the objection to a one word subject?

1. Manufacturing.
2. Household uses of electricity.
3. The Constitution of the United States.
4. Why we celebrate the Fourth of July.
5. The destruction of our forests.
6. Europe.
7. The westernizing of China.
8. How railroads build cities.
9. The fire drill at school.
10. Education.
11. The dead letter office.
12. The clearing house.
13. Business.
14. Honesty in business.
15. Physicians should advertise.
16. Paper.
17. How an electric bell works.
18. Electrifying the railroads.
19. How to make candy.
20. Vocational education in Germany.

Exercise 155—The Divisions of the Subject

After you have selected your subject, decide into what divisions it naturally falls. If it is of the proper length, it probably will divide itself into two or three divisions. Each of these will constitute one-half or one-third of your composition, and within each division illustrations, reasons, and explanatory details will appear. Arrange the divisions in the order in which they naturally come, according to their relative time of happening or according to their relative importance, reserving the most important for the last.

Sometimes this sort of division is difficult to make, because a subject can frequently be treated from different points of view, the point of view deciding the divisions. Sometimes you will find that you have made a number of small divisions, in each of which you can say only one or two sentences. This will at once suggest that you have not found the main parts of the subject, but have made unimportant divisions. Again, it may seem that you cannot divide your subject into satisfactory parts. In that case, you probably do not know enough about it. Think about it again, and, if you find that you really cannot divide it, choose another.

Choose one of the following subjects. Is the title definite and clear? If it is not, change it so that it will be. For example, *Photography* (5) is not a definite title. No one could attempt to explain the entire subject of photography in a few minutes. A better title for a theme would be one of the following: *How to Develop a Negative; How to Intensify* [or *reduce*] *a Negative; Our Camera Club; The Photography Exhibit at the Art Museum; Kinematography; Flash Light Pictures without Smoke or Odor; The Conditions Necessary for a Good Snap Shot Picture; The Advantages of Using a Developing Machine; How My Camera Helped Pay for My Vacation.* Can you suggest still others?

After having selected your title, decide into what divisions the subject naturally falls. For example, let us take (2) below. *A Ball Game* is not a definite title. Instead, let us choose *Last Saturday's Football Game.* As stated above, a subject may be treated from different points of view, the point of view deciding the divisions. Thus, in treating *Last Saturday's Football Game*, we may divide:

a

LAST SATURDAY'S FOOTBALL GAME

I. The first quarter.

II. The second quarter.

III. The third quarter.

IV. The fourth quarter.

b

LAST SATURDAY'S FOOTBALL GAME

I. The excitement for a week before the game.

II. The tension during the struggle.

III. The celebration after the game.

c

THE TWO DECISIVE PLAYS IN SATURDAY'S GAME

I. The long forward pass.

II. The end run to the five-yard line.

Still other divisions may be made if we consider the subject from the point of view of the teams or the players themselves. Can you suggest any such divisions?

In the same way choose one of the subjects given below. Change it, if necessary. Then write out the topic of each division in as few words as possible.

1. An important electrical device.
2. A ball game.
3. Getting dinner.
4. The aeroplane.
5. Photography.
6. How styles change.
7. The back-to-the-farm movement.
8. Why oriental rugs are expensive.
9. Wireless telegraphy.
10. The business course in this school.

Exercise 156—The Outline

If your theme consists of more than one division, before you begin to speak or write you should prepare a definite working plan or outline. It should include enough to suggest the first sentence of each division and the more important details within each. The outline will help you in speaking or writing to arrange the topics so that they will follow one another clearly. If you have an outline, there will be much less danger of including details which do not belong to the subject and of omitting details which should appear.

In the following very simple outlines notice the use of indentation:

1

THE PROBLEM OF KEEPING OUR CITIES CLEAN

I. The cleaning of streets.
(*a*) In summer.
(1) The cost of sprinkling.
(*b*) In winter.
(1) The cost of removing snow.
II. The cleaning of alleys.
(*a*) The disposal of garbage.
III. The smoke nuisance.
(*a*) Smoke consumers.
(*b*) Smoke inspection.

2

PUBLIC GYMNASIUMS

I. Definition of a public gymnasium.
(*a*) Location.
(*b*) Equipment.
(*c*) Management.
II. Benefits to the public.

(*a*) Keeps children off the streets.
(1) Congested districts.
(*b*) Develops them physically.
(*c*) Affords them pleasure.
(1) Outdoor and indoor games.
(2) Bathing at beaches connected with gymnasiums.

One more suggestion is in place here. In writing an outline, be careful that you express similar subdivisions of a topic by similar grammatical elements. For example, in the first outline above, (*a*) under I is a phrase; (*b*) under I should be a similar phrase. It would be incorrectly worded *Winter* or *What the winter problem is*. What is the advantage of such similarity?

Using the divisions you made for one of the subjects under Exercise 155, develop an outline for a theme.

Exercise 157

Choose one of the following subjects; restrict it or expand it, if necessary; select a proper title; write an outline; and then write or deliver your composition, following your outline closely. Notice that the shorter your title the more it includes, and therefore the longer your composition must be to deal adequately with the subject.

1. Giving talks before a class develops self-reliance.

2. Most inventors would not have succeeded without perseverance.

3. The more training a man has, the better chance he has to succeed.

4. Most rich men learned to save early.

5. The value of courtesy in a retail business.

6. The dangers of football.

7. The various methods of heating a house.

8. The sporting page often sells the newspaper.

9. Educational features of the modern newspaper.

10. Our national game.

11. Baseball is a better game than football.

12. The use of machinery has lowered the cost of manufactured articles.

13. How to prevent taking colds.

14. Athletic contests develop courage.

15. Qualities essential to good salesmanship.

16. Our debate with ——.

17. The qualities of a good street car advertisement.

18. A good cartoon.

19. Learning to swim.

20. The trials of washing day.

21. Birds as money savers.

22. Birds as destroyers.

23. Open air as a cure for tuberculosis.

24. Making a raft.

25. Every one should open a savings account.

26. Laziness.

27. Tennis is better than baseball.

28. Our respiratory system.

29. The bad effects of ridicule.

30. The good effects of ridicule.

Exercise 158

Recall one of the books that you have read recently. Name two subjects that it suggests to you and that you can talk about. Write a careful outline for each of them, and be prepared to speak on one.

Exercise 159

Name a subject taken from one of your studies, history for example. Let it be definite enough so that you can tell all the details that you know about it in a speech lasting two or three minutes. Use examples and illustrations to make the subject interesting and clear. Prepare an outline.

Exercise 160

Reproduce an article that you have read in a current magazine. Be careful that you make the material your own before attempting to retell it. Do not under any circumstances try to memorize the article. Understand fully what it says, make an outline of the facts that you wish to reproduce, and then give them as if they were your own ideas. At the beginning of your speech tell the name and date of the magazine from which you are taking the facts.

Exercise 161

As has been said, most of us get our ideas of what is taking place in the world from the articles that we read in current newspapers and magazines. We cannot always form our opinion from what one newspaper on one day says of a particular event. We must read what it says on successive days and, if possible, consult other newspapers on the same subject, for it is well known that not all newspapers are non-partisan. If one in the city is known to be so, that is the paper to read for the material for this exercise. Then, if we can read what one of the magazines says on the same subject, our knowledge will probably be more definite and more nearly true.

Let the class be divided into different sections, representing different kinds of news; for example, national, local, foreign, and business news. Under national news, you can perhaps find articles on national politics, legislative measures being discussed at Washington, rumors of war, immigration; under local news, anything pertaining to the city or the state in which you live; under foreign news, anything of interest to any of the other countries of the world; under business news, the prices of food products, strikes, panics, and their effect on business conditions. These are but suggestions. Such topics change so rapidly that nothing more definite can here be given.

When you have been assigned to one of these divisions, prepare a talk on a topic that you understand thoroughly. Begin your talk with a clear statement of your subject, as explained in Exercise 140; amplify it by details or illustrations; and end with a sentence of conclusion, forecasting the future of your topic or restating what you have proved.

Exercise 162

For a week follow the same current event as recorded in the newspaper, taking notes as you read. Then choose from all your material only those facts that belong strictly to one topic. Write an outline, setting forth the facts in logical order. Deliver the speech, following your outline closely.

Exercise 163

Let the class choose four or six members one week in advance, who are to prepare a debate on a topic of current interest. Let the other members of the class act as judges or volunteer on either side, as the instructor may see fit. Such debates should occur as often as possible.

Exercise 164

About once a month devote a day to the production of a class paper. Let the class choose a name. During the first year let the items be developed into paragraphs. Longer compositions should be reserved for the second year.

SUGGESTIONS FOR ARTICLES FOR THE PAPER

1. A column of interesting business items clipped from leading papers.
2. An important news item that would make a good "story."
3. Original editorials on one or more of the following:
a. Needs or improvements in city, school, or home.
b. Recent city news.
c. Business news.
d. State news.
e. National news.
f. Foreign news.
4. Personal experiences, amusing incidents, or anecdotes, preferably of the business world.
5. For sale advertisements, or "want ads" that the class would understand.

Exercise 165

Criticise the following outlines. Each topic is supposed to represent a division in thought.

1

THE WHEAT HARVEST

1. A group of reapers.
2. Their costumes.
3. The field.
4. Starting the harvest.
5. Carting the sheaves to the barn.
6. The stacks.
7. The field after the harvest.

2

THE TONGUE

1. What it is.

2. It is a good thing.

3. It instructs.

4. Evils done by the tongue.

5. Especially slander.

6. Conclusion.

3

THE NEWSPAPER STRIKE

1. The cause.

(*a*) Strikers want higher wages.

(*b*) Poverty of the families of the strikers.

(*c*) Police have to protect newsboys against strikers.

2. Disadvantages.

(*a*) Newspapers are losing business.

(*b*) Newsboys sympathize with strikers.

3. Riots.

(*a*) Newsboys hurt and newspapers burned.

(*b*) Police cannot watch all sections of city.

4. Conclusion.

CHAPTER XII

PUNCTUATION

WHEN we speak, we make our meaning clear by the expression that we put into our words and sentences. Some sentences we say all in one breath and with not much change in emphasis from one word to the next. We may be pretty sure that such a sentence is short and simple, with all its elements arranged in their natural order. In this respect compare the sentences given below.

Notice that the following sentence is spoken as one word group:

Steam and electricity are making one commercial community of all nations.

A part that is subordinate in idea is subordinate in tone; as,

Steam and electricity, *which are the greatest of all discoveries*, are making one commercial community of all nations.

In the usual order of the sentence the subject comes first. Sometimes for emphasis a participial phrase or an adverbial clause precedes the subject. Such inversion is always indicated; as,

If the grape crop is large, the price of grapes is low.

Sometimes a word or phrase is thrust into the sentence to give clearness or force; as,

If, *on the other hand*, the season is poor, the price of grapes is high.

What, *then*, determines the price of grapes?

We cannot become good speakers until we learn to subordinate in tone those groups of words that are subordinate in idea, and to bring out clearly those groups which, for one reason or another, are emphatic. The same thing is true in music. We cannot become good musicians until we learn phrasing; that is, until we learn to group the notes to form distinct musical ideas. But when we write our thoughts, we cannot indicate the tone in which the words are spoken. We must show in some other way which groups of words belong together, which are important, and which are subordinate in idea. For this purpose punctuation marks have been invented. When we write, we unconsciously speak the thoughts to ourselves; we hear the divisions between the parts of ideas; and, if we understand punctuation, we indicate the divisions.

Questions

1. Why in writing and printing do we separate one word from the next? In ancient writing this was not done.

2. Why do we separate one sentence from the next?

3. We use punctuation marks for the same reason. Explain.

4. The word to keep in mind in punctuation is *separate.* If two words belong together in idea, the two making one idea, allow them to stand unseparated. If they give two ideas, separate them by a mark of punctuation. What is the difference in thought in the two sentences that follow?

(*a*) She is a pretty, energetic girl.
(*b*) She is a pretty energetic girl.

Exercise 166—The Apostrophe (')

The *apostrophe* (') is used—

1. To show the possessive case of nouns (See Exercise 82); as,

The *boy's* writing is excellent.

2. To indicate the omission of one or more letters; as,

I'll attend to the matter.

3. To show the plural of letters, figures, and words that usually have no plural; as,

Your *3's* are too much like your *5's*, your *a's* like your *u's*.

Don't use so many *and's*.

Write sentences in each of which you use one of the following words correctly:

you're	we're	who's	they're
your	were	whose	there
it's	he's	don't	their
its	his	doesn't	

Explain why the apostrophe is used in the following:

1. I've received no reply.

2. This month's sales exceed last month's by one thousand dollars.

3. Politics doesn't affect the matter very much.

4. The mistake was caused by his making his 7's like his 9's.

5. Have you received the treasurer's report? No, I haven't.

Point out the mistakes in the following:

1. For sale, A ladies fur coat.

2. The boy's have gone skating.

3. We wo'nt worry over the political situation.

4. Lets decide now where were to spend our vacation.

5. Dot your is and not your us.

6. Is this book your's or her's?

Exercise 167—Capitals

Capitals are used for—

1. The first word of every sentence.

2. The first word of every line of poetry.

3. The first word of a quotation (See Exercise 169).

4. The first word of a formal statement or resolution; as,

Resolved, That women shall be given the right to vote.

5. The first word of every group of words paragraphed separately in an itemized list, as in an order for merchandise.

6. The pronoun *I* and the interjection *O* (not *oh*).

7. The words *Bible* and *Scripture*, the books of the Bible, all names applied to the Deity, and all personal pronouns referring to Him.

8. All proper nouns, proper adjectives, and words that are considered proper nouns; as,

a. Names of the days of the week, holidays, and months of the year, but not names of the seasons.

b. North, South, etc., when they refer to sections of the country, but not when they refer to a direction or a point of the compass.

c. Official titles or titles of honor when they are used in connection with names, but not when they are used without names; as,

Vice-President Roosevelt, ex-President Roosevelt.
Nominations are now in order for vice-president.

d. Names of political parties.

e. Names of religious sects.

f. Names of important events or documents; as,

The Revolution, The Declaration of Independence.

g. The salutation in a letter; as,

Dear Sir, Gentlemen.

h. Words indicating relationship, when they are used in connection with a proper name, or when used alone as a name, but not when used with a possessive pronoun; as,

We expect Aunt Ellen at four o'clock.
I expect my mother at four o'clock.

9. The important words in the title of a book, play, or composition. Prepositions, articles, and conjunctions are not capitalized; as,

The Call of the Wild.

10. Such words as *Paragraph*, *Article*, or *Section*, when accompanied with a number; as,

Paragraph 26, Article 3.

11. See Exercise 75.

Exercise 168

The *period* (.) is used—

1. To indicate the end of a declarative sentence; as,

The business is prosperous.

2. To indicate an abbreviation; as,

The firm of Clark Bros. has opened a new office at 144 Pleasant St., Erie, Pa.

The *interrogation mark* (?) is used—

To indicate the end of a sentence that asks a question; as,

When did you order the goods?

The *exclamation mark* (!) is used—

To indicate the end of a sentence or other expression that shows strong feeling; as,

Such demands are inhuman!

Frequently, all that shows exactly how the writer wished his thought to be understood is the punctuation. The same words may express different ideas according to the mark of punctuation that follows them. Read the following to show the meaning that the writer wished to convey by each. Explain the circumstances under which each might have been spoken.

1. The price is too high.
2. The price is too high!
3. The price is too high?
4. The crop will not be good. There'll be no corn.
5. Corn! There'll be no corn!
6. You didn't tell him that.
7. You didn't tell him that!
8. You didn't tell him that?
9. You are enjoying yourself.
10. You are enjoying yourself?
11. You are enjoying yourself!

Exercise 169—Quotation Marks (" ")

1. When a speaker's words are quoted exactly, they should be enclosed in quotation marks. This is called a *direct quotation.*

He said, "The business is growing."

Notice that the word *said* is followed by a comma, and that the quotation begins with a capital letter.

2. If the quotation itself is a question, although it forms part of a declarative sentence, it requires an interrogation mark before the quotation mark; as,

Have you been waiting long?
She opened the door and said, "Have you been waiting long?"

3. The same applies to a quotation that requires an exclamation mark; as,

Look!

He cried, "Look!"

4. When the words of explanation follow the quoted words, the punctuation is as follows:

(*a*) When the quotation is a declarative sentence, put a comma after the quotation and begin the words of explanation with a small letter; as,

"The business is growing," he said.

(*b*) When the quotation is a question, conclude it with an interrogation mark, and begin the words of explanation with a small letter; as,

"Have you been waiting long?" she asked.

(*c*) When the quotation is an exclamation, conclude it with an exclamation mark, and begin the words of explanation with a small letter; as,

"Look!" he cried.

5. When the author's words of explanation interrupt the speaker's words, the punctuation is as follows:

(*a*) When the interrupted parts are not naturally separated by any punctuation mark, the comma is used as follows:

I do not believe that the report is true.

"I do not believe," he said, "that the report is true."

Notice in what way the quotation marks show that the words *he said* do not belong to the quoted words.

(*b*) Whatever mark of punctuation would naturally appear between the interrupted parts must be used; as,

(1) I shall buy the Boston ferns; they seem to require but little care.

"I shall buy the Boston ferns," she said; "they seem to require but little care."

(2) Oh! The flames are higher!

"Oh!" she cried. "The flames are higher!"

4. Division into sentences is made within a quotation just as elsewhere. When the thought ends, the sentence must end. The different sentences, however, must not be divided by quotation marks; as,

"The train came in," said he, "half an hour ago. I do not see them in the waiting room. I think they did not come."

5. When a quotation is very long, consisting of several paragraphs, quotation marks should be placed at the beginning of the quotation, at the beginning of each succeeding paragraph, and at the end of the quotation—not at the end of each paragraph.

6. When a quotation occurs within a quotation, the one within is distinguished by single marks; as,

John explained, "After I had told Mr. Brown how I thought the work could be done more easily, he said, 'Thank you for your suggestion.'"

7. Any words quoted from a book or article, or any words quoted with a special significance, such as slang, should be enclosed in quotation marks; as,

The day of the salesman who is satisfied with the "good old way" is fast passing.

8. A formal question, statement, or resolution for a debate is not enclosed in quotation marks; as,

The question we are to discuss is, Shall women vote?

Exercise 170

Punctuate the following, dividing into sentences wherever the sense demands division:

1. Thank you for your suggestion said Mr. Brown

2. Mr. Brown said thank you for your suggestion

3. Thank you said Mr. Brown for your suggestion

4. If you will ask the shipping clerk I volunteered I think you can get definite information

5. How can we enforce the law asked the man

6. The law cried the man how can we enforce the law

7. Tell me said the man how we can enforce the law

8. Tell me this said the man how can we enforce the law

9. The question before us is how can we enforce the law

10. John whispered did you hear his mother say yes you may go

11. As I was walking along the river he continued I heard a voice cry help

12. Halt shouted the captain the bridge is down

13. The captain shouted halt the bridge is down

14. We cannot cross said the captain the bridge is down

15. The bridge is down said the captain and I fear there is no other way to cross

16. Is the bridge down asked the captain does no one know another way to cross

17. The captain said the bridge is down do you know another way to cross

18. What shall we do asked a soldier if the bridge is down

19. Do cried the captain swim that's what we'll do

20. As we were riding along spoke up one of the soldiers I heard a farmer shout you fellows better try the bridge lower down

Exercise 171—Indirect Discourse

In the preceding exercise we saw different forms of direct quotations, or direct discourse. In each case, the speaker's words were quoted exactly. When the substance of the thought is given in slightly different form, we have an indirect quotation, or indirect discourse, in which no quotation marks are used. An indirect quotation is usually a subordinate clause depending on a word of *thinking*, *saying*, *telling*, or the like. Indirect statements are usually introduced by *that*, and indirect questions by *when*, *where*, *why*, *whether*, *if*, *who*, *which*, *what*, and the like. When a sentence is changed from direct to indirect discourse, the person and usually the tense of the direct quotation are changed; as,

Direct: He said, "I do not believe the report."
Indirect: He said that he did not believe the report.

Direct: He said, "Germany is over-populated."
Indirect: He said that Germany is over-populated. (See Exercise 107.)

Direct: She said, "I did my work before I went to school."
Indirect: She said that she had done her work before she went to school.

Direct: "I have finished my work," said the girl.
Indirect: She says that she has finished her work.

Direct: "Why didn't he succeed?" I asked.
Indirect: I asked why he had not succeeded.

Direct: "When may I go?" she inquired.
Indirect: She inquired when she might go.

In the following change the italicized parts to direct quotations. Do not change the paragraphing.

1
THE SEAL'S LESSON

The baby seal said *that he could not swim.*

His mother answered *that he could try.*

The little fellow persisted *that he could never learn.*

His mother looked at him sternly, and said *that every seal must learn to swim.*

He replied *that the water was cold and that he liked the sand better*, but because his mother insisted, he slid into the water whimpering.

After he had gone a short distance, he turned around and called out *that the water was much pleasanter than the sand.*

His mother said *that she knew that it would be so.* She said *that young people must do as they are told because they have not had enough experience to judge for themselves.*

2
A FAITHFUL SERVANT

A certain old time king said *that he needed a servant who could be depended upon.* He said he knew *that such a man is difficult to secure, and in the hope of getting the right one, he would hire two.*

When he had engaged them, he took them to a well and, showing them a large basket, told them *to fill it with water.* He said *that he would return at night to see what they had done.*

The men were very much in earnest when they began the work, but, after pouring five or six bucketfuls of water into the basket, one of them stopped and said *that he did not see any use in doing that because, as soon as he poured the water in, it ran out again, and his time was lost.*

His companion replied *that the kind of work that their master gave them was no concern of theirs; that they were paid to do the work; and, whether it seemed useful to them or not, they ought to do it.*

The first speaker said *that the other man could do as he pleased, but, as for him, he did not expect to waste his time on such foolish work.* Throwing his bucket down, he walked off.

The one that was left continued at the work until about sunset, when he had nearly emptied the well. Looking into the basket, he saw something glittering. Stooping to look more closely, he found in the basket a ring of great value which his bucket had scooped up from the mud at the bottom of the well. He said *that now he knew why the king had wanted the water poured into the basket.*

Shortly afterward, when the king came up with some of his officers and saw the ring in the basket, he knew that the man had obeyed him, and he said *that he knew he could trust him, and as a reward for obedience he would make him master over other servants.*

Exercise 172—The Paragraph in Dialogue

In conversation the words of each speaker, together with the author's words of explanation, form one paragraph. Whenever the speaker changes, the paragraph changes; as,

"Mimer," boldly said the god Odin to the gray old guardian of the well where wit and wisdom lie hidden, "Mimer, let me drink of the waters of wisdom."

"Truly, Odin," answered Mimer, "it is a great treasure that you seek and one which many have sought before but who, when they knew the price of it, turned back."

Then replied Odin, "I would give my right hand for wisdom willingly."

"Nay," rejoined the remorseless Mimer, "it is not your right hand, but your right eye, you must give."—Keary: *The Heroes of Asgard.*

However, when one speaker talks at length, what he says is formed into paragraphs according to the divisions into which it falls. (See Chapter XIV.)

When a short quotation is simply part of a paragraph, it is punctuated as follows:

This, however, was of use to me, the impression continuing on my mind. Often when I was tempted to buy some unnecessary thing, I said to myself, "Don't give too much for the whistle," and I saved my money.

Paragraph the following:

1

On the next morning we had gone but a mile or two when we came to an extensive belt of woods, through the midst of which ran a stream, wide, deep, and of an appearance particularly muddy and treacherous. In plunged the cart, but midway it stuck fast. Then approached the long team and heavy wagon of our friends, but it paused on the brink. "Now my advice is,—" began the captain, who had been anxiously contemplating the muddy gulf. "Drive on!" cried R. But Wright, the muleteer, apparently had not as yet decided the point in his own mind. He sat still in his seat on one of the shaft-mules, whistling in a low, contemplative strain to himself. "My advice is," resumed the captain, "that we unload; for I'll bet any man five pounds that if we try to go through, we shall stick fast." "By the powers, we shall stick fast!" echoed Jack, the captain's brother, shaking his large head with an air of conviction. "Drive on! drive on!" petulantly cried R. "Well," observed the captain, turning to us as we sat looking on, "I can only give my advice; and if people won't be reasonable, why, they won't, that's all!"—Parkman: *The Oregon Trail.*

2

Rebecca walked up the lane and went to the side door. There was a porch there. Seated in a rocking-chair, husking corn, was a good-looking young man. Rebecca was a trifle shy at this encounter, but there was nothing to do except explain her presence; so she asked, "Is the lady of the house at home?." "I am the lady of the house at present," said the stranger with a whimsical smile. "What can I do for you?" "Have you ever heard of the—would you like—er I mean, do you need any soap?" queried Rebecca. "Do I look as if I do?" he responded unexpectedly. Rebecca dimpled. "I didn't mean that; I have some soap to sell; I mean I would like to introduce to you a very remarkable soap, the best now on the market. It is called the—" "Oh! I must know that soap," said the gentleman genially. "Made out of pure vegetable fats, isn't it?" "The very purest," corroborated Rebecca. "No acid in it?" "Not a trace." "And yet a child could do the Monday washing with it and use no force?" "A babe," corrected Rebecca. "Oh! a babe, eh? That child grows younger every year, instead of older—wise child!"—Wiggin: *Rebecca of Sunnybrook Farm.*

Change the following from indirect to direct discourse and paragraph:

When Whittier went on his first fishing trip, it was a day in early summer. The long afternoon shadows lay cool on the grass. The boy said that the flowers seemed brighter and the birds merrier than ever before. When they came to a bend in the river, his uncle said that this was a good place to try. He told the boy to throw out his line as he had seen others do and move it on the surface of the water in imitation of the leap of a frog. The boy did as he was told, but he caught no fish. His uncle said that he should try again. Suddenly the bait sank out of sight, and the boy cried out that he had caught a fish at last. As he spoke, he pulled up a tangle of weeds. His uncle said that he should try again, because fishermen must have patience. In a moment the boy felt something tug at his line, and as he jerked it up, he saw a fine pickerel wriggling in the sun. In uncontrollable excitement he called out to his uncle, telling him to look at the big pickerel. His uncle said that the boy didn't have it yet, and as he spoke there was a splash in the water, and the boy's hook hung empty. His uncle assured him that there were more fish in the river, but the boy would not be comforted. His uncle smiled shrewdly and told Whittier to remember never to brag of catching a fish until it was on dry land. He said that he had seen older people doing that in more ways than one, and so making fools of themselves. He said that it was better not to boast of doing a thing until it was done.

Exercise 173—The Comma (,)

Rule 1.—The comma is used to separate a direct quotation from the words of explanation.

For illustration see the foregoing exercises.

Write the following from dictation; then compare your version with the original:

Literature, the ministry, medicine, the law, and other occupations are hindered for want of men to do the work. To test this statement thoroughly you need only hunt up a first-class editor, reporter, business manager, foreman of a shop, mechanic, or artist in any branch of industry and try to hire him. You will find that he is already hired. He is sober, industrious, capable, reliable, and always in demand. He cannot get a day's holiday except by courtesy of his employer, or of his city, or of the great general public. But if you need idlers, shirkers, half-instructed, unambitious, and comfort-seeking editors, reporters, lawyers, doctors, and mechanics apply anywhere.—*Mark Twain.*

Rule 2.—The comma is used to separate the members of a series.

Exercise 174

Divide the following into sentences and supply the necessary commas:

Abraham Lincoln was a tall strong powerfully built boy he could lift a load cut down a tree or build a fence more quickly than any one else in the neighborhood his perseverance in his boyhood helps us to appreciate the firm true steady hand that guided our country through its great crisis Lincoln unceasingly showed his wise brain his great courage and his kindness of heart his character was not made in a day nor a month nor a year it was built up after years of yearning years of striving and years of hard work.

In the above point out the instances where the comma is used—

1. When several nouns follow one another, all being in the same case.

2. When several adjectives follow one another, all modifying the same noun.

3. When a succession of phrases modifies the same noun.

This kind of succession is called a *series*. Each new member gives a new idea, the comma being used to help the reader to separate one from the next with ease. Notice that the comma is used between the last two members before the coördinate conjunction as well as between the other members.

2

Dear Sir:[4]

You can make no mistake in buying BCL Power Co. bonds now the company supplies power to mines and towns of Colorado Utah and Idaho it furnishes electric light and power to Ophir Ouray Ames Pandora and other towns in Colorado in Utah it supplies light to Mescal Eureka Provo Logan and Bingham it also furnishes power for the street railway systems of Salt Lake City Farmington and Ogden.

The bonds offer such good security good interest and ready convertibility that we expect our allotment to be heavily oversubscribed will you therefore send us your order before Monday

Yours truly,

3

Imagine the scene: a little hollow in the prairie forming a perfect amphitheater the yellow grass and wild oats grazed short a herd of horses staring from the slope I myself standing in the middle like a ring-master in a circus and this wonderful horse performing at his own free will. He trotted powerfully he galloped gracefully he thundered at full speed he lifted forelegs to welcome he flung out hind legs to repel he leaped as if springing over bayonets he pranced and curvetted as if he were the pretty plaything of a girl and finally he trotted up and snuffed about me—just out of reach.

4

Dear Madam:[4]

Our Style Book shows you the best of the season's styles for ladies misses and children it contains illustrations of the latest kinds of long coats of skirts in the most fashionable cuts and materials of hats that are new and particularly becoming and of dresses with the newest sleeves and collars we are especially sure that you will like our waists they are artistic in design stylish in cut and excellent in workmanship they are selected from the leading fashion centers are the creations of the best costumers and always have individuality twenty years of selling goods by mail have given us experience skill and knowledge that make it certain we can please you.

The enclosed coupon is good for fifty cents on a five dollar order one dollar and twenty-five cents on a ten dollar order and two dollars on an order for fifteen dollars or more this offer expires September 30.

Yours truly,

5

Increased wages shorter hours and perhaps lower efficiency for the hours worked have done more to raise the cost of living than almost anything else this higher cost of production we see on the farm in the factory in transportation in merchandising and even in domestic service we cannot double the cost of excavating brick-laying plumbing and decorating and expect not to double the rents that we must pay the cost of building has increased as the demands of laborers increased as their hours of work decreased and as their wages advanced the materials that go into a building the transportation of that material the labor of assembling it and the labor of fashioning it into a building have all advanced in price.

Moreover, high living has a great deal to do with the high cost of living because it has made most of us think that we must have more conveniences more luxuries more clothes and more amusements than our fathers had with a return to the thrift of our fathers with a return to their desire for work we shall no longer feel the grip of the high cost of living there is a real danger to our nation in our extravagance in our indifference to cost in our sweep toward ease and idleness and in our growing antipathy for work.

Exercise 175

Write five sentences illustrating series of words; five illustrating series of phrases; and five illustrating series of clauses.

Exercise 176

Write the following from dictation:

1

THE GOVERNMENT'S LAUNDRY

Some of the paper money in circulation is so dirty that one feels the need of gloves in handling it, and the suspicion that it is germ laden might well be verified. It has often been said that money spreads contagious diseases, nor can such a statement be questioned when one remembers that money goes into every kind of home and is handled by many infected persons. The government has long felt that something should be done to lessen this means of spreading disease, and a machine has finally been invented that will wash and iron the dirtiest bills until they look almost as fresh as new ones. The entire cost of operating the device is hardly fifty cents for each thousand bills, but it is estimated that it will save the government as much as a million dollars a year.

2

LUCK AND LABOR

Luck is ever waiting for something to turn up; labor with keen eyes and strong will turns something up. Luck lies in bed and wishes the postman would bring him news of a fortune; labor turns out at six o'clock and with busy pen or ringing hammer lays the foundation of a competence. Luck whines; labor whistles. Luck relies on chance; labor on character.—*Cobden.*

The selections given above illustrate the compound sentence. Notice the thought expressed in these sentences. There is usually an idea of balance or contrast, and the two halves of the sentence express the two halves of the idea. The two members are usually distinct enough to require a comma before the conjunction. If the conjunction is omitted, a semicolon must separate the two members, as in the second selection above.

Rule 3.—The comma is used before the coördinate conjunction in a compound sentence. If the conjunction is omitted, a semicolon must be used.

Exercise 177

Separate the following into compound sentences and punctuate:

1

Sawdust as a fire extinguisher sounds absurd but recent experiments in Boston have proved it to be successful in quenching fires in tanks of oil and other inflammable liquids the Boston experiments were conducted with tanks of burning varnish but the same principles seem to apply to tanks of burning oil the floating sawdust forms a blanket that shuts off the air from the flames and the lack of oxygen causes the fire to die out the experiments were tried with both wet and dry sawdust and the dry material seemed to extinguish the fire as quickly as the wet.

2

Select the kind of business that suits your natural inclination and temperament some men are naturally mechanics others have a strong aversion to machinery because they do not understand it some men are imaginative others are purely practical some prefer active work others like sedentary employment all should select those occupations that suit them best.

3

Certain Western railroads have long felt the need of a new material for sleepers and they have been experimenting for some time past with cocobolo or Japanese oak the wood is so hard that it is almost impossible to drive spikes into it and screwed spikes in bored holes are used these sleepers will cost a trifle more than those made from American oak but they are expected to last twenty-five or thirty years the reason for experimenting with foreign woods is that native oak is becoming scarce and it is deemed wise to search in time for a substitute.

4

Dear Sir:

We wrote you on the third but as yet no word has come of your decision in regard to the investment you were considering at 475 Second Avenue let us have your order and we shall at once prepare the contract of sale the building is an especially attractive offering at $9,500 and we feel sure that you will find the return from it unusually large.

Yours very truly,

Exercise 178

When an adverbial clause or a participial adjective phrase is put at the beginning of a sentence to secure emphasis, it is called an *initial* clause or participial phrase. A comma separates it from the independent clause to help the reader to see where the subordinate idea ends and where the main idea begins. Rewrite the following from dictation, noticing the punctuation of initial elements:

If a city is to be kept in good condition, every citizen must pay his share of the expense. If the dreadful epidemics are to be exterminated, there must be a good board of health to see that everything is kept sanitary. When the health officers do their work well, the health of the city improves. In order that the decrees of the health department and of the courts may be enforced, there must be a good police department. Besides having these advantages, cities need good streets and good schools. Because all of these good things cost a great deal of money, high taxes must be levied to pay for them.

Rule 4.—An initial clause or participial phrase must be set off from the rest of the sentence by a comma.

Exercise 179

Punctuate the following:

1

Although cotton seed used to be considered worse than rubbish there now come from it every year millions of dollars in profit. Formerly if it was not hauled away to rot it was usually dumped into a neighboring stream and there it did much harm even if we had the space it would be impossible to explain all the products now made from the seed paper and an excellent meal for cattle may be made from the hulls but the most important products are made from the kernels besides making meal for cattle they are readily converted into crude oil according to the degree of refining that it receives this oil may appear as oil for miner's lamps lard compounds or salad oils as an illustration of the way in which modern manufacturers utilize former waste products the cotton seed is supreme.

2

When you sell your old clothes to the ragman do you know that they come back to you as writing paper because the metal buttons buckles and hooks that are often left on the garments cannot be converted into paper they used to be a source of annoyance to the papermaker although the cloth sorters tried to remove them before the garments went into the pulp vats some were overlooked if any found their way into the pulp they tore holes in the paper and often damaged the rollers in order that such danger may be avoided the pulp is now passed through a series of magnetized rakes as the rakes are passed to and fro every bit of metal clings to them when a quantity of such bits of iron is collected it is sent to the foundry to return to us in many new forms.

3

Dear Sir:

Investigating your complaint of the fifth instant we found that the furniture which you ordered on the tenth of last month left our factory on the fifteenth if all had gone well you would have received the articles on or about the twentieth as you surmised the delay in the arrival of the goods is due to a mistake on the part of the railroad company although the goods were properly billed to you they were allowed to go on to Columbus if you do not receive them within ten days' time let us hear from you again.

Yours truly,

4

Dear Sir:

Complying with your request of the 10th inst. I am sending you particulars of the property which I wish to sell as I told you when I was in your office last week the price at which I am holding the building is $20,000 if the buyer prefers not to assume the mortgage of $10,000 I think I can get the mortgagee to agree to accept present payment for the note that he holds against me unless the buyer agrees to pay the unpaid taxes for last year and the assessments levied for improvements already made I shall not consider a sale.

After all preliminary arrangements are made if you will prepare a contract of sale and forward it to me I will have the abstract brought down to date and secured by a guaranty policy.

Since I presume that the prospective purchaser has examined the property and is satisfied to pay the price for it in its present condition I would suggest that you do nothing more toward securing bids for rebuilding the porches.

Yours very truly,

Exercise 180

Write five sentences containing initial participial phrases.

Write five sentences containing initial adverbial clauses.

Exercise 181

The comma is used to separate the month from the year, the city from the county or state, the company from the place in which it is operated, or the like; as,

In December, 1912, I wrote to you from Seattle, Washington.

This use of the comma indicates that words have been omitted, the sentence above really meaning,

In December of the year 1912 I wrote to you from Seattle in the state of Washington.

The same use is shown in such sentences as,

Of the three stenographers Mary received fifteen dollars a week; Ellen, twelve; Susan, ten.

Rule 5.—The comma is used to indicate the omission of words.

Supply the necessary commas in the following:

1. The bonds will be taken over on or before October 1 1934.

2. On January 1 1913 the company had outstanding $4,000,000 of stock of the par value of one dollar a share.

3. The offices are at Salt Lake City Utah.

4. The transaction was officially conducted between the Power Bond & Share Co. New York and the Pacific Power Co. Tacoma Washington.

5. A late announcement of the Census Bureau tells us that the center of population of the United States is four and one-quarter miles south of Unionville Monroe County Indiana.

6. Many mechanical devices in common use may be traced to the patterns furnished by nature. Thus the hog suggests the plow; the butterfly the ordinary hinge; the toadstool the umbrella; the duck the ship; the fungus growth on trees the bracket.

7. The per capita saving in the banks of the United States in 1820 was twelve cents; in 1830 fifty-four cents; in 1840 eighty-two cents; in 1850 $1.87; in 1860 $4.75; in 1870 $14.26; in 1880 $16.33; in 1890 $24.75; in 1900 $31.78; in 1910 $45.05; and it is still increasing.

8. The population in 1820 was 10,000,000 and in 1910 90,000,000.

9. Mexico draws about 55% of her imports from the United States; Nicaragua about 50%; the other Central American states from 35 to 75%; Venezuela 31%; Cuba 52%.

10. In one decade Germany's exports to Latin-America have shown an increase of 222%; those of the United Kingdom an increase of 115%; and those of the United States an increase of 130%.

Write five sentences illustrating Rule 5.

Exercise 182—Explanatory Expressions

There are a number of expressions—words, phrases, and clauses—which are inserted into the sentence for clearness or emphasis. They add a bit of explanation but are not absolutely necessary. In other words, they might be omitted, and the sentence would still be clear. These may be of various kinds but are all similar in use. They should be set off by commas so that the reader will easily see that they are subordinate to the main idea of the sentence.

A. The *appositive* is a word or a group of words inserted lo explain the noun that it follows. (See Exercise 80.)

Explain the use of the commas in the following sentences:

1. William E. Curtis, *one of the world's ablest newspaper correspondents*, in his will expressed the hope that his grandson would continue his life-work, *a recital of the good that men had done and not of the crimes they had committed.*

2. The new device, the adding machine, has greatly lessened office drudgery.

3. Wall street, the great center of business life, fixes stock prices.

4. The people in moderate circumstances, the excellent middle class of a country, suffer most from the strain of high prices.

5. The Montreal Tramways Company, the first company to introduce pay-as-you-enter cars, started its business in the winter of 1861 with a very simple equipment, two horse-drawn sleighs.

6. The Early Gem musk melon, one of the best shipping melons grown, is a cross between the Rocky Ford and the Emerald Green varieties.

7. In making up our collections and bargain offers for this year, we have arranged to put up a "Surprise Box," one hundred packages of selected vegetable and flower seeds.

8. The Chinese Giant, a new variety of sweet pepper, produces branching plants about two feet in height.

9. Amundsen, the discoverer of the south pole, is a native of Norway.

Rule 6.—The comma is used to separate an appositive from the rest of the sentence.

Write five sentences illustrating the use of the comma to set off an appositive.

Exercise 183—Explanatory Expressions

Similar in use to appositives are—

B. Words, phrases, or clauses that separate the subject from the predicate verb, the verb from its object, or the like.

In the natural order of the sentence the verb immediately follows the subject and the object follows the verb. When, for the purpose of explanation, something is inserted between the two, it should be set off from the rest of the sentence by commas. Words that are thus inserted are called appositive or parenthetical expressions and are illustrated in the following:

In Ohio and Kentucky enterprising individuals, *evidently taking the suggestion from the popular rural delivery service*, have established ice cream routes. Ice cream wagons travel the country roads at stated times so that, *with no more trouble than is required to answer the postman's whistle*, dwellers on the farms can now secure the hot weather luxury at reasonable prices. The plan, *so far as one can tell from present indications*, gives promise of meeting with great success.

Rule 7.—Parenthetical expressions should be set off by commas.

Punctuate the following:

1

The politics of the city as well as those of the nation must be kept clean. The most intelligent men of the community not the least intelligent should make our political speeches and be our political leaders. The very opposite we must confess is what we see too often. Many business men steadily pursuing their own ends during the day feel that they cannot devote time to politics. We need not search far to discover that too many of them even if they have the time do not care to give it. At election the most influential business and professional men either through lack of interest or through laziness stay at home instead of going to the polls. The men who are elected in nine cases out of ten are not fit to hold office. The blame belongs every one will agree to those who do not vote.

2

England as most people know is becoming vastly interested in the production of cotton in the Soudan. This state of affairs for more reasons than one is a matter of interest to the American manufacturer as well as to the American cotton planter. Egyptian cotton ranking next to our own sea-island in length and strength of fiber is wanted because of the brilliant finish it gives. For the manufacture of fine goods including sateens India linens and mercerized goods as well as for mixing with silk it has been found very valuable. Cotton growers expect that the enlargement of the Assouan dam will eventually redeem about a million acres from the desert in Lower Egypt and although not more than half will probably be planted to cotton it will increase Egypt's output about twenty-five per cent. Our Department of Agriculture after having experimented for years has developed and acclimated in California a variety of Egyptian cotton superior several experts say to the real Egyptian. It now rests with the planters any one can see to decide whether American manufacturers will get their fine cotton at home or abroad.—*The Wall Street Journal.*

3

For several reasons some of them certainly unworthy people on both sides of the Atlantic are talking of the perils of a "yellow" invasion. It is true that in the past various invasions have been attended with evil but civilization has passed on into an age when migrations even the mightiest that the world has seen are taking place silently and steadily for the good of all. There is no reason to suppose that the overflow and interflow of nations heretofore synonymous with the progress of humanity should bring to us anything but good. Commerce is to lead the van in the new movement of the nations as it has in the past and the merchant consciously or unconsciously is going to anticipate and guide the statesman.—*The Commercial and Financial Chronicle.*

4

The prevailing spirit at least among a certain class of young business men seems to be that the saving of little things in the course of the day consumes time entirely out of proportion to the value of the things saved but like all general rules it is carried too far by young men who could hardly employ their time to better advantage than in saving good though minor materials that would otherwise be lost. The man who originated the idea probably found it correct for himself but like all principles catering to indifference regarding details the idea is too readily adopted by many young men who can ill afford its practice. No one wishes a man to be parsimonious but he should not allow anything to be wasted which can with a reasonable exercise of effort be saved.

Exercise 184—Explanatory Expressions

C. *Independent elements* are words, phrases, or clauses that have no direct grammatical relation with any other word in the sentence. They are really a kind of parenthetical expression, but have less connection with the sentence than those given under B.

The following is an argument against the trusts. The italicized expressions are independent elements. What different kinds do you discover?

Gentlemen, the big problem before us to-day, *therefore*, is the trusts. Shall the people control the trusts, or shall the trusts control the people? *To state the question differently*, shall we all continue to keep a voice in government, or shall we turn our power over into the hands of a few and let their word be law? This centralizing of power, *by the way*, was the evil men tried to remedy by forming republics, and shall we Americans, *do you think*, be willing to sacrifice all that has been gained for us of liberty? *The answer being self-evident*, let us proceed. It seems that the little violator of law can be punished; the big violator cannot be, or, *at any rate*, is not punished. The trusts, *most people know*, are formed to destroy competition. Their reason for destroying competition, *evidently*, is to swell profits by charging all that the trade will bear. The trust, *finally*, is not a method of doing business, but a scheme for levying tribute.

Rule 8.—Independent elements are separated from the rest of the sentence by commas.

Punctuate the following:

1

NEW YORK, May 12, 19—.

Mr. Thomas R. Stevenson,
5010 Prospect Ave.,
Milwaukee, Wis.
Dear Sir:

You are no doubt now planning your summer vacation before you make any new plans however consider the opportunity that we are offering you to see a new and marvelously beautiful world for little more very likely than the cost of an ordinary vacation at the summer hotel to which you usually go.

The idea of summer travel in the Tropics it may be is new to you comparatively few people unfortunately have yet awakened to its possibilities they do not realize at least not fully that the climate in Jamaica Panama and the Central and South American countries is practically the same throughout the year moreover the transportation rates are much lower than they are in the North and the incidental expenses of travel such as carriage fare and the cost of curios are considerably less rough weather too is almost unknown in the summer.

Possibly as you live on the shores of Lake Michigan you have been considering a week's cruise of the great lakes at an expense certainly of $40 or more and along coasts that you have seen doubtless many times before we offer a number of trips varying in length from twelve to twenty-four days and in cost from $50 to $130 to Jamaica Panama and Central and South America thus for ten dollars more you may sail twice as long pass shores much more beautiful visit cities far more strange and return with a new almost magical store of memories.

You are wondering perhaps how it is that we can offer these remarkably low rates the reason briefly told is that our ships carry an exceptionally large amount of freight however do not think merely because our ships carry freight that they are not splendidly equipped for passenger travel on the other hand they are so luxuriously furnished that they are especially fitted for tropical cruises you are missing an unusual opportunity we assure you if you do not more fully investigate our offer.

Yours very truly,

2

We are learning year by year that as a rule financial independence cannot be secured by most men except by saving the savings bank is of course the first place to invest savings because it will receive small sums and pay an interest on them when a man's savings however have reached $1000 for example what shall he do with his money he has not the time or the knowledge probably to watch his investments he wishes therefore to put his money where it will be safe where it will earn a fair rate of interest and if possible where he can on short notice convert it into cash.

3

A man is an investor usually at least by virtue of his savings a woman on the other hand invests because she has received a legacy this may take the form of course of property securities cash or life insurance it is the function of sound investment most people know to surround funds of this nature with strong security the selection of conservative investments it is evident must be made with care those companies naturally that deal in conservative securities are the ones a prospective investor should consult.

4

Not long ago the editor of a financial journal received a letter of inquiry from a woman she had she said only two thousand dollars if she invested it as some of her friends had advised her to do in a well-known security she could not live on the proceeds she had consequently made a connection with a brokerage house and was making a living by buying and selling speculative stocks her list by the way showed a profit of $500 in four months what she wanted to know of course was how she could make the gain a second time in effect she was told to take her profits and run as fast as she could she will not in all probability take the advice and in a few months possibly weeks she will write again for help in rescuing her last few hundred dollars she will have learned at last that the way to keep her money is to save it but she will not by that time in all likelihood have any money to save.

Exercise 185—Explanatory Expressions

D. The *explanatory relative clause.*

Similar to the appositive is the explanatory relative clause. Like an appositive, it is inserted into the sentence for the purpose of explanation and is separated from the rest of the sentence by commas. Because of this similarity, it is sometimes called an appositive relative clause.

Great care must be taken in punctuation to distinguish a clause that may be omitted from the sentence without destroying the meaning from one that may not be omitted. The appositive clause may be omitted. A restrictive clause, because it restricts the meaning of the word it modifies, may not be omitted. Because it is needed for the sake of clearness, it is not separated from the rest of the sentence by commas. To distinguish an appositive clause from a restrictive clause, the former is called a non-restrictive clause.

Notice the difference between the following:

1. The Commonwealth Edison Company, *which controls the electric light and power supply of Chicago*, was organized in 1907 by the consolidation of the Chicago Edison Company and the Commonwealth Electric Company.

The sentence makes complete sense without the relative clause.

2. The concern *that controls the electric light and power supply of Chicago* is the Commonwealth Edison Company.

The relative clause must be used to understand the sentence.

In (1) the relative clause gives an additional idea. In (2) it limits or restricts the meaning of *the concern.* The non-restrictive clause is shown in (1), the restrictive clause in (2).

Dictation to illustrate non-restrictive clauses:

It is estimated that Chicago annually uses 93,450,000 gallons of milk, for which it pays over $28,000,000. To supply this amount 120,000 cows are needed, which are owned by 12,000 dairy farms. Health officers conduct a systematic dairy farm inspection, which has for its purpose the exclusion of diseased milk. Farm owners, who formerly objected to the inspection, now see that cleanliness is profitable. Authorities have discovered that milk, which easily absorbs germs, is dangerous except when produced under sanitary conditions, and now dairies are allowed to sell only clean, pure milk, which is milk given by a healthy cow.

Phrases as well as clauses may be restrictive. In the following sentences decide whether the italicized expressions are restrictive or non-restrictive. State whether they are phrases or clauses. Do any of the sentences need commas?

1. The man *wearing the brown coat* is my brother.

2. My brother bought a new coat *which is brown.*

3. The lesson *that I take at nine o'clock* is English.

4. In English *which I take at nine o'clock* we are studying punctuation.

5. I am going to work in every city *that I visit.*

6. I am going to work in any city *where I can find employment.*

7. I am going to work in Denver *where my uncle lives.*

8. The house *on the hill* is the oldest in town.

9. The house *that is the oldest in town* is used as a museum.

10. The Franklin Museum *which occupies the oldest house in town* is a very interesting place.

11. The town museum is the place *that I like to visit.*

12. The chimney *that was blown down last night in the storm* should have been mended long ago.

13. The old ruined tower *which has long been a picturesque sight in the village* was blown down last night.

14. We counted ten chimneys *that were blown down last night.*

15. The stenography system *that I studied* is Munson's.

16. I think she uses Munson's *which she considers a good system of stenography.*

17. Last year I pursued a course in stenography *which I enjoyed very much.*

18. The book *that we use in class* has a brown cover.

19. The only milk *that is fit to drink* comes from a clean dairy.

20. Systematic inspection has been carried on *which has resulted in securing better milk.*

Rule 9.—A non-restrictive clause should be separated from the rest of the sentence by commas.

Exercise 186

Punctuate the following:

1. We have an enormous crop of cotton the value of which is estimated at one billion dollars.

2. "The root of the mail order evil is the idea which the retail mail order houses have been able somehow to instill into the minds of the buying public that the local merchants ask too much for their goods."

3. Mr. Hilton who was sales manager at that time induced the company to adopt this system.

4. The lecture will be delivered by Mr. Brenton who is the head of the advertising department of Whitlock & Co.

5. Our dog whose fur was wet by his plunge into the lake came running toward us.

6. Genevieve who had always been the leader in the games was not present.

7. A late product of the brain of George Westinghouse who was the inventor of the air brake and numerous electrical devices is an air spring for automobiles. This little article has been patented by Mr. Westinghouse who has the sole ownership. The spring which has already proved popular with automobile owners fits over the end of the regular spring and "makes good roads out of bad ones."

8. Careful selection of investments upon which the safety of your money depends is often difficult. Careful watching of investments which is fully as

essential is much harder. Let us tell you about our Investment Service which does this watching for you and keeps you fully protected.

9. As a direct result of the conference between the railroad and steamship interests of the South-Atlantic and Gulf cotton ports which was held recently at Hot Springs Va. an organization which will be known as the South Atlantic and Steamship Cotton Inspection Bureau has been created. The bureau will have a chief inspector who will supervise the conduct of its business at all ports and will arrange for the employment of the inspectors. According to the rules and regulations copies of which have been received by the cotton agencies and the export departments of the various New Orleans firms any bale that shows external damage from water mud bad bagging or other causes must be condemned and its condition noted and reported.

10. How would you like to wear a hat that has been handed down through six generations in each of which it was a treasured possession? The Italian peasants who love finery are proud to do that very thing. Very few of the poorer people who live in Italy own a hat. When you see a beautifully woven Leghorn hat which is also very dirty on the head of a little peasant child you may be pretty sure that she is celebrating her birthday by wearing the family heirloom. These hats which are sometimes willed to a favorite relative and which in some instances go the round of the family are considered almost priceless. It is a frequent sight along the dusty roads outside the little towns to see untidy old women who are sauntering along twisting twine as they go all vanity under the flopping brim of an antiquated hat. This is almost the only souvenir that tourists' money cannot buy.—*The Chicago Tribune.*

Exercise 187—Explanatory Expressions

E. When the subordinate element that comes at or near the close of the sentence gives an *additional* idea, following the more or less complete idea in the rest of the sentence, it should be set off by a comma; as,

A signature clerk will easily recognize any alteration in a signature, *although thousands of checks pass through his hands daily.*

He gave a statement of the affairs of the company, *explaining that he wished to make a loan.*

Rule 10.—A terminal adverbial clause or participial phrase giving an additional idea should be set off from the rest of the sentence by a comma.

Punctuate the following:

1. Popular-priced goods are the safest for a retail stock however you consider the subject.

2. A sheriff seldom finds large quantities of popular-priced goods on hand when he comes to take possession of any retail store although he usually finds expensive articles.

3. They bring higher prices relatively than the heavier things even when they are disposed of under forced sale.

4. The catalogue houses have little fear for five-and-ten-cent stores because sixty-eight per cent of their business is in big goods such as furniture vehicles sewing-machines clothing and relatively expensive things. They do not wish to increase the sale of popular-priced articles although their catalogue may be full of them because it costs them more to pack one hammer or trowel than the profits can stand.

5. Steel conditions remain about as they have been for several weeks excepting that the price of rails has been advancing for the last few days.

6. Steel men are of the opinion that to increase prices too rapidly would spoil a good market because most of the mills are so filled up with orders that they would not be able to take advantage of increased quotations for some time to come.

7. The steel business for the last three months has been very encouraging as it shows that railroads are dropping their policy of waiting until the last minute to buy. It will probably mean more normal operation of mills instead of spasmodic workings as has been the case for the last few years.

8. Boraxated soap chips will benefit your tableware and your hands making dishwashing a pleasure instead of a task.

9. The man who works to the limit of his physical powers is as foolish as the manufacturer who immediately invests all his profits in his business neglecting to have a reserve fund for unexpected demands.

10. A wide-awake manager tries plan after plan testing and re-testing them until he can apply them to his company's needs.

Write four sentences illustrating Rule 10.

Exercise 188

Punctuate the following letters, supplying a heading and an introduction for each:

1

Dear Madam:

We wish to acknowledge your letter of recent date assuring you that we thank you for the opportunity you have given us of opening a monthly charge account in your name. We shall spare no effort to make every transaction as satisfactory as possible hoping thus to merit a liberal share of your patronage.

Our bills are rendered on the first of each month being payable between that date and the fifteenth.

Yours very truly,

2

Dear Mr. Warner:

In reply to your inquiry I am sending the following information assuring you that I am glad to be of service to you.

The Lancaster Company has apparently abandoned its plan of erecting a new building this year difficulties having arisen it is said in their securing a suitable location. About two years ago the firm purchased a site on the corner of Harrison and Second streets but they sold it again last year taking advantage of a decided rise in real estate values. It is understood we believe that the company will build in the near future even now having two or three possible sites under consideration.

Sincerely yours,

3

Dear Sir:

We offer you the benefits and privileges of our Special Charge Account whereby purchases may be paid for in weekly or monthly installments. You will find this a most convenient arrangement because it permits you to have a charge account without the usual hardship of payment at a fixed time. Moreover a Special Charge Account costs you nothing since our prices are the same whether you pay cash or have purchases charged. Please fill out the enclosed application blank mailing it to us to-day.

You will no doubt enjoy reading the enclosed booklet as it gives much interesting information on fashion tendencies. The illustrations too are unusually attractive although they hardly do justice to the beautiful garments that we sell.

Yours truly,

Exercise 189

Study the punctuation in the following selections from *The Wall Street Journal;* then write them from dictation:

1

TROUBLE IN INTRODUCING STEEL

"Strange as it now seems," said one of Carnegie's "young men," now the vice-president of a large and prosperous corporation in New York, "in the early days of the steel industry we had the greatest difficulty in the world in weaning the old manufacturers away from the use of wrought iron, though they admitted the superiority of steel. They would look at it, test it, and agree that it seemed to possess all the desirable qualities claimed for it, but it was more or less untried by time, and they preferred to stick to the old wrought iron, with which they were familiar.

"I remember one old chap with whom I had wrestled long, but in vain, coming into my office and picking up a long, soft steel rivet, which had been bent double and hammered flat.

"'How many did you break in making this?' he asked, picking it up and examining it curiously.

"'That's the first one we hammered over, and, what is more to the point, we can do it with all steel of that type,' I replied.

"The polite incredulity in his face stirred my professional pride, and I said, 'If I let you go to the mills, pick out a dozen of those rivets just as they come from the rolls, and hammer them with your own hands, will you use that steel hereafter, if it comes up to the test?'

"He said he would, and the rest was easy, for it is much easier not to break than to break that kind of steel. Before long the old man came back with perspiration dripping from the end of his nose but with the light of conviction shining in his eye. The firm had a new customer."

2

CONSERVATION

Leslie M. Shaw, former Secretary of the Treasury, was in New York, attending a meeting of a board of which he is a member. Something was said about the present-day discussion of money power, and Shaw said that it reminded him of a speech he had made in Seattle in the campaign of 1896.

"I was speaking to a filled hall and had almost finished," said Shaw, "when a long-whiskered man arose about the middle of the hall and held up his hand, saying he wanted to ask a question.

"'Go ahead,' I said.

"'How, then, Mr. Speaker, do you explain the unequal distribution of wealth?' was his question.

"When I answered him with, 'In the same way that I explain the unequal distribution of whiskers,' bedlam broke loose.

"As soon as I could get quiet restored, I said: 'Now don't think I returned the answer I did to make fun of your whiskers. You will observe that I have no whiskers, as I dissipate them by shaving them off. Nature gives me abundance of whiskers, and, if I conserved them as you do, I also should be abundantly supplied. Now, it is the same way with money. The man who conserves his money has more than his share, as with whiskers; while the man who dissipates his money is without his allotment.'"

Exercise 190—The Semicolon (;)

The semicolon is used between the propositions of a compound sentence when no coördinate conjunction is used. (See Exercise 176, 2.)

It is not work that kills men; it is worry.

It is important not to overdo this use of the semicolon. Do not use it unless the two principal clauses of the sentence taken together easily form one idea.

Especial care must be taken not to confuse coördinate conjunctions and conjunctive adverbs. The following are conjunctive adverbs: *then*, *therefore*, *consequently*, *moreover*, *however*, *so*, *also*, *besides*, *thus*, *still*, *otherwise*, *accordingly*. When they are used to join principal clauses, they should be preceded by a coördinate conjunction or a semicolon; as,

Fruit was plentiful, and therefore the price was low.
Fruit was plentiful; therefore the price was low.

When there is a series of phrases or clauses, each of which is long and contains commas within itself, the sentence becomes clearer if the members of the series are separated by semicolons instead of by commas; as,

You know how prolific the American mind has been in invention; how much civilization has been advanced by the steamboat, the cotton-gin, the sewing-machine, the reaping-machine, the typewriter, the electric light, the telephone, the phonograph.

Write the following from dictation:

1

No man can deny that the lines of endeavor have more and more narrowed and stiffened; no one who knows anything about the development of industry in this country can fail to have observed that the larger kinds of credit are more and more difficult to obtain, unless you obtain them upon the terms of uniting your efforts with those who already control the industries of the country; and nobody can fail to observe that any man who tries to set himself up in competition with any process of manufacture which has been taken under the control of large combinations of capital will presently find himself either squeezed out or obliged to sell and allow himself to be absorbed.—Woodrow Wilson: *The New Freedom.*

2

If the total amount of savings deposited in the savings banks were equally divided among the population of the country, the amount apportioned to each person in 1820 would have been twelve cents; in 1830, fifty-four cents; in 1840, eighty-two cents; in 1850, $1.87; in 1860, $4.75; in 1870, $14.26; in 1880, $16.33; in 1890, $24.75; in 1900, $31.78; in 1910, $45.05, and it is steadily increasing. Remember the fact that the population had increased from 10,000,000 in 1820 to over 90,000,000 in 1910; the "rainy day" money, therefore, assumes gigantic proportions.

3

In Germany, says *The Scientific American*, wood is too expensive to be burned, and it is made into artificial silk worth two dollars a pound and bristles worth four dollars a pound; into paper, yarn, twine, carpet, canvas, and cloth. Parquet flooring is made from sawdust; the materials may be bought by the pound and then mixed, so that the householder can lay his own hardwood floors according to his individual taste and ingenuity.

4

The country gentlemen and country clergymen had fully expected that the policy of these ministers would be directly opposed to that which had been almost constantly followed by William; that the landed interest would be favored at the expense of trade; that no addition would be made to the funded debt; that the privileges conceded to Dissenters by the late king would be curtailed, if not withdrawn; that the war with France, if there must be such a war, would, on our part, be almost entirely naval; and that the government would avoid close connections with foreign powers and, above all, with Holland.—*Macaulay.*

Exercise 191—The Colon (:)

The colon is always used to indicate that something of importance follows, usually an enumeration or a list of some kind, or a quotation of several sentences or paragraphs; as,

1. Three things are necessary: intelligence, perseverance, and tact.

2. The buffalo supplies them with almost all the necessities of life: with habitation, food, and clothing; with strings for their bows; with thread, cordage, and trail-ropes for their horses; with coverings for their saddles; and with the means of purchasing all that they desire from traders.

3. Quoting from the current number of the —— *Magazine*, he read: (four paragraphs).

Punctuate:

1. For the first fifty miles we had companions with us Troche a little trapper and Rouville a nondescript in the employ of the fur company.

2. About a week previous four men had arrived from beyond the mountains Sublette Reddick and two others.

3. Reynal was gazing intently he began to speak at last "Many a time when I was with the Indians I have been hunting gold all through the Black Hills there's a plenty of it here you may be certain of that I have dreamed about it fifty times" etc.

4. Objects familiar from childhood surrounded me crags and rocks a black and sullen brook that gurgled with a hollow voice among the crevices a wood of mossy distorted trees.

Exercise 192

The colon is used after *thus*, *as follows*, *the following*, or similar expressions; as,

Name the adverbs in the following: He left hurriedly rather early in the morning.

The colon is not used after *namely*, *as*, *that is*, *for example*, *for instance*, and the like. Such expressions are preceded by the semicolon and followed by the comma.

Punctuate the following:

1. The Christmas presents that he wants are the following a toy train a toy automobile a toy circus and a printing press.

2. Do the exercise thus first lunge to the left second raise the arms forward and third wind the wand.

3. We are offering for sale three residences of the size that you wish namely 438 Bishop Ave 1614 Winchester St and 2015 Logan Square.

4. The following are the two that we liked best 438 Bishop Ave and 2015 Logan Square.

5. One use of the comma is to set off an appositive for example Mr Kearne the buyer has left the city.

6. The comma is used to set off an independent adverb as We have not yet decided however when we shall leave.

7. The plan is this I'll do the work and you pay for the materials.

8. The officers are as follows Edward Lawrence for President John Kelly for Secretary and Fred Morrison for Treasurer.

Exercise 193—The Dash(—)

The dash is used to set off parenthetical expressions that have very little connection with the rest of the sentence; as,

In New York the Harlem River tunnel was comparatively a simple one, but the first East River tunnels—the two subway tubes from the Battery to Brooklyn—presented all the difficulties known to subaqueous construction.

These tunnels extend on under the great Pennsylvania terminal building—another of the same decade's accomplishments—to East Thirty-fourth Street.

The dash is also used to indicate a sudden change or break in the thought; as,

1. When the millennium comes—if it ever does—all of our problems will be solved.

2. "I believe—" began the lawyer.

"Believe!" interrupted his client. "I don't want you to believe. I want you to know."

The dash is used before a word that summarizes the preceding part of the sentence; as,

He had robbed himself of the most precious thing a man can have in business—his friends.

After a comma the dash has the effect of lengthening the separation; as,

One thing the Puritans desired,—freedom to worship God.

Exercise 194—Parenthesis Marks ()

Parenthesis marks are used to enclose explanatory expressions that are not an essential part of the sentence; as,

The United States Department of Agriculture estimates that the receipts of cattle at the six leading markets (Chicago, St. Louis, Kansas City, South Omaha, St. Joseph, and Sioux City) from January 1 to August 1 of this year are 15 per cent less than they were in the corresponding period of last year.

Wrong.—Do not use parenthesis marks to cancel a word or a passage. A line should be drawn through a word that is wrong.

Bring to class five sentences that illustrate the correct use of parenthesis marks.

Exercise 195—The Hyphen (-)

The hyphen is used when a word has been divided. It is always used at the end of the line and never at the beginning.

When several short words are taken together to form one word, they are hyphenated; as,

a one-hundred-pound bag of coffee

As a rule, when two words taken together are each accented, they must be written with the hyphen. When only one is accented, no hyphen is used; as,

follow-up, first-class, self-reliant, railroad, steamship

As a rule, nouns which are compounded of a participle and a noun use the hyphen; as,

talking-machine, driving-wheel

When fractions are written out, the hyphen is used; as,

one-third, three-fifths

In other numerals expressing a compound number the hyphen is also used; as,

twenty-one, sixty-six

Exercise 196

Punctuate the following letters, supplying a heading and an introduction for each:

1

Gentlemen:

We are glad to tell you that contrary to the fears expressed in your last letter there are no present indications of sudden changes at least no indications of drops in prices. With the exception of two fruits and one vegetable grapes cantaloupes and cauliflower all commodities sold on the wholesale fruit and produce markets here were quoted yesterday at the prices announced last Friday.

The change in grape prices affected the Red Peru variety in which the supply has almost stopped the price being raised from $1.05 to $1.25 a box. If one may trust the forecast of local merchants the price will probably remain at this higher point until the supply is exhausted. Cantaloupes seem to be a trifle scarce especially the pineapple variety the price of which was raised from $1.10 to $1.30 a crate. Cauliflower was raised to $1.35 a dozen heads the staple price probably for the rest of the season.

Excepting these items we shall be glad to receive any orders at Friday's quotations.

Yours truly,

2

Gentlemen:

Your order of the 20th instant forwarded from our Trenton office came this morning. We regret to say however that we do not carry the Sanito brand of canned goods as we do not consider the grade first-class. If the Monsoon brand which is generally acknowledged to be excellent will serve your purpose we can fill your order at once.

We are now in a position to supply the trade with Mrs. Keller's coffee of which we have fortunately secured several thousand packages at a very low price. If you wish any at $2.50 per dozen packages less than half the retail price you will notice let us hear from you at once.

Yours truly,

3

Dear Sir:

We acknowledge your letter of October 5 but we regret that as yet we have no information in regard to the excess charge of $1.02 which you were obliged to pay on the express shipment of one piece 27 yds. of plaid silk chiffon. We have taken up the matter with the mill however and as soon as we receive their report we shall write you again.

Asking your indulgence meanwhile we are

Yours truly,

CHAPTER XIII

THE CLEAR SENTENCE

BUSINESS men like to talk of brevity. They tell you that a talk or a letter must be brief. What they really mean is that the talk or the letter must be concise; that it must state the business clearly in the fewest possible words. Don't omit any essential fact when you write, but don't repeat. If you can express an idea in ten words, don't use twenty. In a later exercise we shall meet the sentence, *The size of the crops is always important, and it is especially so to the farmer, and this is because he has to live by the crops.* The writer of that sentence was very careless. He had a good idea and thought that, if he kept repeating it, he would make it stronger. Just the reverse is true. The sentence may be expressed in a very few words: *The size of the crop is vitally important to the farmer.*

If you wish to secure conciseness of expression, be especially careful to avoid joining or completing thoughts by these expressions: *and, so, why, that is why, this is the reason, and everything.*

In this chapter we shall consider some of the larger faults that should be avoided in sentences.

Exercise 197—Unity of the Sentence

Give the definition of a sentence.

How many thoughts may one sentence express?

What is likely to happen when two thoughts are joined by *and?* What, then, is the danger in using the compound sentence?

The compound sentence is good to use to express certain ideas, especially contrast; as,

It is not work that kills men; it is worry.

It is not the revolution that destroys the machinery, but the friction [but it is the friction].

The sentences which most clearly and easily give us one thought are the simple and the complex sentences.

Compare the following sentences. Which of them leave *one* idea in your mind?

The tongue is a sharp-edged tool.

A sharp tongue is the only edged tool that grows keener with constant use.

A sharp tongue is like an edged tool, and it grows keener with constant use.

Exercise 198

The following is wordy. Rewrite it, condensing as much as possible. Use simple and complex sentences rather than compound, expressing in each only one thought.

In the early summer the corn crop frequently seems to be very poor, and so reports begin to circulate that corn will be high in the autumn, but when the autumn really comes, Wall Street, that great center of business life, begins to see that the reports have been greatly exaggerated and that crops really will be very good, and so business begins to pick up. The size of the crop largely settles the volume of the next season's business, because so great a part of the world's business activity is made up of buying and selling the actual potatoes and corn and wheat and cattle or the products made from these, and when the crop is poor there are a great many people concerned, because they will be poor just as the crops are poor, and this applies to the farmer as well as to the dealer.

The size of the crops is always important, and is especially so to the farmer, and this is because he has to live by the crops. A man may be living in the city and working for a salary and begin to see that his work is not supporting him, and if he is an ambitious man, he will change his occupation. This the farmer cannot do because he has made an enormous investment; in the first place, he has invested in his land, and then in his seed and farm implements, and this investment often means all the available money the farmer has, and often it means a mortgage on his farm. He puts the mortgage on his farm in hope of getting a good crop, and when his hope is not realized, he is in trouble, because he may lose his whole farm if he cannot pay the installments of interest due on his mortgage; but then, on the other hand, if we consider the other side of the question, when the crop is large, the situation is altogether different. Even if the farmer has put a mortgage on his farm, he gets enough money from his produce to pay the debt of that mortgage, and he need not worry how he is to live during the next winter.

The town merchants depend on a good crop, because, if the farmer has not a good return from his fields, he will have almost no ready money, and so he cannot buy much clothing or household furnishings. In Iowa, for instance, there is a little town in the center of a corn-raising community, and it is here that the farmers congregate to do their buying, and in this town there is quite a large department store, and it is run by a woman. She does most of her buying in the autumn and she prefers to do it personally, and so she likes to make a trip to New York for the purpose, but she never sets out until she knows that the corn crop is good. And the reason for this is that she knows that it will cost her hundreds of dollars to make the trip East, to stay at a good hotel, and to spend the requisite length of time choosing her purchases at the different wholesale houses, and she knows that if there is no corn crop she will sell very few coats and hats and lace curtains, and it will never pay her to run up her expenses into the hundreds of dollars, but she will buy as best she can from the drummers, and buy only a little, and thus the size of the crop determines how much the farmer can buy, and, therefore, how much the wholesale and retail dealers can sell.

Exercise 199—Subordination in the Sentence

Sentences containing compound predicates may be made more direct in thought if one of the verbs is changed to a participle or an infinitive, because the predicate will then express only one action; as,

1. The carpenter *threw* down his hammer *and walked* out of the shop.

2. *Throwing* down his hammer, the carpenter walked out of the shop.

3. I *went* downtown *and applied* for the position.

4. I went downtown *to apply* for the position.

Change the following sentences so that one action is denoted by the predicate of each:

1. A teamster drove out of the alley east of the theater and swung his horses directly in front of a Madison street car.

2. The tongue struck the front of the car and bored a hole in the fuse box.

3. The fire spread and burned the roof of the car.

4. The half dozen passengers were badly frightened and got out quickly.

5. Several people ran and turned in a fire alarm.

6. In a few minutes the fire engines arrived and began to fight the flames.

7. Crowds came from all directions and silently watched the flames.

8. The people poured out of the theater and cheered the firemen.

9. The half dozen passengers soon recovered and stood on the curbstone in the crowd.

10. The firemen did their work quickly and departed amid the cheers of the crowd.

Exercise 200—Combination of Short Sentences

Sometimes short sentences are bad because two or three of them are needed to express one complete thought. If that is the case, they should be combined, the most important detail being put into the principal clause, and the other details into modifiers, as in the preceding exercise.

Make use of—

1. Adjectives.
2. Adverbs.
3. Participial phrases.
4. Infinitives.
5. Relative pronouns.
6. Subordinate conjunctions.

Below, the first and second sentences together make one thought, which is expressed in the third.

John is a good reporter.
That is why he earns a good salary.
Because John is a good reporter, he earns a good salary.

Combine the sentences of each group below into a single sentence, either simple or complex, omitting as many words as possible but no ideas:

1. We stayed at home for two reasons: first of all, we thought Baltimore might be unpleasantly warm. Then, the other reason was that we thought we ought to economize.

2. In China the wedding takes place at the bridegroom's house. This has been decorated with strips of bright red paper, and they have the word "Hsi" on them. This means "Live in happiness."

3. First in the procession come the standard bearers. They are hired for the occasion. These men have red coats put on over their dirty clothes. The men they hire are usually beggars.

4. Six years ago I went sailing on Lake George with my father. I was ten years old at that time. Two other men went along with us. The boat that we went in belonged to my father and these men.

5. The wind was high and it would come in gusts. This made it hard to sail. It shifted the sails so quickly that it would throw the boat over on one side.

6. Several times the boat leaned over at an angle of forty degrees. This let the water come in on that side. When this happened, we all had to jump to the other side. We did this so that the boat would right itself.

7. The heart is the most important organ in the body. This is because if the heart stops beating, you cannot live. Besides, all the other organs are connected with it. It is something like the main spring in a watch.

8. This is a good machine. And since that's the case, I don't see why it is that it doesn't work as it should.

9. In every business there are many bad debts. Some can be collected and others cannot be. This is because the men who made them were given credit, and they didn't have any money.

10. The night was dark, and there were no stars. The fishermen stood on the shore, and they gazed at the wild sea. A storm had arisen, and they could not go out in their boats.

Exercise 201

As in the preceding exercise, rewrite the following, omitting as many words as possible, but no ideas. Use shorter, simpler expressions wherever possible.

1

Uncle Sam now has an aerial navy, but it's a small one, and foundations of it were recently laid. This was done when contracts were signed for the delivery of three aeroplanes and they are the first aeroplanes that the United States bought. These aeroplanes are of the latest development. They are all capable of rising from land or water. They are able also to land on water or on the deck of a ship, and they can carry at least one passenger and are equipped with wireless outfits. Two of them are Curtis machines and the third is a Wright, and they ranged in price from $2,700 to $5,500.

2

The United States produces more steel than any two European countries, and it is continuing to produce more. Moreover, it has the productive capacity to produce more than any other three or four countries put together. This capacity is being still further increased. At the present time, there is one very important steel company. It is very large, and seems to wish to monopolize the entire iron and steel industry. Even at this time it owns half the principal plants that are now producing steel and iron, and controls half the trade of the entire steel and iron industry, and when such a thing happens, it is a matter of international concern.

3

Condense the following into a single sentence, either simple or complex:

The iron and steel industry is very important, and it includes a great deal. First, the ore has to be mined, and then the work includes everything up to making the finest wire for musical instruments. Or, to put it another way, you can say from smelting the ore to building a battle ship. This is a very interesting occupation and, as said before, very important. There is hardly anything more interesting or important except agriculture.

Exercise 202—Dangling Expressions

Sometimes a sentence is not clear because it contains a participle which does not modify anything in the sentence. A participle is part *verb* and part *adjective*. As a verb, it expresses the idea of the verb from which it is derived. As an adjective, it must modify a noun or a pronoun. The important point is that this noun or pronoun must be expressed in the sentence and not lie in the mind of the writer, as it does in the following:

Riding from Saugatuck to Holland last year, the country showed unmistakable signs of lack of rain.

Here the writer means, *We saw that the country*, etc., but he says that the country rode from Saugatuck to Holland.

Again, an expression may be used which is really an incomplete clause. Do not use such a clause, unless the understood subject is the same as the subject expressed in the independent proposition.

Wrong: When almost exhausted, the camp was reached.
Right: When almost exhausted, we reached the camp.

Recast the following sentences, correcting the dangling expressions:

1. You should not stop studying your lessons until thoroughly prepared.

2. In talking to the postman yesterday, he said that his route had been changed.

3. Owing two months' rent, the foreman laid me off.

4. Before becoming a physician, the law sets a very severe examination.

5. Having eaten our luncheon very hastily, the typewriters were soon clicking merrily again.

6. The difficulty could easily be settled, going about it in the right way.

7. Although determined to get my money, the task was harder than I had expected.

8. Having installed an adding machine, our office work could be done in half the time.

9. On entering the car, the first thing that caught my attention was the sign at the end.

10. Silk should be washed with warm water and a mild soap, being careful not to rub it.

11. The house was redecorated, making it clean and homelike.

12. The book should be carefully studied, reviewing each chapter after it is read.

13. Going to work this morning, an accident happened.

14. Having entered college, Mr. Brown watched his son's progress with pride.

15. Soon after abandoning the boat, it sank.

16. They say he will be lame, caused by a fall on the ice while skating.

17. While trying to break the half mile record, his back was injured.

18. Many people object to football, because in tackling the boys' hearts are weakened.

19. He did not wish to take up an extra study, thus lessening his chance of being eligible for athletics.

20. While a child, my father often told me stories of Indian days.

21. Absorbed all day in superintending his work, in the evening the newspaper brought him political news enough to fill the hours between dinner and bed-time.

22. Discussing the happenings in the ward with an old crony, his daughter would often sit near him listening.

23. He is failing in his work, caused by his laziness.

24. Although a good tonic, I did not gain weight while taking it.

25. In the new telephone, upon lifting the receiver, a ticking sound is heard.

26. Leaving the window open when she went to lunch, of course the papers were disarranged on her return.

27. Dictionaries must be returned to the desk after using.

Exercise 203—Pronouns with Uncertain Antecedents

Sometimes the meaning of a sentence is not clear because the pronouns have uncertain antecedents.

1. Sometimes a pronoun may refer to either of two antecedents; as,

Wrong: He gave his brother John the umbrella and then *he* left.
Right: He gave the umbrella to his brother John, who then left.

2. Sometimes the sentence must be entirely recast and a direct quotation used before the pronouns can be made clear; as,

Wrong: Tom told his father that *his* suit case was lost.
Right: a. Tom said, "Father, your suit case is lost."
b. Tom said, "Father, my suit case is lost."

3. Sometimes the pronoun refers to a word that has not been expressed or to an *idea.* In that case, the antecedent must be supplied; as,

Wrong: If any one wishes to contribute to the cause, let him send *it* in the enclosed envelope.
Right: If any one wishes to contribute to the cause, let him send *his contribution* in the enclosed envelope.

Wrong: I wouldn't wear mittens. Nobody does *that* nowadays.
Right: I wouldn't wear mittens. Nobody wears *them* nowadays.

4. A sentence containing an indefinite *they* or *it* is corrected thus:

Wrong: Don't *they* have street cars where you live?
Right: Are there *no* street cars where you live?

Recast the following:

1. She asked her mother if she could go, and she said she thought she ought to stay at home.

2. John told James he was sure he did not know the office that he meant.

3. George told his father his watch had stopped.

4. The manager asked the clerk to bring his book.

5. A light touch is important in a typewriter, because it makes it easy to write upon it.

6. The size of the crops is important to the farmers, because they have to live by them.

7. They decided to reorganize the company, which is always a difficult task.

8. They went into the hands of a receiver, which is an indication that the affairs of the company had been poorly managed.

9. There is a boat on the lake over which there is a pleasant view, in which there is a club for working girls.

10. He stole some money which brought about an investigation.

11. She asked her aunt how old she was.

12. John is famous for telling anecdotes, and he got it by remembering every story he reads.

13. The sleighing party last night was a success, which is not always the case.

14. He told a lie, which is a bad thing to do.

15. They engaged a gardener, which doubled their monthly expenses.

16. Why don't you get some of that new fur trimming for your blue dress?

17. They had an accident on the street car this morning.

18. In the newspaper it said that the lecture would begin at 8:15.

19. They don't find iron in Illinois, do they?

20. Do they have the original paintings in our art gallery?

21. It says "Closed" on that door.

22. It doesn't mention a bank draft in this book.

23. They have a great many foreigners in New York City.

24. John accompanied his brother to the city where he bought a typewriter.

25. I had expected to take the 9:30 train, but I couldn't do it.

26. Going up to the horse he put a lump of sugar into his mouth.

27. In letter writing one should always be exact and arrange them in the customary form.

28. Those hooks are not rust-proof because the back of my dress is stained with it.

29. The telephone is a great convenience to all. They are now used in almost every house.

30. As we came down the road, it sounded like a train, which, as we approached, grew louder and louder.

Exercise 204—Misplaced Modifiers

Sometimes a sentence is not clear because a modifier does not stand close to the word it modifies.

Wrong: I can't *even* do the first problem.
Right: I can't do *even* the first problem.

Change the order of words in the following sentences, placing each modifier as closely as possible to the word which it modifies. Some of the sentences are incorrect because they contain split infinitives. (See Exercise 92.)

1. I only waited for him about ten minutes.

2. She stood at the window, trying to close it with a troubled face.

3. The city is supplied with water from cold springs which flow nearly a hundred million gallons of the purest liquid that ever burst from the earth, daily.

4. The famous S. F. ice cream is made in this factory containing fifty per cent pure cream.

5. A man should not be allowed to cast a vote, who cannot read and write.

6. After taking the medicine for a short time, the appetite is improved, and a desire is created for food, that has not existed before.

7. In real value, this magazine towers head and shoulders over all others to the woman who is in charge of her home.

8. There are pages of fashion news and embroidery hints and news articles of the day that will appeal to the husband and father as the others do to the wife and daughter as well as departments for the children.

9. The number of the sewing machine is 37A with a drop head.

10. They neither are gentle nor well-mannered.

11. I only heard about the trouble yesterday.

12. He left the same station at which, thirty years before, he had arrived very humbly, in his own special car.

13. He urged his brother to buy a home in his letter.

14. The lighting system has been developed to a really remarkable degree of perfection for the trains.

15. The dynamo is so arranged that when the train is standing still or only traveling twenty miles an hour, the lamps are lighted from a storage battery.

16. The batteries must be large enough during the run to carry the entire lighting load.

17. Please send me 6 Dining Tables No. 46 that extend to ten feet as soon as possible.

18. Large trees grow on each side of the house which is a rambling affair shutting out the light.

19. They decided to give a bonus to the one doing the best work, amounting to fifty dollars.

20. We had almost got to the corner before we saw the fire.

21. I don't ever remember having seen so big a fire.

22. Remember to thoroughly oil the machine.

23. Do you need to in any way alter the machine?

24. If we expect to completely fill the order to-day, we need more help.

Exercise 205—Omission of Necessary Words

Sometimes a sentence is not clear because a word has been omitted that is necessary to the sense; as,

Wrong: The two officers that they elected are the president and secretary.
Right: The two officers that they elected are the president and *the* secretary.

Wrong: His writing is as good or better than yours.
Right: His writing is as good *as* or better than yours.

Wrong: The library is where we go to read.
Right: The library is *the place* where we go to read.

State the difference between the following typewriter ribbons:

1. A red and blue and black ribbon.
2. A red and a blue and black ribbon.
3. A red and blue and a black ribbon.
4. A red and a blue and a black ribbon.

Supply the omitted part in each of the following:

1. I always have and I'm sure I always shall be considerate of others' feelings.

2. They have a stenographer and bookkeeper, who are kept busy all day.

3. I believe he has already or will soon begin the work.

4. The cushions of the rocker are much softer than the armchair.

5. The arrangement of your flat is much more convenient than our house.

6. The number of shelves in your sideboard is just the same as our china closet.

7. I think the articles you ordered will arrive as soon or sooner than you expect.

8. She is as tall or taller than you.

9. When your message arrived, I had already or at least had decided to begin cutting the goods.

10. It may not be better but it is fully as good as the other article.

11. I think you cook fully as well if not better than your sister.

12. His poems hold a place in our hearts second only to the Bible.

13. Your idea is as good if not better than mine.

14. We decided to make the change both for the sake of health and economy.

15. You will find the armchair fully as comfortable, if not more so, than the rocker.

16. The river is where we had the most fun.

17. I know you better than Mary.

18. She went to the park but I didn't care to.

19. We didn't object to the scheme as much as you.

20. A conservatory is where there are all kinds of flowers.

Exercise 206—Shift in Construction

Sometimes the meaning of the sentence is obscure because there has been a shift in construction. Do not change subject, person, tense, or any grammatical form without a good reason. Remember that *and* is a coördinate conjunction. If there is an adjective before *and*, there must be an adjective after it. If a clause precedes, a clause must follow. In other words, *and* joins two members of exactly the same structure. *And* may not join one word and a phrase, nor may it join a prepositional and a participial phrase. Both members must be alike. In the following extract, parallel constructions are used correctly. Be able to tell what kinds of elements are used and how they are parallel.

To eat your cake and keep it too; to wear a gown with the air of originality and distinction, and keep a full purse; to have your house display taste and refinement, and be praised as an economical housewife; to dress your children daintily, and save money for their education—use ABC transfer patterns. By their aid you can make an inexpensive waist look like a French blouse, have table linen of unrivaled elegance, and dress your babies in the most approved style. These patterns cost,—some ten, some fifteen cents. They cover the entire field of dress,—waists, tunics, panels, infants' clothes, underwear, men's apparel, and neckwear; and of household articles,—towels, table-linen, and pillow tops.

Recast the following sentences, correcting the shift of construction in each:

1. In the large department stores every clerk is to report on her way to lunch and coming back.

2. When one hears a cry of "Fire," your first thought is to run.

3. He seemed fond of his work and to have skill in doing it quickly.

4. I decided on taking the trip and to keep my expenses within fifty dollars if possible.

5. X Y Z Cleaner is good for softening water and other household uses.

6. Because of the rise in the price of meats and owing to the fact that grocers charge more for butter and eggs, people find it hard to live.

7. The office is well-heated and with plenty of light.

8. The crowds began to watch the fire and cheering loudly.

9. I heard the opera last year and have gone again this year.

10. It was wonderful to see how fast they worked and their accuracy.

11. I can't decide whether to take up stenography or if bookkeeping is better.

12. He taught us the principles of letter writing, and somewhat of advertising was taken up.

13. Hoping that the work progressed, and unless a landslide occurred, the Americans expected to remove 5,000,000 cubic yards each year.

14. The study of the earth has always been stimulated by two fundamental passions of humanity—a desire for wealth and because of their curiosity.

15. He insists on our taking the trip and to go without further delay.

16. In reviewing, it is well to go over each part of the course carefully, and you should make a note of every point which you do not understand, and let each ask those questions which he himself cannot answer.

17. Mr. Fitzmorris is a man of great technical skill and who has handled the situation capably.

18. It will cost her hundreds of dollars to make the trip East and spending the requisite length of time choosing her purchases at the different wholesale houses.

19. He had assumed control of the office, planned the advertising, and the finances were also directed by him.

20. We have decided to go on the excursion to the Capitol and at the same time visiting Uncle John.

Exercise 207

What prevents clearness in the following?

1. The Federal Government began an investigation into fire conditions in Europe in 1907, through our consuls.

2. It cost $2.39 a year for fire in the United States between 1901 and 1910, for every man, woman, and child, and Germany does not even pay nineteen cents.

3. The number of our fires is increasing, which is worse.

4. In ten years our population has increased 73 per cent and 134 per cent is the increase in fires.

5. Having considered the details, the conclusion is easily drawn that fire is a disgrace.

6. He only gets to the office at ten o'clock.

7. Having settled the plan of attack, the rest was simple.

8. The manager warned him not to make the mistake again and adding that mistakes are costly.

9. To keep flannels from shrinking, wash in the following way, and you will find it very satisfactory.

10. To open a fruit jar run a knife under the edge and it comes off easily.

11. I didn't even finish half the questions.

12. Electric lights are economical, clean, and give more light than gas.

13. You should buy your suit now, both for the sake of economy and style.

14. If in doubt as to the best word, a book of synonyms should be consulted.

15. The comma fault is where, two principal clauses are run together without a coördinate conjunction.

Rewrite the following so that it will be correct, concise, and clear:

The Europeans were anxious for trade with the East, for they were dependent upon them for spices and luxuries. The three routes were through the Mediterranean Sea, over the Suez Peninsula, down the Red Sea, and across to India. Another was through the Mediterranean and then through Arabia. The other was from the Mediterranean and then through the Black Sea and then by land to India. It became necessary to seek a new route because the Turks held Constantinople, and all vessels had to pass through the Mediterranean, and the Turks held this by pirates. The first explorers were working under the leadership of the King of Portugal, and they solved the problem by going around Africa and then to the Indies, but this was too long, and so explorers tried other ways, and the result was the discovery of America.

CHAPTER XIV

THE PARAGRAPH

The sentences developing each of the divisions of a composition make one *paragraph*. A paragraph, therefore, is the treatment of one of the natural divisions of a subject. The length depends on the topic to be treated. Two cautions may be given:

1. Do not write paragraphs containing only one sentence. Such paragraphs do not represent divisions of the subject. They are simply statements which have not been expanded as they deserve, or they are sentences that should be placed with the preceding or succeeding sentences in order to make a good paragraph. Some business men in their letters and advertisements use the one-sentence paragraph too frequently to concentrate the attention of the reader. A writer divides his composition into paragraphs in order to aid the reader to follow the thoughts he is presenting. When the reader sees the indentation that indicates a new paragraph, he thinks that the writer has said all that he intends to say on the topic in hand and now intends to open a new topic. It is confusing to find that the new paragraph is simply another sentence on the same topic as the preceding paragraph. Notice the jerky effect of the following extract from a letter:

We are sending you a copy of our latest catalogue, which gives illustrations and prices of all our stock.

The illustrations are all made from actual photographs and are faithful in representing the shoe described.

Bear Brand Shoes are shipped in special fiber cases, thus lessening freight bills and eliminating the annoyance of shortage claims because they cannot be opened without immediate detection.

Errors of any kind should be reported without delay.

Imperfect or damaged goods must be returned for our inspection; otherwise no allowance will be made.

2. Do not go to the other extreme, writing paragraphs of great length. Much depends, of course, on the matter to be treated, but, as a rule, in a student's theme a paragraph should be not longer than one page. If one of the divisions of your subject is necessarily long, subdivide it, allowing a paragraph to treat each of the subdivisions.

Whether it is to be long or short, a paragraph must treat but one topic; from the first sentence to the last, it should be the development of one idea. Moreover, this topic must be revealed to the reader in no unmistakable way.

Sometimes the subject is so simple that the topic may easily be gathered from the details given, but usually it is well to have one sentence that in a brief or general way states the topic. This is called the *topic sentence.* It may be at or near the beginning; in this case the rest of the paragraph defines or illustrates what it states. It may, however, be found at almost any point in the paragraph, not infrequently acting as a sentence of conclusion, summing up the details that have been presented.

A paragraph that begins with a topic sentence sometimes ends with a sentence of conclusion. The first sentence states the topic, the following sentences explain or illustrate it, and the last sentence summarizes or otherwise indicates that the topic has been completed. This form has been called the *hammock* paragraph, because it has a solid "post" at each end with a mass of details "swinging" between. It is a good form to use in writing paragraphs on given subjects, when each paragraph is to stand alone, complete in itself, not forming part of a longer composition. The practice of writing such paragraphs induces clear, forceful thinking.

Exercise 208

Study the following paragraphs for—

1. Topic sentence, if there is one.
2. Development of the topic.
3. Sentence of conclusion, if there is one.

1

The problem in many large firms is how to develop office efficiency to the highest possible degree. In this respect the monthly examination scheme has been found a great success. The examination consists of a list of questions about merchandise and business procedure. The questions are given out on the last Saturday of the month, and the answers are returned for criticism on the following Wednesday. The employees are told that they may consult as many authorities as they wish, but each man must write his own paper. A poor percentage in three of these tests usually means dismissal. Thus the inefficient are dropped, and the ambitious who have studied are recognized. The vice-president of one concern that uses this system says that it is a strong reminder to his men that they must make themselves worthy of the organization. Besides maintaining an even standard of efficiency, the plan has resulted in developing a number of valuable executives, whose latent powers were brought out by the rigidness of the tests.

2

Every month the department head in one big eastern concern, watch in hand, times a large force of typists individually, testing how rapidly they can write a letter of 200 words from their shorthand notes. Rapidity, punctuation, spelling, and neatness are carefully recorded. This plan has had a desirable influence in bringing stenographers up to grade in their daily work, because a good examination mark is reduced one-half by careless daily work, and a poor examination mark correspondingly raised by excellent daily work. When both examination average and daily average are excellent, the stenographer's salary is increased; when both are below good, the stenographer is dismissed. In this way the standard of stenographic work is kept high.

3

In his effort to succeed many a young business man overlooks the detail of business courtesy. He does not realize the value that a buyer places upon that commodity. The more experienced man, however, knows that courtesy does more to hold a buyer than do bargain sales. In our large cities merchants have incurred great expense to fit up rest rooms where customers may spend an idle hour, write letters on stationery that is provided, and read the latest magazines. In the rural districts, where such luxuries are often impossible, the merchant provides chairs for his customers and a place for stationing their teams. The country merchant, however, can often accomplish his object more quickly than the city dealer by spending an hour gossiping with his customers. He recognizes the fact that buyers are flattered when the proprietor himself takes the time to say a few words to them. He knows just as well as his city competitor does, that if a buyer feels at home in his store, sales are practically guaranteed.

4

The rural landscape of Norway, on the long easterly slope that leads up to the watershed among the mountains on the western coast, is not unlike that of Vermont or New Hampshire. The railway from Christiania to the Randsfjord carried us through a hilly country of scattered farms and villages. Wood played a prominent part in the scenery. There were dark stretches of forest on the hilltops and in the valleys; rivers filled with floating logs; sawmills beside the waterfalls; wooden farmhouses painted white; and rail-fences around the fields. The people seemed sturdy, prosperous, independent. They had the familiar habit of coming down to the station to see the train arrive and depart. We might have fancied ourselves on a journey through the Connecticut valley if it had not been for the soft sing-song of the Norwegian speech and the uniform politeness of the railway officials.

—Van Dyke: *Fisherman's Luck.*

5

The plan of the *Spectator* must be allowed to be both original and eminently happy. Every valuable essay in the series may be read with pleasure separately; yet the five or six hundred essays form a whole, and a whole which has the interest of a novel. It must be remembered, too, that at that time no novel, giving a lively and powerful picture of the common life and manners of England, had appeared. Richardson was working as a compositor. Fielding was robbing birds' nests. Smollett was not yet born. The narrative, therefore, which connects together the Spectator's essays gave to our ancestors their first taste of an exquisite and untried pleasure. That narrative was, indeed, constructed with no art or labor. The events were such events as occur every day. Sir Roger comes up to town to see Eugenio, as the worthy baronet always calls Prince Eugene, goes with the Spectator on the water to Spring Gardens, walks among the tombs in the Abbey, and is frightened by the Mohawks, but conquers his apprehension so far as to go to the theater when the "Distressed Mother" is acted. The Spectator pays a visit in the summer to Coverley Hall, is charmed with the old house, the old butler, and the old chaplain, eats a jack caught by Will Wimble, rides to the assizes, and hears a point of law discussed by Tom Touchy. At last a letter from the honest butler brings to the club the news that Sir Roger is dead. Will Honeycomb marries and reforms at sixty. The club breaks up, and the Spectator resigns his functions. Such events can hardly be said to form a plot; yet they are related with such truth, such grace, such wit, such humor, such pathos, such knowledge of the human heart, such knowledge of the ways of the world that they charm us on the hundredth perusal. We have not the least doubt that if Addison had written a novel on an extensive plan, it would have been superior to any that we possess. As it is, he is entitled to be considered not only as the greatest of the English essayists, but as the forerunner of the great English novelists.

—Macaulay: *Essay on Addison.*

Exercise 209

Prepare a paragraph developing each of the following topic sentences:

1. The kitchen was a cheerful place. (Tell all the details that will explain the word *cheerful.*)

2. In the kitchen the preparations for the feast went on merrily. (Give the details that will help one get the picture.)

3. Examinations are helpful to the student. (In what ways are they helpful? If possible, use examples to illustrate the point.)

4. Winter is more enjoyable than summer. (Contrast the pleasures of the one with those of the other, showing that those of winter are more enjoyable.)

5. Riding a motorcycle is apt to make a boy reckless. (Develop by using examples.)

6. A man must like his work if he is to succeed in it.

7. Farm lands vary in price.

8. The farmer feeds the world.

9. Every department store should have regular fire drills.

10. Every sale ought to be an advertisement.

Exercise 210

Paragraph the following so that the paragraphs will represent the divisions in thought. If there are any topic sentences, underline them.

1

I have often noticed that every one has his own individual small economies, careful habits of saving fractions of pennies in some one peculiar direction, any disturbance of which annoys him more than spending shillings or pounds on some real extravagance. An old gentleman of my acquaintance, who took the intelligence of the failure of a Joint Stock Bank, in which some of his money was invested, with a stoical mildness, worried his family all through a long summer's day because one of them had torn (instead of cutting) out the written leaves of his now useless bankbook. Of course, the corresponding pages at the other end came out as well, and this little unnecessary waste of paper (his private economy) chafed him more than all the loss of his money. Envelopes fretted his soul terribly when they came in. The only way in which he could reconcile himself to such a waste of his cherished article was by patiently turning inside out all that were sent to him, and so making them serve again. Even now, though tamed by age, I see him casting wistful glances at his daughters when they send a whole inside of a half-sheet of note paper, with the three lines of acceptance to an invitation written on only one of the sides. I am not above owning that I have this human weakness myself. String is my foible. My pockets get full of little hanks of it, picked up and twisted together, ready for uses that never come. I am seriously annoyed if any one cuts a string of a parcel instead of patiently and faithfully undoing it fold by fold. How people can bring themselves to use India-rubber bands, which are a sort of deification of string, as lightly as they do I cannot imagine. To me an India-rubber band is a precious treasure. I have one which is not new—one that I picked up off the floor nearly five years ago. I have really tried to use it, but my heart failed me, and I could not commit the extravagance. Small pieces of butter grieve others. They cannot attend to conversation because of the annoyance occasioned by the habit which some people have of invariably taking more butter than they want. Have you ever seen the anxious look (almost mesmeric) which such persons fix on the article? They would feel it a relief if they might bury it out of their sight by popping it into their own mouths and swallowing it down; and they are really made happy if the person on whose plate it lies unused suddenly breaks off a piece of toast (which he does not want at all) and eats up his butter. They think that this is not waste. Now, Miss Matty Jenkins was chary of candles: We had many devices to use as few as possible. In the winter afternoons she would sit knitting for two or three hours—she could do this in the dark or by firelight—and when I asked if I might not ring for candles to finish stitching my wristbands, she told me to "keep blind man's holiday." They were usually brought in with tea, but we burnt only one at a time. As we lived in constant preparation for a friend who might come in any evening (but who never did), it required some contrivance to keep our two candles of the same length, ready to be lighted, and to look as if we burnt two always. The candles took it in turns; and then, whatever we might be talking of or doing, Miss Matty kept her eyes habitually fixed upon the candle, ready to jump up and extinguish it and light the other before they had become too uneven in length to be restored to equality in the course of the evening.

—Adapted from Mrs. Gaskell's *Cranford.*

2

Dear Madam:

We are sorry to say that we have no more house coats No. SP62 in size 38 at $4.50. As we advertised, SP62 is not a regular stock number, but represents a collection of $5, $6, and $7.50 coats remaining after the holiday sales and reduced to insure their being sold before spring. At the opening of the sale there were only a few coats in size 38, and they were sold almost at once. In our catalogue, pages 68 to 71 inclusive, you will find descriptions of all our stock house coats. On page 68 you will see No. 450HC, our regular $4.50 coat. If you would like us to send you one of these in size 38, we shall forward it to you at once. However, if you would like a $5, $6, or $7.50 coat, you will, no doubt, send us the difference in price on receipt of this letter. Of course, the more expensive garments are made of better materials, but all our coats show the same excellent workmanship. The best way for you to get the exact shade of trimming that you wish is to send us a sample of the goods that you would like to match. We assure you that we shall take all possible care to send you the proper color.

Yours truly,

Exercise 211

Paragraphs may be developed in different ways. For example, if you were going to write on the process of making a layer cake, you would explain in detail the different ingredients in the mixture, the proportion of each, and the steps in the process before the product could be sold as a layer cake.

By the use of explanatory details develop the following:

1. Making a kite.
2. Making a baseball.
3. Making fudge.
4. How to play checkers.
5. The manufacture of soap (or any article in a grocery).
6. The manufacture of a tin can.
7. The manufacture of pins.
8. Every man must have an ambition.
9. Why I intend to enter business.
10. The greatest modern invention.

By the use of examples to illustrate your point develop the following:

1. Electricity is making housework easy and pleasant.
2. Many sons of poor parents have won great wealth.
3. The wireless apparatus has saved many lives.
4. A boy can show that he is a good citizen.
5. Young Americans have little respect for authority.

By the use of comparison and contrast develop the following:

1. Improvements in modern lighting systems.
2. Improvements in modern heating systems.
3. Improvements in modern means of locomotion.
4. Two kinds of work, pleasure, or study.
5. Why I intend to have a business of my own.
6. The study that I like best.

By explaining cause and effect develop the following:

1. The advantages of public gymnasiums.
2. The success of loose leaf devices.
3. The objections to football.

Exercise 212

Develop the following into paragraphs; in each case be able to show what method or methods you have employed:

1. A man who cannot read and write English should not be allowed to vote.

2. Postal savings banks inspire the savings habit.

3. Women—the mothers of children—should vote.

4. Women should not vote because they do not read the newspaper.

5. The effect of school slang is bad.

6. I wish I had seen the coronation of George V. Every fairy story I had ever read would suddenly have become real.

7. Canada would gain by reciprocity with the United States.

8. The United States would gain by reciprocity with Canada.

9. Our forests should be preserved.

10. The waste of lumber by forest fires results from carelessness.

11. The waste of lumber in cutting railroad ties is too great.

12. The rotation of crops enriches the soil.

13. Apples are more easily gathered than cherries.

14. Efforts should be made to keep the birds in our city parks.

15. Every boy should learn a trade.

16. Peddlers should not be allowed to call their wares.

17. Great crowds gathered in the city during aviation week (or any celebration).

18. The electric toaster is good for hurry-up breakfasts.

19. Ironing with an electric iron is more convenient than with the old-fashioned kind.

20. The wireless apparatus makes sea voyages safer than before.

21. A mixed diet is best.

22. Cats should be exterminated because they spread disease.

23. The parcel post will decrease the profits of the express companies.

24. A good book is opened with expectation and closed with profit.

25. Merchants should charge for delivering purchases.

26. The object of the Child Welfare Exhibit is to promote the best interests of children.

27. One of the best enactments of our time is the Child Labor Law.

Exercise 213—Smooth Connection

We may as well confess at the beginning that smooth connection between sentences and paragraphs is a hard thing to learn. Primarily, it depends on clear thinking. In Exercise 135 we saw that the idea of one sentence must grow out of the idea of the preceding one. It is the same with paragraphs. The thought must develop gradually from one to the next. Each paragraph, we know, represents a unit within the larger unit of the composition; each represents a division of thought. Not infrequently the thought of one division differs considerably from the thought of the next. The tying together of such units is sometimes hard. It may be done in one of the following ways:

1. By repeating at the beginning of the new paragraph or sentence part of the preceding paragraph or sentence.

2. By using pronouns to refer to what has gone before.

3. By using connecting links, sometimes called *transition words* because they indicate the transition from one division to the next. Besides those mentioned in Exercise 135, we may use a numeral connection, as, *in the first place*, *in the second place;* or an expression much like a numeral, as, *furthermore*, *in the next place;* or an expression showing that an adverse idea is to be presented, as, *on the other hand*, *however*, *in spite of this*, *nevertheless*. But whatever you do, choose the right link, especially if you use such a one as *possibly*, *probably*, *perhaps*, *certainly*, *surely*. Use the one that expresses your idea exactly. Have none rather than the wrong one.

In the following the first and second paragraphs are connected according to (1) above; the second and third are connected according to (3) above.

There comes to every prosperous man a time when he wishes to know the best way of securing a steady income from his accumulated savings without the burden of responsibility of managing some property in order to gain his income. The merchant may not wish to put back into the business all the earnings he gets from it, and yet he wishes to prepare for his old age.

The farmer may wish to give up active work, but he realizes how soon his broad acres may deteriorate through soil-robbery when he rents his property "on shares." With such a problem before him the thoughtful man makes an effort to *learn* how to act to secure a good *income* all his life.

One of the first things he *learns*, if he studies the situation carefully, is that there is a wide difference between an *income* derived from one's business ability, such as the profit secured from running a store, factory, jobbing house, or farm, and the income which is derived as the result of money "working" by itself. In the first case, a man must of necessity keep up his business responsibilities; in the other, once he has selected a safe investment, practically all he has to do is to collect his income from time to time as it falls due. There is in the latter no depreciation of land, buildings, machinery, or the like; no insurance payments to worry about; no crop failures to consider.

It is evident, then, that if one wishes to put surplus money away—say the proceeds from the sale of a business or a farm—and get a steady income from it without bother or worry, the most important thing to consider is how to go about it to select something which, once purchased, will turn out to be a safe investment.

Exercise 214

In the following paragraphs taken from Robert Louis Stevenson's *The Philosophy of Nomenclature*, point out all the transition words that join (1) sentence to sentence, and (2) paragraph to paragraph:

To begin, then: the influence of our name makes itself felt from the very cradle. As a schoolboy I remember the pride with which I hailed Robin Hood, Robert Bruce, and Robert le Diable as my name-fellows; and the feeling of sore disappointment that fell on my heart when I found a freebooter or a general who did not share with me a single one of my numerous *praenomina.* Look at the delight with which two children find they have the same name. They are friends from that moment forth; they have a bond of union stronger than exchange of nuts and sweetmeats. This feeling, I own, wears off in later life. Our names lose their freshness and interest, become trite and indifferent. But this, dear reader, is merely one of the sad effects of those "shades of the prison house" which come gradually betwixt us and nature with advancing years; it affords no weapon against the philosophy of names.

In after life, although we fail to trace its working, that name which careless godfathers lightly applied to your unconscious infancy will have been moulding your character and influencing with irresistible power the whole course of your earthly fortunes. But the last name is no whit less important as a condition of success. Family names, we must recollect, are but inherited nicknames; and if the *sobriquet* were applicable to the ancestor, it is most likely applicable to the descendant also. You would not expect to find Mr. M'Phun acting as a mute or Mr. M'Lumpha excelling as a professor of dancing. Therefore, in what follows, we shall consider names, independent of whether they are first or last. And to begin with, look what a pull *Cromwell* had over *Pym*—the one name full of a resonant imperialism, the other mean, pettifogging, and unheroic to a degree. Who would expect eloquence from *Pym*—who would read poems by *Pym*—who would bow to the opinions of *Pym?* He might have been a dentist, but he should never have aspired to be a statesman. I can only wonder that he succeeded as he did. Pym and Habakkuk stand first upon the roll of men who have triumphed, by sheer force of genius, over the most unfavorable appellations. But even these have suffered; and, had they been more fitly named, the one might have been Lord Protector and the other have shared the laurels with Isaiah. In this matter we must not forget that all our great poets have borne great names. Chaucer, Spenser, Shakespeare, Milton, Pope, Wordsworth, Shelley—what a constellation of lordly words! Not a single commonplace name among them—not a Brown, not a Jones, not a Robinson; they are all names that one would stop and look at on a door-plate. Now, imagine if *Pepys* had tried to clamber somehow into the enclosure of poetry, what a blot would that name have made upon the list! The thing is impossible. In the first place, a certain natural consciousness that men have would have held him down to the level of his name, would have prevented him from rising above the Pepsine standard, and so haply withheld him altogether from attempting verse. Next, the booksellers would refuse to publish, and the world to read them, on the mere evidence of the fatal appellation. And now, before I close this section, I must say one word as to *punnable* names, names that stand alone, that have a significance and life apart from him that bears them. These are the bitterest of all. One friend of mine goes bowed and humbled through life under the weight of this misfortune; for it is an awful thing when a man's name is a joke, when he cannot be mentioned without exciting merriment, and when even the intimation of his death bids fair to carry laughter into many a home.

So much for people who are badly named. Now for people who are *too* well named, who go topheavy from the font, who are baptized into a false position, and who find themselves beginning life eclipsed under the fame of some of the great ones of the past. A man, for instance, called William Shakespeare could never dare to write plays. He is thrown into too humbling an apposition with the author of *Hamlet.* His own name coming after is such an anti-climax. "The plays of William Shakespeare?" says the reader—"O no! The plays of William Shakespeare Cockerill," and he throws the book aside. In wise pursuance of such views, Mr. John Milton Hengler, who not long since delighted us in this favored town, has never attempted to write an epic, but has chosen a new path and has excelled upon the tight-rope. A marked example of triumph over this is the case of Mr. Dante Gabriel Rosetti. On the face of the matter, I should have advised him to imitate the pleasing modesty of the last-named gentleman, and confine his ambition to the sawdust. But Mr. Rosetti has triumphed. He has even dared to translate from his mighty name-father; and the voice of fame supports him in his boldness.

Exercise 215

Turn back to Exercise 210, 1. How are the different paragraphs that you have made connected?

CHAPTER XV

BUSINESS LETTERS

NOT long ago the head of one of the biggest mail order firms in this country said: "Business needs the boys and the girls. Do not let them think they can be but cogs in the great system of wheels. More to-day than at any previous time the world needs men and women who can speak and write *themselves* into English. Four hundred million dollars is wasted every year in unprofitable advertising alone, and as much more in bad handling of good prospects and loss of customers through inefficient letters. We look to the future generation to conserve a part of this enormous loss. If a single page advertisement in a single issue costs $7500, what you say on that page is important. Look into any current magazine, and you will be tremendously impressed with the importance of English in this branch alone, not to mention its importance in letter writing."

There is no greater power in business to-day than the ability to use convincing English in correspondence and in advertising. Any one who can write good letters, letters that the reader feels he must answer, has success ahead of him, because the market of a good letter is practically unrestricted. Wherever a letter can penetrate, it may create desire for an article and make sales.

But what is a good letter? Nothing more than a bit of good English. Can you write clear, direct, crisp, yet fluent English? Then you can write good letters—but not till then.

In modern business the letter has become the advertiser, the salesman, the collector, and the adjuster of claims. An advertisement must be attractive; it must arouse the interest of the one who sees it. A salesman must understand human nature; he must forestall objections by showing the customer how he will gain by buying. The collector and the adjuster of claims must be courteous and at the same time shrewd. If a letter is to meet all of these requirements it cannot be dashed off at a moment's notice. It must be thought out in detail and written carefully to include all that should be expressed. This means, especially in a sales letter:

1. An unusually worded opening that puts the writer's affairs in the background and the reader's gain in the foreground. Begin with *you*, not *we*. The reader is interested in himself, his own progress, his own troubles, and not in the possessions of the writer, except as the writer can show that those possessions affect him.

3. A clear, simply worded explanation of the purpose of the letter.

3. Proof of advantages to the reader.

4. Persuasion or inducement to act now.

5. Conclusion, making this action easy.

Above all, if a letter is to be good, it must not be too short. In the pursuit of brevity too many pupils in business English make the mistake of writing altogether too little to get the reader's attention; and if his attention is not aroused, the letter fails. The letter should be long enough to suggest interest in the welfare of the reader and enthusiasm for the subject under discussion.

Enthusiasm in business involves knowledge both of your project and of your customer. You cannot attempt to write a letter of any kind unless you know the facts that require it. Perhaps it is a complaint that you must try to settle. Without a knowledge of the facts, of the truth or the untruth of the claim, how can you write the letter? Sometimes it requires both time and study to gather the necessary details, but they must be gathered.

When you have your details and begin writing, be sincere. You must be so absolutely in earnest that the reader will at once feel and begin to share your enthusiasm.

Knowledge of the person to whom you are writing is fully as important as knowledge of your subject. You must get his point of view, understand his character, and appeal to the qualities that you recognize in it, to the desires or ambitions, that it shows. To a certain extent all of us are alike. There are certain fundamental interests that we all possess; these may safely be appealed to at almost all times. But our employment, our habits of life, our ways of thinking make us different. The same argument, probably, will not always bring satisfactory replies from a manufacturer, a farmer, a judge, a minister or priest, a carpenter, and a woman. Some people like to receive a long letter that goes carefully into detail; others will not take the time to read such a letter. Each customer must be studied. This is so difficult a matter that no one can expect to learn it all at once.

Finally, from the first word to the last be courteous. No matter how righteous your indignation, be courteous. You cannot afford to lose your temper. Courtesy does not imply flattery nor a lack of truth. Your letter can be strong and yet polite in tone. Lose your temper, and your letter will probably fail. Keep your temper, show thoughtfulness for the reader's interest, and your letter will more likely fulfill its purpose.

Exercise 216—The Form of the Letter

Before we look at some actual letters to judge of their effectiveness, we must learn the conventional form of a letter, the parts which many years of use have shown to be necessary. There are six parts to a formal or business letter:

1. The heading, which includes the writer's address and the date.

2. The introduction, which includes the name and the address of the one to whom you are writing.

3. The salutation; for example, Dear Sir:

4. The body of the letter, the important part.

5. The courteous close; for example, Yours truly,

6. The signature.

Each part ends with a period except the salutation, which ends with a colon, and the courteous close, which ends with a comma. The various groups of words within the heading and the introduction are separated by commas.

Why does the salutation end with a colon?

Why does the courteous close end with a comma?

The Arrangement

In the following, notice the spacing. If the heading is short, it is put on one line; as,

Heading Hilliard, Fla., June 30, 1914.

Introduction Mr. Thomas Barrett,

Boston, Mass.

Salutation Dear Sir:

Body ....

....

....

*Courteous close*Yours truly,

Signature Samuel Garth

If the heading is long, arrange it in one of the following ways:

1

334 Lexington Ave., Chicago,
May 19, 1915.

Mr. Thomas Barrett,
Boston, Mass.
Dear Sir:

2

334 Lexington Ave.,
Chicago, Ill., May 19, 1915.

3

334 Lexington Ave.,
Chicago, Ill.,
May 19, 1915.

4

334 Lexington Ave.,
Chicago, Ill.,
May 19, 1915.

The superscription on the envelope is arranged and punctuated like the introduction in the letter, except that the punctuation may be omitted from the end of lines.

There is a growing tendency to "block" the different parts of a letter; that is, to begin each item of each part directly below the first, with no indentation.

There is also a tendency to use no abbreviations (except for titles like *Mr.*), the name of the month and of the state and the word *street*, *avenue*, or *building* being spelled out.

NOTE.—The punctuation as shown in the examples given above is that in more prevalent use. Certain writers, however, advocate the omission from the formal parts of the letter of commas at the end of lines and of periods (except to show abbreviations).

Arrange the following headings, supplying capitals and punctuation marks:

1. 55 water st mobile ala june 16 19—

2. calmar iowa september 1 19—

3. 453 marquette building chicago ill jan 5 19—

4. 123 salem st springfield mass june 23 19—

5. highland park grand haven mich may 3 19—

6. 220 broadway new york n y february 15 19—

7. 78 main street portland oregon december 10 19—

8. 32 lincoln st kansas city mo oct 2 19—

9. room 15 1321 pennsylvania ave washington d c sept 2 19—

10. 25 chestnut st philadelphia pa april 14 19—

11. 212 tribune building new york n y march 2 19—

12. 98 dorchester ave boston mass feb 12 19—

13. 24 milk st boston mass June 14 19—

14. 231 west 39th st new york city march 4 19—

15. 345 newark ave jersey city n j (supply date)

16. 44 fifth ave detroit mich sept 1 19—

17. 102 west 42d st denver colorado (date)

18. Explain the difference between (16) and (17). Notice that the name of the street in each case is a numeral. Why is it spelled out in (16) and not in (17)?

Exercise 217

Supplying the name of the firm and the business engaged in, write letter heads using the items given in Exercise 216. For example:

BARRETT, BROWN & CO.
Groceries
55 Water Street
Decorah, Iowa, — 19

When may & be used?

What is the advantage of using a letter head?

In making letter heads, imagine you are a printer. Arrange the items so that they may show to the best advantage. Let your lines of printing or writing be of different lengths. Add any details that you wish, such as trade-mark designs or the names of officers.

Arrange and punctuate:

1. citronelle business mens association citronelle alabama may 2 19— mr john harvey 19 e monroe st rochester n y dear sir

2. 173 broadway new york June 10 19— mr walter thomas 191 e main st waltham mass dear sir

3. 25 broad st maplewood n h messrs hausen & ottman 18 la salle station chicago ill gentlemen (supply date)

4. john randolph & co druggist 14 jefferson st charleston s c jan 8 19— gerhard mennen & co newark n j gentlemen (letter head)

5. 43 south 5th ave madison wis aug 8 19— the white mountain freezer co nashua n h gentlemen

Address an envelope for each of the above, using the following as a model.

> **Barrett, Brown & Co.,**
> **55 Water Street,**
> **Decorah, Iowa.**

Exercise 218—Cautions

The Heading

Always date your letters.

Give your full address, even if you are certain that the one to whom you are writing knows it.

The Introduction

The person addressed must always be given a title. If you address one man, use *Mr.;* if a firm, use *Messrs.;* if a woman, *Miss* or *Mrs.* If a man has a title like *Professor* or *Doctor*, it should be used, and *Mr.*, of course, omitted.

Hon. (Honorable) is used for a person who holds, or who has held, a public office. It is a very formal title.

Esq.(Esquire) is a legal form used by some correspondents in addressing any man. It is an English usage. It always follows the name, and, if it is used, *Mr.* is omitted. In this country *Mr.* is preferable.

In writing to a man in his official capacity, the following form is correct when there is no street number or when the title is short. Notice that *Mr.* is omitted.

G. N. Fratt, Cashier,
First National Bank,
Racine, Wis.

The following is correct when the title is long:

Mr. John Frederick Pierce,
Ass't. Engineer of Bridges and Buildings,
607 White Building, Seattle, Wash.

Notice that in the last example, the city and the state are put on the same line as the street in order to make the three lines of about the same length. Four lines might have been used.

The Salutation

If you address one man, the salutation is *Dear Sir;* as,

Mr. John Pierce,
Seattle, Wash.
Dear Sir:

If you address a firm, the salutation is *Gentlemen;* as,

Messrs. Brownleigh & King,
Portland, Oregon.
Gentlemen:

If you address a woman, married or single, the salutation in business letters is *Dear Madam;* as,

1

Mrs. John Pierce,

Seattle, Wash.
Dear Madam:

2

Miss Florence Pierce,
Seattle, Wash.
Dear Madam:

A more familiar form of salutation is either of the following:

1

Miss Florence Pierce,
Seattle, Wash.
My dear Miss Pierce:

2

Miss Florence Pierce,
Seattle, Wash.
Dear Miss Pierce:

In using *Hon.*, the salutation is usually *Sir.*

The Courteous Close

The courteous close corresponds in tone to the salutation. If the salutation is *Dear Sir*, *Gentlemen*, or *Dear Madam*, the courteous close should be one of the following:

Yours truly,

Yours very truly,

Very truly yours,

Respectfully yours,

Yours respectfully,

Sincerely yours,

Very sincerely yours,

If the salutation is *Sir*, the courteous close should be *Respectfully yours* or *Yours respectfully*.

If the body of the letter and the courteous close do not agree in tone, the effect is often ridiculous. Suppose, for instance, that the courteous close of (2) under Exercise 220 were *Yours respectfully*. What would be the effect?

The Signature

If an unmarried woman is signing a business letter, she should avoid confusion by prefixing (Miss) to her name.

A married woman should sign her own name, as, *Alice Pierce;* she should indicate her title, as *Mrs. John F. Pierce*, either below the other or at one side.

No other title should be prefixed to a signature.

If a letter is signed by the name of a firm, the signature of the one who dictated the letter is usually added; as,

Yours very truly,
Smith Lumber Co.
by ——

This sort of signature gives a letter the "personal touch." Explain.

Folding a Letter

Business letter paper is about eight by ten inches. In folding a letter sheet, (1) turn the lower edge up to about one-eighth of an inch from the top; press the fold firmly, keeping the edges even; (2) turn the paper so that the folded edge is at your *left* hand; (3) fold *from* you a little less than one-third the width of the sheet; (4) fold the upper edge *down* toward you so that it projects a trifle beyond the folded edge. Without turning it over, pick it up and insert it in the envelope, putting in *first* the edge that was folded last.

Write the address and the salutation for:

1. A business house in your town.

2. Mr. John R. Tobin, president of the Detroit State Bank, Detroit, Mich.

3. Miss Mabel Gunther, Shullsburg, Wis.

4. Professor C. M. Watson, Harvard College, Cambridge, Mass.

5. John F. Campbell, Manager Bond Department, First Trust and Savings Bank, Boston, Mass.

6. Taylor and Critchfield, Chicago, Ill.

7. Mrs. Thomas D. MacDonald, 126 E. Second Street, Washington, Ia.

Write the courteous close and the signature for:

1. A letter from a business house in your town signed by F. R. Wilson.

2. A letter from Miss Mabel Gunther (2 above).

3. A letter from Professor C. M. Watson (4 above).

4. A letter signed by John F. Campbell (5 above).

5. A letter from Taylor and Critchfield signed by you yourself.

6. A letter from Mrs. Thomas D. MacDonald (7 above).

Exercise 219—Ordering Goods

If an order includes a number of separate items, it is usually written on a separate sheet of paper. Firms often supply blanks for this purpose. If the order is short, it forms part of the letter. In any case, each item is placed on a separate line, so that the items may be checked as the order is filled. In the following, notice the arrangement and the punctuation:

Hamilton, Montana, Feb. 16, 1914.

Messrs. MacBride & Dickens,
New York, N. Y.
Gentlemen:

At your earliest convenience please ship me the following via the Northern Express Co. from St. Paul:

6 doz. A 68 assorted sizes Men's Black Caps	@	1.50	9.00
5 doz. D 71 Men's Cotton Handkerchiefs	@	.60	3.00
5 doz. X 30 Men's Linen Handkerchiefs	@	2.00	10.00
			$22.00

Enclosed find a draft on New York for twenty-two dollars.

Yours truly,
S. D. Jensen

Write the letters outlined below:

1. Order fifty copies of the Business Arithmetic that you are using. How shall you pay for them?

2. Clip from a newspaper an advertisement of groceries. Imagine that you are a housekeeper, and spend ten dollars to the best advantage, ordering several articles.

3. Bring in an advertisement of household necessities—linens, tinware, etc. Spend five dollars, buying several articles.

4. Bring in an advertisement of furniture. Write a letter ordering enough to furnish a parlor or a dining room. Have the amount charged to your account.

5. A magazine offers one of several books as a premium with a year's subscription. Answer the advertisement.

Exercise 220—The Tone of the Letter

Undue familiarity or an evidence of loss of temper will at once frustrate the object of a letter. A dignified letter never shows either. Just what constitutes a dignified letter is hard to define but fairly easy to feel. This much is certain: it must be simple in structure, direct in its wording, and so sincere in feeling that no one will doubt its truth. Any extravagance of language, therefore, has no place in a dignified letter.

Study the following to see whether they show dignity:

1

Tuesday, 5 P.M.

Miss Sarah Howard,
Denver, Colorado.
Dear Madam:

I have a great piece of CONFIDENTIAL news for you.

Take advantage of the remarkable offer our company is making to you, and it will mean thousands of DOLLARS in your pocket. Understand that this offer is not open to every one. You have been especially selected. You are the only one in your town who will hear of this remarkable offer.

2

Elsworth, Brown & Co.,
120 Jefferson Ave.,
Detroit, Mich.
Gentlemen:

What is the matter with our last order? Have you people gone out of business, or are you asleep? If we don't get that order by the third, you'll never hear from us again.

3

A letter to Mrs. Bixby, written Nov. 21, 1864.

Dear Madam:

I have been shown in the file of the War Department a statement of the Adjutant General of Massachusetts that you are the mother of five sons who have died gloriously on the field of battle. I feel how weak and fruitless must be any words of mine which should beguile you from the grief of a loss so overwhelming. But I cannot refrain from tendering to you the consolation that may be found in the thanks of the republic they died to save. I pray that our Heavenly Father may assuage the anguish of your bereavement, and leave you only the cherished memory of the loved and lost and the solemn pride that must be yours to have laid so costly a sacrifice upon the altar of freedom.

Yours very sincerely and respectfully,
Abraham Lincoln

Exercise 221

In writing the following letters, be definite and courteous:

1. You have advertised your eight-room, furnace-heated house for sale for $3,500. A letter of inquiry desires particulars. Answer it.

2. You live on a side street, which for the last week has not been lighted. Write to the editor of the paper, or to a town official, whichever you think would remedy the matter. Be courteous. A letter to an editor is begun: To the Editor of ——.

3. The cars on which you ride every day are very dirty. Write to the mayor. He is addressed: Hon. ——.

4. You wish to have a telephone installed. Make application.

5. Two weeks ago you wrote (4). Still you have no telephone. Write again, stating the substance of (4) and asking the reason for the delay.

6. Write the telephone company's reply. Be very courteous. What good reason could you give for the delay?

7. You understand that your Congressman has the privilege of recommending a young man for the entrance examinations of your state university. Write to him, asking that he recommend you. Remember that he is a stranger to you. What should you tell him?

Exercise 222—Mistaken Ideas in Letter Writing

It is too bad that, to a number of people, the term *business letter* conveys the idea of a colorless, stilted composition full of trite and almost meaningless business formulas. No one reads such a letter unless he has to, and surely that is not the kind one should practice writing. Below are given a few of the expressions that should be avoided.

I. Sometimes a writer tries to impress a reader with the volume of business he is doing by showing haste in his correspondence; as, in

1. Omitting the subject; as,

Wrong: In reply to your question will say ——
Right: In reply to your question I will say ——

2. Omitting articles and prepositions; as,

Wrong: Direct package care Western Canning Co.
Right: Direct the package in care of the Western Canning Co.

3. Using abbreviations

a. Of the introduction. Write out the introduction in detail, both name and address. Abbreviating this part of the letter is highly discourteous.

b. In the body of the letter; as,

Wrong: The Co. sent a no. of large orders last year.

c. Of the courteous close; as,

Wrong: Yours etc.
Wrong: Yours resp'y.

4. Using a phrase as a sentence; as,

Wrong: Yours of the 6th at hand and contents noted.

It is much better to refer indirectly to the receipt of a letter; as,

In the order you sent us on Aug. 5 ——

The same sort of mistake is seen in the all too frequent closing:

Wrong: Hoping that we hear from you soon,
Yours truly,

Right: Hoping that we hear from you soon, we are
Yours truly,

Why use such an expression at all? Avoid *hoping, trusting, awaiting,* or any other artificial closing.

II. Sometimes a writer makes an effort to be extremely courteous, but fails because he uses hackneyed wording; as,

1. *Kindly.*—A good word in itself but greatly abused.

2. *We beg to state.*—Never use *beg* in this sense. You have no right to beg attention; earn it.

3. *Your favor, your esteemed favor, your valued favor.*—Say, *Your letter.*

4. *Will you be so good as to.*—Belongs in the class with *beg to state.* Make your requests courteously, but directly.

5. *Would say.*—Avoid this expression.

III. Sometimes in an effort to be clear a writer uses *same* as a pronoun; as,

Wrong: If the books are not satisfactory, return same.

This is one of the worst of the distinctly business blunders. *Same* is never a pronoun. Write to a man as you talk to him and you will not use *same* in this way. (See Exercise 88.)

IV. Sometimes in order to get attention a writer will use a liberal sprinkling of dashes and capitals, probably in imitation of advertising copy. Better than such artificial means is the attraction of a well worded letter.

Criticise the following letters, pointing out all the expressions that should be improved. Rewrite the letters.

1

Gentlemen:

We beg to acknowledge your esteemed favor of Apr. 6. In regard to shoes received by you in poor shape as per complaint, would say that on receipt of same will try to locate cause of trouble. If due to defect in manufacture, will credit you with value of same.

Hoping this is satisfactory to you,

Yours truly,

2

Dear Sir:

Yours of March 18 at hand. Referring to matter of short weight, I beg to call your attention to C & A car 87324, which you loaded for us March 7 at your Auburn mine, gross weight 121,400 lbs. This car was check weighed at Peoria March 11 on your company's scales and showed gross weight 113,200 lbs. or shortage 8,200 lbs. Having investigated car, I find same was in good order and no indication of leakage, and it would appear to be a case of carelessness at time of loading. Therefore will request you to kindly send me cr. memo, on 8,200 lbs.

Yours truly,

Exercise 223—The Sales Letter

The object of the sales letter is to make the reader buy. How can you do it? To begin with, get his point of view—that of the user. Then imagine that he is present and talk to him on paper. Get his interest with your opening sentence. Explain what you have to sell. Show him that he needs it. Whet his desire to possess it, and, finally, make it easy and imperative for him to order today.

The opening paragraph is all-important. It may make or mar a letter. If it is stilted or lacks directness, if it hasn't the personal, natural tone that makes the reader feel you are talking to him, or if it is stereotyped in its wording, the letter will probably go to the waste-basket.

Contrast the two letters that follow. Both were written to accompany a catalogue. Notice that the first begins and ends in a stereotyped way; has too few details to arouse interest; asks for an order but has no inducement to give one now; and, throughout, lacks the personal, convincing tone that makes the second a good selling letter. Notice that the second begins with *you*, not with *we*, and keeps the same *you* attitude to the end.

Turn back to the five essentials of a letter given on page 230. See if you can differentiate the five in the second letter.

1

Dear Sir:

In compliance with your request of recent date we are sending you our latest general catalogue, inasmuch as we do not know which department catalogue you wish. We also have specialized books for jewelry, furniture, hardware, and drygoods. On request we shall be glad to send any one of these also.

We carry the biggest line of Variety Store Leaders in the country, and our goods are always of the best. We take particular pains to acquaint our customers with the latest thing in the trade, and to give business-getting suggestions. Our Co-operative Bureau cheerfully answers all inquiries.

Trusting we shall hear from you with an order, we are

Yours truly,

2

Dear Sir:

Under separate cover you will receive a copy of our latest general catalogue, published especially for owners of Variety Stores. We are sending you the general catalogue because we do not know whether you are interested in a particular department. However, if your business specializes in any one class of goods—such as jewelry, furniture, hardware, or drygoods—we shall be glad to supply you with the departmental book you need. On the enclosed postal card simply check the one you wish, and mail the card to-day. We shall forward the catalogue at once.

You may know that we always have on hand between two hundred and two hundred and fifty different Variety Store Leaders, affording you a wide selection of high-class goods of the finest materials, the neatest workmanship, and the latest styles at very low prices. After glancing over the catalogue you will agree with us that in every department of our huge business a dollar has full purchasing power.

A unique feature of our business, moreover, is the Co-operative Bureau, which you will find a decided help in building up your business. Each week the Bureau sends out a Bulletin, acquainting our customers with important business events in the larger trade centers, with suggestions for new advertising and selling methods, with notices of new stock additions that make especially good leaders, and with advice how best to display them. The Bureau invites correspondence and sends customers, absolutely free of charge, advice on new store arrangements, window decorations, and advertising plans.

Your first order makes you a co-operating member and entitles you to all the privileges of the Bureau and the services of an institution with wide experience and with a recognized reputation for square-dealing. Fill out the enclosed order blank, mail it to-day, and receive this week's Bulletin by return mail. It contains several splendid suggestions for novel, inexpensive advertising.

Yours truly,

The letter given above is personal and yet dignified. Usually that is the best style to use, and the one that we wish to practice writing. Sometimes, however, results can best be obtained by using the colloquial or even jocular tone illustrated in the following letter sent to a retailer in Ottumwa, Iowa:

Dear Sir:

We sell cheese, a new brand, the finest kind you ever tasted, put up in the most attractive package, to sell at the most attractive price. Called Par Excellence Creme, wrapped in silver foil with a gold label, it sells for fifteen cents and costs you ten. Ever hear a better proposition?

Better buy now before your rival gets ahead of you. Everybody's calling for it. Why? Because we're advertising everywhere. It has been out only one month, and yet sales have trebled our highest expectations. Half the sales of a new cheese depend on the package and the price; the other half depend on the quality. All three are right in Par Excellence Creme.

Mr. S. R. King, our Iowa representative, tried to see you last week, but, unfortunately, he was unable to find you in. Now, he carries a full line of our samples, and it's worth the time it takes just to see how good they look, even if you don't care to buy. How about it? Don't you want to see them? Mr. King will be in Ottumwa next Wednesday.

Yours truly,

This style is commonly called "snappy." It has its advantage, but should be used only rarely. Above all, if you do use it, avoid the dash. Notice how the dash spoils the following:

Dear Sir:

Have you ever eaten that king of nuts—the budded or grafted paper shell pecan—the nut whose kernel is as nutritious as beef and as sweet and delicious as honey—the nut that is so delightfully palatable and so wholesome, the discriminating epicures of two continents have set their seal of approval on it—creating a demand that literally cannot be supplied—even at prices ranging as high as a dollar a pound.

To use the dash in this way seems to imply that you do not understand punctuation or sentence structure. If the paragraph is rewritten, removing the dashes and dividing into sentences, we get a much stronger appeal. The dash makes for weakness rather than for strength because it suggests hysterics.

Dear Sir:

Have you ever eaten the king of nuts, the budded or grafted paper shell pecan? The kernel is as nutritious as beef and as sweet as honey. It is so wholesome and so delicious that discriminating epicures of two continents have set their approval on it, creating a demand that literally cannot be supplied, even at prices ranging as high as a dollar a pound.

A very good way to open a sales letter is to get the attention by a bit of narration containing direct quotations, as shown in the following:

Dear Sir:

"It saves seven per cent."

So said Mr. John H. Samuels, a manufacturer of Birmingham, Ala.

He had watched his bookkeepers at their work, and it seemed to him that their main business was turning and flattening the springy pages of the bulgy ledger. Ten seconds were wasted, he said, every time a page was turned—almost every time an entry was made—and hardly more than two minutes were needed to make the entry. That was enough. Each of his twenty men was wasting seven per cent of his time.

"Try hinged paper," suggested the head bookkeeper.

Accordingly, Mr. Samuels tried several kinds of hinged paper, only to find that the hinged section tore, broke, or cracked. The time that the clerks now saved in flattening the leaves they wasted in rewriting the pages that had torn out.

He had no more faith in hinged papers by the time that he saw the advertisement of the Benton hinge. "As strong as the rest of the paper!" he scoffed. "We'll see about this!"

"Send me a sample," he wrote us. "If your ad tells the truth, you get my order."

We sent it. He tested it. He pulled it, crumpled it, ruled on it, erased it on both sides, and even creased it. But it did not break.

Very cautiously and doubtingly he tried the paper in one ledger for one month. He found that the book rolled flat whenever it was opened, that no hinge tore, and that every page could be used from binder to outer edge.

"It does the work," he told our salesman at the end of the month. "It saves seven per cent. Send me a consignment."

If you, too, are paying seven per cent of your bookkeepers' salaries for waste motion, let us send you a sample. It will cut down your expenses as it cut down Mr. Samuels'.

Remember that you put yourself under no obligation to us. You take no risks. Simply promise to use the paper if we send it free.

Yours truly,

Exercise 224

Study the following letters and letter openings for good and bad qualities:

1

Dear Sir:

People who have not had much of what the world calls "good luck" find it hard to believe an opportunity when it comes—they don't feel sure about it—on the other hand, people who have had many opportunities have a natural confidence that every opening presented is intended for them and they grasp it with an assurance that begets success.

You may be one of those who have not had many chances to do what you would like to do and therefore not sure that my offer is an opportunity. For that reason let us again go over the points of advantage. . . .

2

Dear Sir:

I am taking the liberty of writing you again because I fear you do not fully realize the value of the proposition I am offering you. Why, man, it's the opportunity of a life-time! . . . (extended for three pages.)

3

Dear Sir:

If we wanted to know just what kind of person you are, do you know where we'd go to find out? We'd ask your old friends and neighbors, who know all about you from close association.

If you want to find out about us—what we are doing and what improvements we are making in southern Florida—the best place to get this information is from the people of Florida, who know the facts from first-hand observation. The enclosed clipping is an editorial expression—not a paid advertisement—from the Ft. Meyers Press. The editor is under no obligation to us and is merely expressing the opinion of the people here. . . .

4

New York, Right Now.

A DEAL OF IMPORTANCE

It affects YOU! It is so important I must forego the pleasure of a personal letter in order to write 5,000 people to-day—500 of whom—the wide-awake ones who read this letter through—will be able to coin it into dollars—real money—money you can spend.

What we now offer you has never before been offered by any body in the world. It is a combination we are fortunate enough, just at this time, to be able to offer you, because of an important deal we have just closed—a deal that may easily spell dollars to you. Read every word of this letter—it may be—possibly is—the only thing to make you a successful and wealthy man. . . .

5

R F D 4 Logansport, Ind.
8-26-11.

Mr. M. H. Smith, etc.
Dear Sir:

I acknowledge getting your telegram over the telephone yesterday, and if I had been in funds would have answered by return telegram, but such is life. I accommodated a friend by loaning him $750, which will probably be paid the last week of never. I thank you for the offer, and when I am in funds will call on you either personally or by letter.

Very truly yours,

Exercise 225—Opening an Account

Imagine that you are manager of a wholesale dry goods house. You have received an order from P. H. Powley, 23 Water street, Franklin, Mich. As you do not know Mr. Powley, write him, stating in as courteous a way as possible that, since this is his first order, he must either furnish references or send a remittance. Make your letter direct and personal. Include some good selling talk.

The exercise above illustrates the method that might be adopted in case of a small order. If Mr. Powley had sent a large order, the wholesale house would no doubt consult a financial agency to discover his financial condition; his *rating*, it is called. If his name were not found in the book of the agency, the wholesale house would require Mr. Powley to send a correct account of his financial standing; that is, a list of his assets and liabilities. If he refused, they would not do business with him. Why? The principal financial agencies are Bradstreet and Dun. Besides these, there are many mercantile agencies. They give any information that is required concerning a business man. All such information is confidential.

In connection with this exercise study the letters that follow:

Request to Open an Account

Madison, Wis., Sept. 16, 1915.

Wilson, Brighton, & Co.,
68 Broadway, New York.
Gentlemen:

Until recently I was in the employ of Samuel Stratton & Co. of Milwaukee, but I have now started a business of my own, for which I should like to open an account with your house. As to my business ability and financial standing, I refer you to my late employers, Samuel Stratton & Co. of Milwaukee, and to the Madison State Bank of this city.

If on investigation you decide to accept me as a customer, will you please send the goods on the enclosed order, deducting your usual discount for cash? Upon receipt of the goods and of the invoice, I shall at once forward a sight draft on the Broadway National Bank of your city.

Respectfully yours,
George R. Scott

Reply No. 1

Dear Sir:

In seeking information through the usual outside channels for basing credit for you, we find our reports have not been sufficient in detail to permit us to arrange this matter satisfactorily. These reports all speak very highly of you in a personal way, but do not give us the required information financially.

We assume you want our goods for your Christmas trade. It is imperative, therefore, that we ship immediately. We suggest that on this order you send us a draft, in consideration of which we shall be pleased to allow you a special discount of 4%. Understand that we suggest these terms on this first order only, as we feel confident that we can easily arrange a credit basis for future shipments. We sincerely trust you will take no offense at the above suggestion, as we have made it in your interest.

Yours very truly,

REPLY NO. 2

Dear Sir:

Thank you for the order you sent us yesterday. Its size confirms the belief we have always held that D—— is a rapidly growing business center, the right place for a retailer to settle and prosper.

After careful consideration of your letter, however, we have decided to hold back your order for a short time. You cannot regret this more than we do. We do not like to lose your account, and yet, under the circumstances, we feel we cannot send you the order. We hope you can sell the property you mentioned in your letter and thus clear up the balances against you. Then we shall gladly open an account for you.

We are especially sorry we cannot send the order at once, as you no doubt need your fall stock now. Don't you think it would be the best solution if you would send us your remittance for $250 now, so that we may send the goods? We know what it means to buy in the open market so late in the season. We assure you that on receipt of a remittance the order will go through immediately.

Yours truly,

Exercise 226

1. Order from the Grand Rapids Furniture Co., Grand Rapids, Mich., 5 mahogany rockers, 1 Turkish rocker, 2 brass beds, 12 dining room chairs, 2 dining room tables. Supply catalogue numbers and give shipping directions.

2. The Grand Rapids Furniture Co. replies, acknowledging the receipt of the above order (give date) but stating that you did not mention how you would pay for the goods. On receipt of a certified check to cover the amount, or of the names of two reliable references, they will be pleased to send you the order. Make this a good sales letter.

Exercise 227

1. You are a florist of Rockford, Ill. Write to S. M. Porter & Son, 155 S. State Street, Chicago, saying that this fall you are opening a new department of Landscape Gardening. Judging by advance orders, you will need approximately 200 shade trees, maples and poplars; 200 fruit trees of various kinds; and several hundred flowering shrubs. You will probably duplicate the order in the spring. Ask for terms, saying that you would like to open an account. Give two references.

2. S. M. Porter & Son reply, acknowledging your order, and saying that they will be pleased to do business with you on sixty days' credit, terms 50 and 5%. If this is satisfactory, they will add your name to their books. Make it a sales letter.

Exercise 228

1. Samuel Radford of Douglas, Mich., wishes to buy a motor boat. He orders of the Modern Steel Boat Co., manufacturers of high grade motor boats, Detroit, Mich., boat No. 172. page 425, catalogue No. 10. The price as listed is $192. He accepts the offer they made him —— (date), of —— (terms) and encloses a certified check for the amount. He gives full shipping directions. (Be sure you can do this.) He asks how cheaply he can obtain cushions for the boat.

2. The company reply: They have shipped the boat. (Is this sufficiently detailed?) A set of new cushions to fit the boat costs $25. They have a set of secondhand cushions in excellent condition for $15. If Radford desires either of these, he should wire at once at their expense.

3. Telegraph his decision.

Exercise 229

1. Messrs. Lee and Watkins, druggists of Gallon, Ohio, wish to open an account with Pierce, King & Co., 17 S. Albany St., Baltimore, Md., for the purchase of large orders on ninety days' credit. They say they do a very large business as they have the only drug store within a radius of several miles. They give several names as references. Write the letter.

2. You are a traveling salesman for Pierce, King & Co. They write you at the Union Hotel, Columbus, telling you of the foregoing letter, a copy of which they enclose, and asking you to investigate the standing of Messrs. Lee and Watkins.

Reply that you visited the drug store in question on a Tuesday (give date), because in your experience the early part of the week is very quiet in the business of small towns. Say that two clerks were kept busy constantly and that several people spoke of the enormous business done on Saturdays and market days. The firm has good credit in the town. You are satisfied that the gentlemen in question are reliable.

3. Write from Pierce, King & Co. to Messrs. Lee and Watkins, acknowledging the receipt of their letter —— (date) and expressing pleasure in being able to enter their name on the firm's books. Write as courteous a letter as you can.

4. Imagine that the salesman's reply (2) had been unfavorable. Write to Messrs. Lee and Watkins, refusing them credit but trying to get their cash business.

Exercise 230—Letters Requesting Payment

It is better not to make threats in a collection letter except as a last resort, and then the threat should be carried out. It is advisable in a first letter of the kind to take for granted that a customer is honest and that the failure to pay is an oversight. If some inducement for further purchases is included in the letter in the form of good selling talk, a remittance will probably be sent, and perhaps another order as well.

If the customer, however, takes no notice of the first letter, a second, making the request for payment more urgent, may follow. The tone of the second letter and subsequent letters will depend on the value that you put on the customer's trade. Finally, if he ignores all of these letters, dally no longer. Say that if payment is not made by a certain date, you will draw on him at sight. If he does not honor the draft, put the matter in the hands of your attorney.

Study the following letters. Select from them those that you think would make a good series:

1

Dear Sir:

Ten days ago we mailed you a statement of your account, which was due at that time. As we have heard nothing from you, we have concluded that the letter must have miscarried. We are, therefore, enclosing a duplicate of the former statement. We trust that it will reach you safely and have your prompt attention.

Yours very truly,

2

Dear Sir:

Evidently you, too, are experiencing the increase in business that our customers in general are reporting. In the rush of orders you probably have overlooked the fact that your account with us is three weeks over-due. Your remittances hitherto have been very prompt, and we trust that this reminder will be treated equally promptly.

By the way, have you found that the Holeless Socks are coming up to our guarantee? From all parts of the country we are getting flattering reports in the form of big orders. We feel that they merit their popularity, and with the extensive advertising campaign that we have inaugurated they are bound to continue in favor.

We are especially prepared at present to give you an attractive price, enabling you to realize large profits on these socks. If you need more of them, we can make shipment at once.

Yours very truly,

3

Dear Sir:

In looking over our accounts, we find that your purchases have lately been increasing considerably and that your payments have been few and unimportant. Statements have been sent regularly, we believe, but have probably been overlooked because of the stress of your other affairs. Such things, of course, can happen with any of us, especially when we have many other matters to look after.

We have always valued your account, and we greatly desire our pleasant relations to continue. As the amount that you owe us is now long over-due, we would appreciate your returning the enclosed bill to be receipted during the next few days.

Yours very truly,

4

Dear Sir:

Your attention has twice been called to your account for $——, but for some reason you do not reply to our letters.

Our terms, as you know, are thirty days, and we cannot allow a longer extension except by special arrangement. We have borne the matter very patiently, realizing that unusual conditions sometimes prevent one's doing as he desires. At the same time, it is entirely out of reason that your account should still be owing at this time. May we not expect your remittance by return mail?

Should we not hear from you by the 15th, we shall draw on you, and, if you have not remitted in the meantime, please provide for our draft upon its arrival.

Yours truly,

5

Dear Sir:

On March 15 we drew on you for $250. Our draft has been returned to us by the Blank Bank, unpaid.

Your account is long past due, and, although we are willing to do almost anything to accommodate our customers, we feel that in your case the time for concessions has passed. We desire your check at once for the balance due us.

You are credited with using considerable money in your business, and it would seem that you should without difficulty be able to take care of amounts such as you owe us. If we do not hear from you by April 1, we shall send a second draft. If you permit this to be returned unpaid, we shall be compelled to take action to force collection. We wish to express the hope, however, that you will not allow this to be done.

Yours truly,

Exercise 231

Letter (2) above is written primarily to get a check for the over-due account and incidentally to get another order. Suppose that the customer sends an order and no money. You do not wish to extend further credit until the old balance is paid. Write a tactful letter, saying that you will hold back the order until you receive a check to pay the over-due account.

Exercise 232

Write the letters in the following transaction:

1. J. F. Brookmeyer, Peru, Ind., is a dealer in shoes. He opened an account with you a month ago. He has purchased shoes to the amount of $250. You rendered an account on the first of the month, two weeks ago. Write a letter saying that you do not carry over accounts from month to month, as your small margin of profit makes it impossible for you to carry an irregular account. Make it a courteous sales letter as well as a collection letter.

2. J. H. Brookmeyer sends a certified check for the full amount, apologizing for the delay.

Exercise 233

1. John R. Phillips, 32 New York Building, Seattle, Washington, owes you $470. Write him, saying that you need the money. Give a good reason. Make it a courteous, friendly letter.

2. Mr. Phillips has not answered (1). Write him again, saying that if you do not get a remittance by ——, you will draw on him at sight.

3. Your bank notifies you that your draft has been returned unpaid. Write Phillips, asking for an explanation. Say that unless you hear by ——, you will bring suit.

4. Phillips writes an apologetic letter, giving illness as the reason for his non-payment. He says he was in the hospital and did not receive letters (1) and (2). He encloses fifty dollars and promises to pay at least half the balance next month, the full amount within sixty days. Write his letter.

5. Accept this offer.

Exercise 234—Answering Complaints

1. A mail order house discovered that its files contained the names of 10,000 people who had once been customers but who had not bought anything for the last two or three years. Write a letter in the name of the manager frankly asking why the customer has stopped buying. Advertise the stock.

2. One correspondent in reply demands a return of $16, which he had paid for a coat that was "not worth a cent." How would you reply to this letter so that the one making the complaint would send in an order? Write the letter.

In connection with this exercise study the following letter:

Dear Sir:

We wish to acknowledge your letter of April 16, in which you say that on April 14 you received a bill for five S & Q Railway bonds, which Mr. Wensley had sold you on the 11th at 100 and interest; that you sent us your check for the amount on the same day; and that on the 16th, two days afterward, you received a letter from us, offering a new block of these bonds at 99 and interest.

This complication was brought about through a peculiar chain of circumstances, an explanation of which, we feel, is only just both to you and to us. When Mr. Wensley came to the office on Saturday, the 12th, he told us that he had your order for five of these bonds at 100¼ and interest. The market price was then 100 and interest, and we were very glad to give you the benefit of the more favorable price. At that time we had no intimation that more of these bonds were coming on the market. Quite unexpectedly on Monday we received notice from our Boston office that they had in view a new block of the bonds. Even at that time we did not know definitely that we would get them. On Tuesday, again quite unexpectedly, we were instructed by our Boston office that the bonds had been secured and were to be offered immediately at 99 and interest. So suddenly did the entire transaction take place that we were unable to prepare a new circular, and on Tuesday night we merely sent out a letter, telling our customers that we had an additional block of these bonds. In fact, the new circular will not be ready until about noon of to-morrow.

We realize that you should have been informed of the new price. The bonds, however, came on the market so quickly and in taking care of the details of the offering we were so busy that the matter, unfortunately, was overlooked. We are glad, therefore, to make adjustment of the price now by having our banking department send you our check for $50.

It is unnecessary for us to say, we presume, that we regret this occurrence and to assure you that had we known of the new bonds on Saturday we would have advised you to hold off your purchase until the offering was ready. We feel that you know us and the policy of our house well enough to be sure that we would not willfully take advantage of you in this way. We trust that the arrangement that we have made satisfactorily straightens out the matter.

Yours very truly,

Exercise 235

1. What is the advantage of the policy shown in the following suggestion from *System?*

The manager of a retail establishment says: "We never refuse to refund money. If a dissatisfied customer returns a purchase, before we ask what the trouble is we refund his money gladly. When he is free to walk out of the store with his money, we try to find the source of the trouble. Generally we can adjust the difficulty and make a sale."

2. State the advantage in the policy of a large clothing concern which follows the sale of every suit or overcoat with a letter to the customer, asking him whether the purchase is proving satisfactory.

3. Write such a letter.

Exercise 236

1. Conrad H. Harwood of 122 Winter Street, Vandalia, Ill., writes to Wilson, Black & Co., manufacturers of shoes, 100 Second Street, Lynn, Mass., asking why they are not sending his order of —— (the goods ordered) of —— (date). He is losing sales because of the delay. If the goods are not received before ——, Harwood will cancel the order.

2. Wilson, Black & Co. acknowledge the receipt of Harwood's letter and say that this is the first notice they have received of such an order. The first letter must have miscarried. They have shipped the goods. Be very courteous.

Exercise 237

1. C. F. Gardner, a merchant of 432 Puyallup Ave., Tacoma, Wash., has received notice from the C.M. & P.S.R.R. freight office that a box of goods has arrived from Messrs. Fiske & Jones, Detroit, Mich. Gardner ordered the goods a month ago. He writes Messrs. Fiske & Jones that he refuses to accept the goods because of the delay. He has bought elsewhere in the meantime.

2. Fiske & Jones apologize for the delay and explain that it was due to the unreliability of one of their shipping clerks, who has since been discharged. They had known nothing of the matter until Gardner's letter of complaint arrived. They assure him that he will never suffer another such inconvenience.

3. Fiske & Jones telegraph the C.M. & P.S.R.R. to return the goods at Fiske & Jones's expense. Write the telegram.

Exercise 238—Letters of Application

A letter of application usually has three parts. In writing such a letter, first, tell where you saw the advertisement and apply for the position; second, tell your qualifications and give your references; third, end the letter appropriately, possibly asking for an interview.

This is a difficult kind of letter to write. Not only should it be neat in appearance and clearly written, but it should also be so carefully worded that it will show enough of the writer's individuality to distinguish it from a form. Be neither hesitant nor bold, but tell your qualifications in a simple, straightforward way.

Study the following letters. Are they convincing? Do they show the personality of the writers, or are they mere forms?

1

Gentlemen:

Your advertisement in to-day's Record for a salesman who knows the tea and coffee business interests me. I should like you to consider my application for the position.

Since my graduation from the Blank High School, four years ago, I have been employed as salesman for the Economy Wholesale Coffee Co., a firm doing business in this city and its outlying districts. During these four years I have gathered a wide knowledge of the principles of the buying and selling of coffees and teas and of the grades and blends of both, just the training, it seems to me, that you wish to secure.

You may depend upon my taking an active interest in your business, because I have an intense desire to advance. I myself vouch for my honesty and earnestness, and Mr. Robert Brown of the firm mentioned above has assured me that he will supply you with any information that you may wish as to my character or ability. He endorses my desire to secure a broader opportunity.

If the position that you have to offer is one in which there is a real future for an energetic, capable man, I should like to have an interview with you.

Yours very respectfully,

2

Dear Sir:

I am answering your advertisement in to-day's Record for a clerk because I wish to get started in the wholesale dry goods business, my idea being to work into the sales department. If the position that you advertise affords such an opportunity, I wish to apply for it.

I have had a little experience in the retail dry goods business, having worked as clerk for Mr. Amos Jones of this city during the past two summers. What I have seen and learned of the business makes me feel that I have ability as a dry goods salesman. I shall be glad to work hard in a clerical position if only I get a chance to learn and to advance.

I am eighteen years of age and have just graduated from the Blank High School, where I took the four-year commercial course. This, as you know, includes business arithmetic, bookkeeping, and some business practice. During the last two years I was business manager of the high school paper. This position gave me considerable experience in handling details rapidly and in soliciting advertising. It is this latter experience that makes me feel that I would have success in selling.

I am confident that I can please you, and I should be grateful if you will grant me an interview. Mr. Amos Jones, 815 E. 47th St., will be glad to give you any information that you may wish as to my work, and if you desire I can furnish other references.

Yours respectfully,

Exercise 239

Apply for the following positions:

1. OFFICE MAN—who can handle correspondence and general office work for growing North side manufacturing company. Good opportunity for the right man. State experience and salary expected. Address A. H. Stanton, 17 Elm St.

2. MAIL ORDER MAN—up-to-date, experienced; must have ability and be capable of handling a large volume of correspondence; must also be a pusher and systematizer. In reply give references, age, and detailed experience. Address X. W. 291 News.

3. AMBITIOUS YOUNG MEN—who are willing to start at the bottom to learn steel and iron business; must be high school or college graduates, or have equivalent education, and furnish exceptional references; very good opportunity for the future. Address A. F. 361 Times.

4. BRIGHT YOUNG MAN—for office work in large manufacturing plant, Northwest side; must be neat, quick, and accurate at figures. State age, experience, and salary expected. Address J. F. Holtz & Co., 320 W. Exchange St.

5. OFFICE CLERK—a girl who can write a plain, rapid, legible hand; desirable, permanent position, and excellent chance for advancement. Give

age, experience, if any, and where formerly employed. Salary $6.00 to start. Address T. P. 514 Chronicle.

6. HELP WANTED—salesman having established trade on rubber or leather footwear in Michigan, northern Indiana, northwest Ohio, or eastern Wisconsin. Good chance to become connected with live middle-western jobbing house. Give late experience. Address G724 Boot and Shoe Recorder, Boston, Mass.

Exercise 240—Contract for Painting Iron Work

1. James W. Walker & Co., 325 Second St., Pittsburgh, are receiving bids for painting the iron work of the bridge to be constructed over the Cheesequake Creek at Morgan Station, New Brunswick, N. J. The Barnard Emerson Co., of Harrisburg, Pa., write saying they would like to figure on the work. They ask James W. Walker & Co; to send plans and specifications. Write the letter sent by the Barnard Emerson Co.

2. James W. Walker & Co. reply that they are sending plans and specifications. They say that bids must be in by March 10. Write the letter.

3. The Barnard Emerson Co. write that page two, line four, of the specifications for the bridge to be constructed (state in detail) reads "and paint all beams underneath two coats of dark green," and page four, line ten, reads "all upright beams above and underneath to be painted two coats of light green between shades three and four." They ask which is correct. Write the letter. Be exact.

4. James W. Walker & Co. reply that page two, line four, is correct. Explain in detail.

5. The Barnard Emerson Co. agree to do the work on (repeat exactly what bridge you mean) for three thousand dollars. They guarantee to finish the work by April 30, according to the specifications. They will forfeit fifty dollars for every day after that date until the bridge is finished. Write the proposal or bid.

6. James W. Walker & Co. write, saying that they accept the bid above and that they enclose duplicate contracts, one of which they have signed and which the Barnard Emerson Co. is to keep. The other the Barnard Emerson Co. is to sign and return to James W. Walker & Co.

Exercise 241—Contract for the Delivery of Property

1. The Arlington Coal Company, Old Colony Building, Chicago, Ill., write to the Red Rock Coal Company, Auburn, Ill., saying that they need several cars of egg coal per week throughout the year. They ask if the Red Rock Coal Co. wish to offer some on contract. If so, they must state how the coal is screened, and give their lowest price. Write the letter.

2. The Red Rock Coal Co. reply that they will offer egg coal for shipment at the rate of two cars per week throughout the year, at $1.15 per net ton, cars f.o.b. mines. If a contract were drawn up for three or more cars per week, they would give the coal for $1.12½ per net ton. They say their egg is an excellent steam producing coal and gives general satisfaction. It is shipped from the Red Rock mine via the Chicago & Alton Railroad, freight rate being 82¢ per ton. Write the letter.

3. The Arlington Coal Co. write that the Red Rock Coal Co. may send a one year contract drawn in triplicate for three cars of egg coal per week at $1.12½ per net ton, cars f.o.b. mines. Of course it is understood that the usual clauses regarding accidents or other unavoidable happenings on either side will be inserted. Write the letter.

Exercise 242—Contract for Construction

NEWS ITEM.—Bids will be received until Dec. 12 by the Chairman of the Board of Public Works, North Bend, Washington, for the construction of a solid concrete bridge over the Snoqualmie River at North Bend; double arch, with one pier in the river; span of arch 92 feet; width of bridge 50 feet. Plans may be had by addressing the Chairman.

The McClaine Construction Co., of Spokane, Wash., send in a bid for $25,000, guaranteeing to use Atlas Portland cement, crushed rock for the coarse aggregate, and torpedo sand for the fine aggregate, the concrete to be reinforced with the Kahn system of reinforcement as set forth in the specifications. The company specify, further, that they shall be paid extra for excavation, on the scale of 25¢ a yard for earth, 75¢ a yard for loose rock and hard pan, and $1.00 a yard for solid rock. Write the letter that they send.

Exercise 243—Form Letters

It frequently happens in business that you receive a number of letters requiring practically the same answer. In such cases, the best plan is to have one letter that is as good a letter of its kind as you can write. Use that as an answer to all those to which it can be made to apply. You may have to add a bit of information or change a word here and there, but, practically, you are using the same form for all the letters. When you have mastered the form, the answering of letters of this class will be a simple matter. The letter accompanying a catalogue may easily be a form. (See the second letter in Exercise 223.)

The danger, however, is that the use of form letters tends to make work mechanical. When letters are different, they must receive different replies. A form letter should never be used just because it is easy to use when it does not really apply.

Mandel Bros., Chicago, Ill., announce their annual sale of silk remnants. Make this a good advertisement that will reach several classes of customers. Have in it as one item white wash silk of heavy quality, 36 inches wide, at 47 cents a yard.

1. Make out a sales letter for the above.

2. Several mail orders have been received in excess of the supply. Make out a form letter that could be sent when the money is returned. What is the advantage of a form letter in this case?

Exercise 244—Circular and Follow-up Letters

There is a class of letters that usually originates in the advertising department of a firm. They are not sent out to answer inquiries, but to solicit new customers and to keep old ones. Such letters are printed in large numbers in imitation of typewriting, and the introduction and the salutation are afterward carefully filled in on the typewriter. The intention, of course, is to make the recipient feel that he has received a personal letter. Firms are generally careful to fill in the signature in pen and ink. These are called *circular* letters. (See the last letter in Exercise 223.)

These letters are very important and each year more numerous. Frequently a series of them is written, each one expanding one argument in a series of arguments. If all the letters are read, one after the other, you have a complete list of reasons why you should buy the particular article which the letters advertise. These letters are sent out regularly, so that the effect of one may not quite wear off before the next arrives. It is frequently the case that not until the third or fourth letter is sent out does any reply come. Such letters should be definitely planned in order to present arguments that are true and attractive. They must be simply and clearly written. They are called *follow-up* letters.

The following series of follow-up letters was intended to be sent to women who keep no maids. The series was planned to contain five letters. Write two more, using different appeals from those in the letters here given.

Dear Madam:

Do you remember the fairy tale of Little Two-Eyes?

A fairy, out of pity for the child's hunger, spread a table before her each day as she was watching the goat in the field, and when her appetite was satisfied all the child had to say was, "Table clear yourself," and the dishes magically disappeared.

"This is a beautiful way to keep house," was Two-Eyes' verdict, and every woman, thinking of her own distaste of dirty dishes, will agree.

"How I hate dishwashing!" You have said it hundreds of times—after every meal, probably.

"I like to cook and bake," you declare. "They are really interesting. There is fun in trying new recipes—but the dishes!"

You enjoy giving luncheon and dinner parties. It is a delightful way of meeting one's friends. Moreover, you are justly proud of your skill in cooking, and you like to show your beautiful china. But what a damper it is on your spirit of good-fellowship, after the guests are gone, to have to spend an hour or more washing the dishes. Then you would like to say, with the child in the story, "Dishes wash yourselves!" Wouldn't you?

Well, you may. For thirty days—ninety meals—we will put the Fairy Dishwasher in your home, without charging you a penny.

The machine is simplicity itself. Wheel the cabinet into your dining room, alongside your serving table, and, as a course is finished, without rising from your place, stack the dishes into the washer. When you have finished the meal, wheel the cabinet into your kitchen, make the connection, and turn the switch. In a few minutes the dishes are washed and dried. Having friends in to dinner is fun when the Fairy washes the dishes.

Let the Fairy do yours. Simply return this letter to us in the enclosed envelope, making sure that your name and address are correct, and we'll send you the Fairy. Use it three times a day for thirty days. Then if you think you can get along as well without the machine, all that you need to do is to send us a postal card, telling us so. We'll take back the Fairy and ask no questions.

But send to-day.

Yours very truly,

2

Dear Madam:

Did you ever envy another woman's smooth, white hands? You looked at hers, and then you looked at yours; you sighed and thought, "It's dishwashing."

But what can you do? Haven't you tried everything to make dishwashing less drudgery? Haven't you tried patent soaps and tepid water, only to find that the dishes were not clean? Haven't you tried dish mops, scrapers, and rubber gloves, only to find that the mop and the scraper saved but one hand? As for rubber gloves, as likely as not, the first time you used them they were caught on the prong of a fork and were thereafter useless. Yes, you've tried everything; haven't you?

No, you haven't. You have not tried the only sure help that there is. Stop your drudgery and let the Fairy wash your dishes.

For thirty days—ninety trials—we will put the Fairy Dishwasher in your home, absolutely free of charge, guaranteed to wash and sterilize your dishes in boiling water, without a touch of your hand.

Do your manicuring while the Fairy does the dishes.

Pay no money, but send the enclosed postal card to-day. It will bring the Fairy at once.

Very truly yours,

3

Dear Madam:

An extra hour of leisure every day! What is it worth to you?

Think what you could do if some one would give you an extra hour of leisure every day. There's the book you would like to read, the call you ought to make, the embroidery you wish you could finish. There are the thousand and one things that a housekeeper continually wishes she could do—but where can she get the time?

And yet you waste at least an hour each day washing dishes when the Fairy Dishwasher will not only save you the time but rid you of a distasteful task. You pay 16²/₃ cents a day for five months and the Fairy does your dishes every day; you buy yourself an extra hour every day,—you are an hour ahead every day for the rest of your life.

Is it worth the price?

Remember that we allow you to use the Fairy for thirty days—ninety meals—before you pay a penny. Then for five months you send us five dollars a month, and we guarantee that you will declare it the best twenty-five dollars that you ever spent.

Send the enclosed postal card to-day. It will bring the Fairy and a booklet of full directions.

Very truly yours,

Exercise 245

You have bought a big tract of land in Alabama. You wish to sell a part uncleared, to set out a part in pecan trees, and to devote a part to truck farms. Write three letters to the same man, making each one stronger than the one before. Keep in mind the five essentials of a good letter. (See page 230.)

1. Offer the uncleared land at a very low price. Offer as many inducements as you can, such as desirability of location, fertility of the soil, and comparison in price with other land in the same neighborhood.

2. You received no response from (1). Try to sell the section in which you are planting pecan trees. What inducements could you offer that might reach a man who was not affected by (1)?

3. You received no response from (1) or (2). Try to sell a truck farm. What inducements could you offer that might lead a man to buy a truck farm when he had no interest in either uncleared land or pecan trees?

Exercise 246

1. The *Modern Magazine* offers a set of Mark Twain's complete works absolutely free if you subscribe for one year for the *Modern Magazine* and the *Household Magazine* at the regular price of $2 for the *Modern Magazine* and $1.50 for the *Household Magazine.* This offer expires —— (date). Write the letter.

2. You have not responded. The *Modern Magazine* feels that you could not have understood its offer. These are no cheap books. To prove this, the firm is willing to send you the books to allow you to examine them before you send any money. If you accept them, pay the express agent; if not, return the books at the expense of the *Modern Magazine.* Remember that this offer expires —— (date).

3. You have not responded. The magazine extends the time. Give a reason for the extension of the time.

What criticism can you make on (3)?

Exercise 247

A druggist was obliged to move from his corner store four doors east on a side street. He decided to advertise by sending a series of follow-up letters embodying the following ideas:

1. Change of location because ——.

2. Stick to your druggist because he holds the key to your health.

3. What is the reason that my trade is staying with me? (Prizes for the best answer.)

4. The reasons why trade stays with me—what my patrons say.

5. The pure food question—why we must handle only fresh drugs.

6. We are registered pharmacists—what this means to you.

7. Why our sales expense is smaller now than formerly—how you profit.

Exercise 248

A furniture house selling goods on monthly payments decides to advertise by sending a series of follow-up letters, using the following reasons why you should buy, one in each letter:

1. Variety of stock; assurance that they can please, no matter what you wish. Amplify.

2. Reliability of the firm.

3. The small profit on which they run their business gives you an excellent opportunity of buying good values at low prices.

4. Buying on the "easy payment" plan enables you to have the use of your furniture while you are still paying for it.

Why is (4) a poor argument?

Exercise 249

Write a series of letters to sell an electric washing machine, using the following items:

1. The machine is ball bearing; therefore very easy to work. You can sit down while you do your week's washing. The only work required is hanging the clothes out of doors.

2. It saves laundry bills.

3. Summary of (1) and (2). The investment required is not large. Special plans for payment.

4. The machine is durable.

5. Summary of the above. The following figures show that during the time that has elapsed since (1) was received the machine might have been paid for out of the money spent for laundry bills.

PART III
BUSINESS PRACTICE

CHAPTER XVI

MANUFACTURE

THE following chapters will furnish exercises in composition, both oral and written, based upon the various phases of business. They are intended to show the application of the principles underlying manufacturing, buying, and selling. Of course, we cannot expect to go into great detail in any one of the divisions. That must be reserved for future study, perhaps reserved until the time that you enter a particular business. We must remember that our first consideration is the study of English, the problem of clear-cut expression. Underlying clear-cut expression is clear-cut thinking. It cannot be repeated too often that without a definite thought there can be no definite wording of the thought. To say, "I know, but I don't know how to tell it," shows a lazy brain. Learn to exercise your thinking powers so that you can force them to stay upon a subject until you have thought it out carefully and can express it. All of the oral exercises in the following chapters require careful preparation. This does not mean that they should be written out before the recitation, but it does mean that they must be carefully thought out. The preparation need not take a particular form. The main thing is that you know exactly the points that you wish to make before you begin to speak. If the exercise calls for a paragraph, have clearly in mind the plan by which you expect to expand your thought. Perhaps you expect to begin with, or to lead up to, a topic sentence. Remember that this may be done in several ways. Choose whichever plan seems best. If the exercise does not call for a particular form, such as a paragraph or a debate, you are left free to develop your thought in the way that you think fits your subject best and to the length which you think it demands.

There are many different kinds of businesses. We shall not attempt to consider any except the most common and fundamental. Some, like farming or mining, consist in bringing forth certain products from the ground. Such products are called raw materials, of which an example is wheat. Some raw materials are sold and used unchanged, but most of them go through the process of manufacture in order to be directly usable. The miller is an example of a manufacturer, because from wheat he makes flour. In this chapter we shall study the principles underlying manufacture.

The exercises do not by any means exhaust the subject. Each one is to be considered as a nucleus about which others are to be grouped. If you live in a manufacturing district, other subjects will easily suggest themselves. If you have studied Industrial History or Commercial Geography, you probably have in mind a number of topics for discussion. If you know but little about raw materials, read some of the books suggested in Exercise 257. At all events let your work be definite. Whatever statements you make be able to substantiate by an illustration of something that you have seen or heard or read.

Exercise 250—Manufacture

Almost all the things we eat, wear, and use every day are manufactured articles. Each one of them requires its own particular process in the making, involving the necessity in most cases of complex and expensive machinery, of expert workmen, and of still more expert management. Take, for example, the shoes we wear, in the manufacture of which an amazing number of complicated machines and of expert workmen is necessary. According to the United States Department of Labor, men's rough shoes go through eighty-four distinct processes performed by skilled workmen and automatic machines. No less amazing is the amount of work turned out by these machines. It has been estimated that the McKay machine, which attaches the soles to the uppers, sews up in about one hour and a half one hundred pairs, an amount which it would take ninety-eight hours, or about eleven whole working days, to sew by hand.

Each manufacturing business has peculiarities, machinery, methods, and even a language of its own; sometimes men must spend years in the study of the technicalities of certain manufacturing businesses before they become expert in them. It is evident that we cannot take up any one of them here except in so far as the principles of one apply to all, and these can be set down only very briefly.

The first essential to successful manufacturing is correct buying. In fact, in some businesses this is so essential that the buyer gets a larger salary than the manager himself. We can see the reason for this when we consider that a good buyer must understand not only the materials that he buys, but also the manufacturing processes, so that, knowing the process through which the raw materials will go in his particular business, he will buy those materials that will make the most profitable manufactured articles.

The next essential, and in most cases the most important one from the manufacturing standpoint, is a management capable of producing the best product at the least cost. The managers decide what shall be produced and how; they hire the workmen and decide what each shall do; they decide what shall be done by hand and what by machinery; and they choose the machines. Sometimes they go even so far as to determine exactly the method in which each task shall be done, and whenever they see that it would be advantageous to install a machine, they do so. Pursuing this policy, a Chicago yeast concern not long ago put in three machines for wrapping the small yeast cakes, eliminating the services of 140 girls and cutting the cost of wrapping to three-fifths of what it had been. In the steel business the early success of Andrew Carnegie and the famous Bill Jones was largely due to the fact that on several occasions they did not hesitate to break up half a million dollars' worth of machinery and replace it with newer and more efficient kinds.

The third essential to manufacturing success is aggressive marketing of the product. From the standpoint of money success this is probably the most important consideration; so important is it, in fact, that it will be more fully discussed in the chapter following.

Exercise 251—Manufactured Articles

Oral

1. Define the word *industry*. When is a business called an industry? (Consult an unabridged dictionary.)

2. *a.* Name several raw materials.

b. Name some industries whose business it is to produce raw materials.

3. Name some companies or industries whose business it is, or whose principal function it is, to manufacture from raw materials.

4. Name some companies or groups of companies that make articles more useful by transporting them to places where they are needed.

5. Name some wholesale houses. In what does their business consist?

6. Name several kinds of retail businesses. In what does their business consist?

7. Name some companies that manufacture only one article.

8. Name some companies that manufacture more than one article, but all of the same class. This is the largest group.

9. Name some companies that manufacture several different kinds of articles.

10. Name some companies which, in manufacturing one product, make a secondary or by-product.

11. Name a number of by-products and what they are by-products of.

Oral or Written

In each of the following emphasize the labor involved, not the machinery used; prepare outlines:

1. Select any manufactured article that you have seen on a grocer's shelves, and trace it through (2), (3), (4), (5), and (6) above, from the raw material until the product is in the housekeeper's hands. If possible make your information exact by visiting a factory in which the article is made. The information contained in advertisements of well-known articles may help you.

2. Trace the labor that is necessary to put a loaf of bread on the table.

3. Trace the changes that the mineral undergoes to be suitable for the making of edged tools, such as knives or axes.

4. Trace the changes that cotton must undergo before it is suitable for wearing as a dress or a pair of stockings.

5. Trace the changes that wool undergoes before it can be worn as a sweater or a winter coat.

6. Trace the changes that the skins of animals undergo before they can be worn as a muff.

7. Trace the changes that silk undergoes before it can be worn as a neck-tie.

8. Trace the changes that hemp undergoes before it can be used as a rope.

9. Trace the changes that hides undergo before they can be worn as shoes.

10. Trace wood from the tree to a piece of fine furniture or to the case of a musical instrument.

11. Trace the steps in the process of making maple sugar.

12. Trace the steps in making a piece of glazed pottery.

13. Trace clay to bricks.

14. Trace flax to a tablecloth.

15. Trace the steps necessary to make a five dollar gold piece.

Exercise 252

Subjects for Themes, Oral or Written

The following are suggestions for theme subjects on manufacture. Develop one or more as the teacher directs.

1. Household uses for asbestos.
2. Making turpentine from wood.
3. A convenient electrical device.
4. The advantages of the fireless cooker.
5. The advantages of concrete as a building material.
6. The way to make a plaster cast.
7. How iron castings are made.
8. Artificial flowers from feathers, paper, or cloth.
9. How a suction sweeper works.
10. The safety match.
11. The uses of wood pulp.
12. Patent roofing.
13. The manufacture of plate glass.
14. Utilizing cotton seed.
15. The advantages and the disadvantages of using baking powder.

Exercise 253

Suggestions for Debates

1. The average young man has a better chance to succeed in business than in a profession.

2. A manufacturing business offers a better opportunity for a young man at the present time than a mercantile business.

3. Manufacturing industries would suffer if immigration were restricted.

4. The labor union should be abolished.

5. The labor union has no right to restrict the number of apprentices.

6. The profit-sharing plan produces greater efficiency in the working-force.

Exercise 254

Imagine that you are Stanley M. Benner, 171 South St., Buffalo, N. Y., proprietor of a factory making men's shirts and collars.

1. Write an order to The American Printing Mill, 1038 Canal St., Passaic, N. J., for several bolts each of percale, madras, corded madras, and silk striped madras. Use catalogue numbers.

2. Write another order to The Trescott Silk Mill, 976 River St., Paterson, N. J., for several bolts each of No. 62, No. 14, and No. 20 shirting silks, No. 62 being a striped silk and the others figured. Be definite in ordering the colors that you wish.

3. You have received an order from Spencer & Mitchell, 1925 Pearl St., Albany, N. Y. Write a letter, thanking them for the order and explaining when and how the goods will be sent.

4. You have received an order from William F. Atwood, 590 Jackson St., Wilmington, Del., for a certain style of collar on which there has been a run. Write a letter, explaining that it will take about three weeks to fill the orders that you now have for this collar and that you therefore cannot send Mr. Atwood's goods before the end of the month.

5. The goods have arrived from The Trescott Silk Mill. You find, however, that two bolts of No. 14 are badly soiled. Write a letter, saying that you are returning the bolts and asking to have the matter adjusted.

6. A. W. Trescott, President of The Trescott Silk Mill, replies, expressing regret that the goods were soiled and saying that two clean bolts of No. 14 are being sent at once. Write his letter.

7. You have on hand about 50 gross men's striped madras collars, for which there is no longer a call. Write to Markham Bros., wholesale jobbers, 1765 Greenwich St., New York City, asking what price they will offer for the lot.

8. Accept their offer of $1.50 a gross for the collars.

9. A customer sends a cash order for goods at last year's prices, 10% below present prices. Write a politic reply.

10. Owing to the mildness of the winter, you fear that you will not sell your stock of men's flannel shirts. Write a circular letter, offering the shirts in lots of 25 dozen each, assorted sizes and colors, at a 35% reduction in price. Address one letter to. Frederick H. Howard, a dealer at 775 Cedar St., Harrisburg, Pa.

11. A teamsters' strike has delayed your shipments. You have received so many complaints of the non-arrival of goods that you decide to prepare a form letter that will answer all the complaints. Address one letter to William A. Spaulding, 2937 Waterman St., Providence, R. I.

12. Miss Sarah MacComb has a small dry goods store in Norwich, Conn. She has owed you $125 for six months. You have been lenient with Miss MacComb because you know that she has had difficulty in meeting her bills. However, you feel that she should pay at least a part of her indebtedness to you. Write a courteous letter, longer and more persuasive than if it were to go to a man, demanding payment but retaining the customer's good will. This is a difficult letter to write. Prepare it carefully.

Exercise 255

1. You have been manager of the Forsyth Furniture Co., Grand Rapids, Mich. You have financial backing for $25,000 and are looking for a location for a factory of your own. Write the same letter to the Secretary of the Chamber of Commerce of Great Falls, Mont.; Memphis, Tenn.; Houston, Texas; Indianapolis, Ind. Ask the Secretary to tell you the prospects for such a factory in his city, and what inducements the city will offer you. (By writing to different cities, the teacher can obtain their booklets and their special offers to manufacturers.)

2. Investigate the conditions in one of the cities mentioned above and reproduce the letter that the Secretary wrote.

3. Of the four cities, Great Falls appeals to you as the best location for your factory. Write again, asking the Secretary especially about the water power facilities offered and the rates charged for electrical power.

4. He replies that Great Falls has the most extensive power in the United States, the hydro-electric power being ready for delivery in any quantity at exceptionally low rates. He tells of the many factories that are already located in Great Falls because of its water power facilities.

5. Great Falls is your choice. After your factory is built and your machinery installed, write to the Secretary of the Sand Point Lumber Co., Sand Point, Idaho, asking him to submit figures for a contract for supplying all your fir lumber. Tell him you think you will use about a million board feet a year.

6. The Secretary replies, offering you a contract on the following terms: For all amounts under 250,000 feet a year, a rate of 12 cents a foot; under 500,000, 11 cents; over 500,000, 10 cents. All goods are to be billed at the highest rate and rebates made at the end of the year, terms of payment being 90 days, 5% for 30 days.

7. Write to the Central American Supply Co., Tehuantepec, Mexico, ordering 50,000 feet No. 1 Mahogany Veneer. Have it charged to your account, which you have previously opened.

8. Write to Gregory Bros., wholesale dry goods merchants, 12141 Nicollet Ave., Minneapolis, Minn., ordering 15 bolts No. 7 Green Denim; 10 bolts No. 09 Green Panne Velvet; 50 yds. No. 216 Tapestry; 50 yds. No. 16 Tapestry; 100 bolts Green and 100 bolts Brown No. 5 Guimpe. Instruct them to ship the goods at once and draw on you at sight through the First National Bank of Great Falls. (See page 344.)

9. Write to the Excelsior Varnish Co., Merchants' National Bank Building, St. Paul, Minn., ordering articles such as varnish, stains, oils, enamels, and finishing wax.

10. Write an order to a St. Louis firm for leather.

11. Write an order to a Spokane firm for springs.

12. Find out where a Great Falls merchant would buy oak and birch, and write an order for each.

13. Write to the Hanover National Bank of New York City (because you happen to know the cashier of that bank), explaining that you are having a very decided increase in your business and that, in order to take care of the demand, you require a loan of $10,000. Explain further that the rates are too high in Great Falls for you to take a loan there. Say that you are enclosing a statement of your assets and liabilities.

14. A dealer in Portland, Ore., writes, complaining that he has not yet received the goods that he ordered ten days ago. Write an appropriate reply.

15. You receive an order, one item of which is 3 doz. oil mops, which you do not carry. Reply that you have referred the matter to —— a firm which you can recommend highly.

Exercise 256

Topics for Investigation and Discussion

Principles involved in manufacture:

1. The location of a factory.

a. Where necessary raw materials can be obtained easily and cheaply.
b. Where land is not expensive.
c. Where the coal or water supply will make power inexpensive.
d. Where transportation facilities are good.

2. The advantages of using machinery in manufacture.

a. Relative amount of work turned out.
b. Relative cost of work turned out.
c. Relative cleanliness of work turned out.
d. Relative uniformity of work turned out.

3. The number of working hours.

Some factories have made the experiment of reducing the number of working hours from ten to eight without reducing the wages of the workers. They have found that the quantity of work turned out is increased and the quality improved. Can you explain why?

4. The advantages of the profit-sharing plan, both for employer and for employee.

This is a plan by which a certain per cent of the profits of the business is divided annually among the employees. (See a very interesting article in *System* for March, 1911, or read *Profit-sharing between Employer and Employee* by N. P. Gilman.)

5. Specialized labor.

There was a time when a man made all the parts of a pair of shoes. Why in modern factories does he make only one part? Which system tends to make shoes of uniform workmanship? Is uniformity a good quality in manufacture? This principle applies to any kind of factory.

6. Special products.

Suppose that you manufactured a large number of styles of millinery, or novelty, footwear. Would you expect your profits on these to be larger or smaller than on your staple styles? Give reasons and illustrations.

7. Why is there a struggle between labor and capital?

8. What is the cause of strikes?

9. Are strikes a good thing for manufacture?

10. A visit to a shoe factory (or any other factory).

Exercise 257

Books that will Suggest Topics for Talks

If you have access to a public library, you can probably obtain some of the following books. They are all simple and interesting, and any of them will suggest several topics for talks.

ALLEN, N. B., Industrial Studies.

BAKER, R. S., Boys' Books of Inventions.

BARNARD, CHARLES, Tools and Machines.

CARPENTER, F. G., How the World is Fed; How the World is Clothed; How the World is Housed; Geographical Readers.

CHAMBERLAIN, J. F., How We are Fed; How We are Clothed.

CHASE, A. and CLOW, E., Stories of Industries (two volumes).

COCHRANE, C. H., The Wonders of Modern Mechanism.

COCHRANE, ROBERT, Romance of Industry and Invention.

DOUBLEDAY, RUSSELL, Stories of Invention.

FORMAN, S. E., Useful Inventions.

GIBSON, C. R., The Romance of Modern Manufacture.

LANE, M. A. L., Industries of To-day.

LITTLE CHRONICLE CO., Industries of a Great City.

MOWRY, W. A. and MOWRY, A. M., Inventions and Inventors.

PARTON, J., Captains of Industry (two series).

ROCHELEAU, W. F., Products of the Soil; Minerals; Manufactures.

TOWLE, G. M., Heroes and Martyrs of Invention.

WILLIAMS, A., How it is Made.

Exercise 258

Study the punctuation of the following; then write from dictation:

1

It is stated that practical experience with gas mantles made of artificial silk—that is, silk made from wood pulp—has proved them to be far superior to those made of cotton, especially where the mantles are exposed to excessive vibration. Several German towns are said to be obtaining exceptionally good results from these new mantles used in conjunction with pressure gas, and it is asserted that the mantles are in good condition after being used for seven or eight weeks. Artificial silk, according to reports, has also been used experimentally by several manufacturers of incandescent gas mantles in the United Kingdom. The reports are all very encouraging, except that there seems to be one difficulty that is purely mechanical—the knitting of the artificial silk. The knots and other imperfections in the yarn cause a considerable amount of waste. However, the knitting-machine makers are experimenting to overcome it.—*Daily Consular and Trade Report.*

2

As the production of wool in this country, although approximating 320,000,000 pounds a year, does not begin to meet the demands for the raw material, there is a yearly importation of from 156,000,000 to over 300,000,000 pounds. When each new census reveals the fact that there are fewer sheep of shearing age in the country than there were ten years before, the question of wool production becomes one of still greater importance. A solution may be found in a Peruvian product. A variety of cotton grows in Peru whose long, rough, crinkly fiber mixes so readily with wool that manufacturers use it in connection with wool in manufacturing "all wool" goods. It grows on a small tree that yields two or three crops a year for seven or eight years. The area, however, in which it is being successfully cultivated in Peru is so limited that the annual output is only about 16,000,000 pounds, of which the United States takes approximately 5,500,000 pounds. As the region in which it thrives is practically rainless, perhaps a way may be found to persuade the rough Peruvian to make a home for itself in the hot and arid regions of our Southwest. It would be a triumph of agriculture, certainly, to raise vegetable wool in regions not fitted for real sheep.—*The Wall Street Journal.*

3

THE CASTING OF METALS

As is well known, some metals are unsuitable for casting, while others, like iron, can readily be cast into any desired shape. The property of casting well, it is said, depends upon whether the metal contracts or expands in solidifying from the liquid form. Iron, like water, expands in solidifying, and hence the solid metal may be seen floating in the liquid iron about it. The expansion causes it to fill the die into which it is poured, and so it can be cast easily. Gold and silver contract in cooling, and are, therefore, not suitable for casting.—*Harper's Weekly.*

CHAPTER XVII

DISTRIBUTION

CORRECT buying and the most efficient methods of manufacture play a large part in the successful carrying on of a business, but the most important consideration is the successful marketing or distributing of the product after it has been manufactured or bought. Very few products are so superior in quality that they sell themselves purely on merit. Competition in business to-day is so keen that, in order to find a market for his product, a merchant must create a demand for it. Thus at its very foundation, distribution is merely a process of creating a demand and then filling that demand. For instance, the retail merchant is concerned with bringing the customers to his store rather than to his competitor's across the street. The wholesale merchant is concerned with having the retailers handle his goods rather than those of another firm. The mail order merchant is concerned with getting the farmer's business before some other dealer gets it. The salesman is concerned with writing the order before a rival from another house writes it.

In the first place, the merchant must handle those things that his customers consider necessary or desirable. Overcoats cannot be sold in August, ashsifters on the equator, nor electric fans in Iceland. Different peoples, different times, and different conditions create different demands, and it is the merchant's business to study those demands and to fill them. In the second place, he must leave no stone unturned in endeavoring to make his product more desirable than that of his competitors. This may mean extensive advertising campaigns, expensive displays, outlay for costly catalogues and booklets, the expenditure of money for inducements to bring customers, or the hiring of expert salesmen. In fact, thousands of plans are carried out every year in this endeavor to increase trade.

The getting of new and additional business, however, is only one of the important considerations that the merchant must always have in mind. He must also keep what business he already has by maintaining the standard of his goods and by giving his customers satisfactory service. One of the first essentials in this question of service is promptness and exactness of delivery. In this the merchant must depend very largely on the transportation companies, and therefore a brief study of these facilities will be especially in place at this point.

Transportation

Transportation is an essential item in the problem of distribution. If you wished to drink a cup of coffee and found that none could be had except in

Brazil, you would begin to realize how much the steamship company and the railroad company have done in transporting and hauling it where you might buy it. The same is true of our oranges from California and Florida, our apples from Washington and Oregon, and our grain from the Middle States. In fact, in the case of many products the most important item is not growing them, but bringing them to market, since the transportation charges are often much greater than the actual cost of producing. Thousands of barrels of apples rot on the ground every year because their quality does not warrant the high transportation charges, the lack of transportation rendering them useless. In a smaller measure, the delivery wagons in our cities and towns are essential to us because they save us the trouble of carrying our purchases about. Thus, the element of transportation enters into our lives every day, saving us inconvenience, bringing to us necessities that we demand and luxuries that we like, and, at the same time, increasing the price of commodities.

Common carriers, as transportation companies are called, are of two general classes:

1. Those operating on water—the steamship companies.
2. Those operating on land—the railroad companies.

THE STEAMSHIP COMPANY

Steamship companies operate three general kinds of lines: (1) lines consisting of the largest and fastest steamers which carry only passengers, mail, and valuable parcels; (2) lines using slower steamers which carry both passengers and freight; and (3) lines employing vessels—steamers, sailing vessels, and barges—which carry only freight. The cost of hauling cargoes by water is in every case less per mile than that of carrying the same quantity of goods on land. It costs, for example, over four times as much to carry a bushel of wheat from Chicago to New York by rail as it does to carry it across the Atlantic. It is for this very reason that the traffic on our navigable rivers, the Ohio and the Mississippi, and on the Great Lakes is so heavy. Whenever a cargo can be shipped as well by water as by rail and there is no hurry for delivery, it is shipped by water. However, because so much of our freight must be rushed from place to place, the railroads get the bulk of the inland traffic.

THE RAILROAD COMPANY

The services of the railroad company embrace the hauling of freight, the carrying of passengers, and the transporting of express and of mail. The hauling of freight is the most important item in the railroad business, about three-quarters of the total income being derived from this source. Each year over one billion tons of freight are turned over by shippers to the railroads, who use almost two and one-half million freight cars to carry it. About one-half of this tonnage is minerals, mainly ore and coal; about one-seventh consists of manufactured articles; and one-twelfth of agricultural products. Commodities are grouped into from ten to fourteen classes, on each one of which the freight rate is different from that of the others. By freight rate is meant the cost of shipping a certain unit, usually 100 pounds or a ton, from one place to another; it is dependent on the distance. There are certain bulky commodities like coal, livestock, lumber, grain, and cement, which are almost always handled in carload lots. They are not included in the freight classification, but have a special ex-class freight rate. Freight rates depend also on whether the goods are shipped by slow or *local* freight or by fast or *through* freight.

There are a hundred different kinds of papers used in carrying on the railroad freight business. Only four of the most important will be considered here. When a shipper turns over his goods to the railroad company at its freight depot, he gets from the agent a *receipt for freight*, which is merely a receipt for the goods he has turned over. In the ordinary course of business these receipts are exchanged at the company's office for a *bill of lading* in triplicate. The original and one copy are given to the shipper. The second copy is kept by the railroad. This bill of lading may be of two kinds, *straight* or *order*. If a straight bill of lading is given, the original is sent to the person to whom the goods are shipped, who is called the *consignee*, who on the presentation of the bill of lading is entitled to the goods after paying the charges. An order bill of lading is much like a check, in that it can be assigned to another person. Like the straight bill it states the name of the consignee or the person for whom the goods are intended and his address, but the consignee cannot get possession of the goods until he has paid for them. To collect payment, the shipper attaches to the order bill of lading a draft for the amount of the goods and the freight, and through his bank and the bank of the consignee the amount is collected. The consignee then gets possession of the order bill of lading, which entitles him to possession of the goods. This is more fully explained on page 344. The railroad's most important paper is the *way bill*, which shows the conductor or the agent of the company just what articles are included in the shipment, so that it can be checked when unloaded. When the goods arrive at their destination, the consignee is notified and is sent a *freight bill* showing the freight charges. When he presents his bill of lading and pays the charges, the *freight bill* is receipted and the goods are his.

In quoting prices on goods, manufacturers and distributors usually designate whether they will pay the freight or whether it is to be paid by the consignee. In the latter case the price is quoted f. o. b. at the place from which the goods are shipped, which means freight on board at that point. That is to say, if a distributor located at Detroit quotes his automobiles f. o. b. Detroit, he means that he will see that the goods get into the railroad company's hands at Detroit, but that the consignee pays the freight from Detroit to the destination. The latter is the common practice in shipping.

In the following exercises we shall treat the subject of distribution under four heads:

I. The Retail Merchant.

II. The Wholesale Merchant.

III. The Mail Order Merchant.

IV. The Salesman.

I.—THE RETAIL MERCHANT

Exercise 259

Oral

You are opening a grocery store. Remember that your object is to sell the largest possible amount of goods. Develop each of the following suggestions:

1. What kind of location would you desire?

2. How would you have the front of your store painted? Would you try to make it stand out from the rest?

3. Do you think it would pay you to have the interior newly and brightly redecorated? To put in the best and brightest lights?

4. What quality of stock would you select? The same for all neighborhoods? Give your reasons. Would advertised brands bring you more trade?

5. Do you think window display would pay? Would you recommend freak or ordinary displays? Price-marked or non-price-marked? Give your reasons.

6. Does the delivery wagon pay? Would it be advisable to buy a new wagon and a good horse? What other considerations would enter?

7. Would you sometimes cut the price of some necessity to draw people? Give reasons for your answer.

8. Is it a good thing to have a general cut-price-sale to bring customers to your store? Even if you lose money by it?

9. Would you give credit? Would the class of people you served come into consideration?

10. Is the use of trading stamps and premiums good policy?

11. Why do you often find a meat market in connection with a grocery?

12. There are two kinds of retail meat markets: (1) the one that sells goods which can be retailed at a low price, and (2) the one that sells superior goods at a higher price. Which policy would you follow and why?

13. Could a retailer combine the two spoken of in (12)? Consider cost, space, satisfaction of the customer.

14. Would you advertise by means of handbills? By circular letters?

15. What would you do if another grocery opened across the street from yours?

Exercise 260

Written

1. You have bought Burton & Sanders' grocery at Fort Wayne, Indiana. Send out a circular letter advertising the new White Front Grocery and telling what the policy of the new management will be. Explain that the opening sale will begin next Monday and that a special feature of the sale will, be twenty pounds of granulated sugar for eighty cents with a two dollar order.

2. At the same time have an article appear in a local newspaper, telling that Burton & Sanders have sold their store to you and that you are making extensive improvements, especially in sanitary means of handling provisions. In addition, let the article give an account of your business career in another town. Would such an article be of value to you? Write it.

3. Write to Peabody, Harper & Co., Rush Street Bridge, Chicago, Ill., saying that you would like to open an account with them. Give as references a bank in your town and one in Logansport, where you used to live. Ask Peabody, Harper & Co. what terms they can offer you.

4. You have decided to advertise in a local paper. Write to the advertising manager, asking him for yearly rates for a half-column every evening and a quarter-page every Friday.

5. Find out what are the advertising rates of a paper in your town and answer (4).

6. Reproduce a letter that a woman living in town sends, ordering two dollars' worth of groceries and requesting that you send, in addition, the twenty pounds of sugar you advertise in (1). She encloses a check for $2.80.

7. You are in receipt of a letter from Peabody, Harper & Co., answering your inquiry in (3) and offering you sixty days' credit and 2% discount for payment within ten days. Write the letter.

8. Send an order to Peabody, Harper & Co. for $200 worth of groceries. Among the items let there be 6 cases of canned tomatoes, first quality, at $1.75 a case. Ask them to send the goods by the Pennsylvania R. R.

9. Your business is increasing and you need another clerk, (a) Write an advertisement for one. *(b)* Apply for the position.

10. Write a short circular advertising an inexpensive novelty that a grocer might sell. These circulars are to be wrapped with purchases.

11. Peabody, Harper & Co. write, confirming your order in (8) and enclosing a straight bill of lading.

12. When the goods arrive, you find no tomatoes among them. Write a complaint to the wholesale house.

13. Peabody, Harper & Co. reply to your letter in (12), apologizing for the mistake, explaining how it occurred (supply an explanation), and telling you that they have sent one case by express at their expense. The rest will follow by freight.

14. The tomatoes sent by freight do not arrive. Write to the grocery company, asking the latter to send out a "tracer"; that is, to request the railroad company to trace the goods on its lines.

15. The grocery company telephones the railroad company, requesting the latter to trace the goods and to report. The grocery company also writes a letter confirming its request. Write the letter.

16. (*a*) The railroad company reports that by mistake the goods were carried through to Lima, but that they are being returned to Fort Wayne. (*b*) The grocery company informs you of the developments and hopes that the delay has caused you no great inconvenience. Write both letters.

Exercise 261

1. You wish to get a partner to open a meat market in connection with your grocery. Write to a friend in Lafayette, Ind., who you think will be interested, proposing the plan. Tell him of the opportunities, as you see them, of business in Fort Wayne and the surrounding country. Tell him that with $4,000 additional capital you and he could set up a much larger establishment, invest in a motor wagon, and thus secure the trade of the outlying districts.

2. Your friend replies that the proposal appeals strongly to him, but that he has only $2,000 in cash. However, he holds a mortgage for $2,000 on —— (state the location of the house) in Lafayette, and, if he can sell the mortgage, he will be glad to avail himself of the offer.

3. After the partnership is formed, your partner writes to Orr & Locket, 14 W. Randolph St., Chicago, Ill., ordering the following to be shipped by Pennsylvania R.R.: 1 Refrigerator No. 361; 2 Meat Blocks No. 3; 1 Scale No. M. 30; $^1/_6$ doz. Saws No. 33 (16 in.); $^1/_6$ doz. Saws No. 33 (22 in.); $^1/_4$ doz. Knives No. 955; $^1/_4$ doz. Knives No. 490; $^1/_6$ doz. Steels No. 82; $^1/_6$ doz.

Cleavers No. 09; $^1/_4$ doz. Block Scrapers. He explains that he is the same man who formerly had a meat market in Lafayette.

4. Orr & Locket acknowledge the receipt of the order, enclose the invoice, and offer him 5% discount for payment within 30 days. Write the letter.

5. A Detroit manufacturer sends you f.o.b. prices on his motor wagons. Investigate the prices and write the letter.

6. Order one of them. (Remember the f.o.b. item.)

7. He writes confirming your order, saying that the car is now in the shipper's hands and that his bank has sent the order bill of lading with draft attached to the First National Bank of your city. Write the letter. (See page 344.)

8. At the same time the shipper's bank sends a letter to the First National Bank of your city enclosing the order bill of lading with draft drawn on you for collection. A copy of this letter is also mailed to you. Write it.

9. You telephone your bank to draw on your account for the amount of the draft and to send you the bill of lading. You confirm this understanding by a letter. Write it.

10. Your bank writes, confirming the telephone conversation and enclosing the bill of lading and a receipt for the correct amount. You present your bill of lading, pay the freight charges, and get your motor wagon. Write the letter the bank sends.

11. The automobile manufacturer has meanwhile received through his bank a credit for the amount you paid for the car and writes acknowledging its receipt. Write the letter.

Exercise 262

Choose four or six members of the class, one-half of whom are to argue in favor of the policy indicated in the plan outlined below and one-half of whom are to argue against it.

A certain grocer opened a store with the determination of doing a strictly cash business, and of making no deliveries unless the purchaser paid for the delivery. This was his plan as suggested by *System:*

1. To those who would carry their own purchases he sold everything for cash much lower than any other grocer in town sold it.

2. If the customer bought very bulky goods, or if he did not wish to be his own delivery man, the grocer charged him for delivery a certain

percentage of the total of his cash purchases. Yet the customer bought more cheaply than he could buy in any other grocery in town.

3. Those who wished to pay once a month instead of at every visit he advised to deposit a certain sum of money with him as banker and to buy against that, paying cash prices and receiving 3% interest on the amount left on deposit.

II.—The Wholesale Merchant

Exercise 263

Oral

Each of the following should be developed into a paragraph:

1. You are a manufacturer and wholesale distributor with a factory on the outskirts of a town; would you have a warehouse in the center of the town? Give reasons for your answer.

2. What would be the advantage of having your warehouse near the railroad freight depots? Near the docks?

3. What would be the advantage of being located in a large city with many railroads and with water transportation facilities—Chicago, for example?

4. Speed gets orders. With this in view, what would you recommend with respect to the equipment for handling? What would you suggest about the number of people through whose hands the order would have to go before being shipped?

5. If you were looking for big trade in a big city, what kind of stock would you carry? Musical instruments? Clothing?

6. Would it be a good plan to make a specialty of certain brands for leaders and to quote a special price on them?

7. If you were just starting a wholesale hardware or grocery business, state which you think would be the better policy: (1) to concentrate on one kind of goods in one territory and to take on other kinds and territories later, or (2) to work all kinds of goods as widely as possible from the very beginning. Explain fully.

8. Would you bear part of the expense of retailers' advertising, especially of window displays, provided they handled your goods?

9. Would it be good business for the salesmen of the firm to suggest selling methods to retailers and to plan window displays for them? Give your reasons.

10. Do you think it would increase sales to offer a money prize to the retailer selling the largest amount of a certain kind of your goods, the sale of which you wished materially to increase?

11. Tell which you think would be the better policy: (1) to undersell your competitors for a time and then, when you had the trade, to raise your prices, or (2) to set one price and maintain it from the beginning. Give your reasons.

12. If you were getting out a new brand of carpenters' tools, where would you advertise? Would you conduct an extensive national campaign?

13. If you were bringing out a new soap or washing powder, where would you advertise? Would you conduct an extensive national advertising campaign? What would your answer be if you were introducing a new brand of crackers?

14. Would bringing out novelties from time to time help the sale of your staple articles? Explain.

15. Do you think it would pay to send circulars to the housewives of a certain locality to get the local grocers' trade? After you had the local grocers' trade?

Exercise 264

Written

1. You are Thos. H. Peabody of Peabody, Harper & Co.'s wholesale grocery. Prepare a circular letter, announcing your removal to a new building. The letter will be printed in imitation of typewriting and the introduction filled in later on the typewriter. Remember you are seeking patronage. Address one letter to Walter T. Barth, 350 E. Water St., Milwaukee, Wis.

2. Write an advertisement to appear in the January number of *The Grocer and Country Merchant*, a grocers' trade journal. It will announce your change of location.

3. You receive an order from a retailer in which he asks for a certain brand of coffee that you do not carry. Write a letter telling him you do not handle that brand and offering him another. Make the letter as courteous as possible.

4. Write an advertisement for (1) a bookkeeper; (2) a stenographer.

5. Answer (1) or (2) above.

6. Write an advertisement for a traveling salesman.

7. Answer (6) telling why you think you could sell groceries although you have had no experience.

8. Write a circular letter to send to the trade setting forth the merits of a new brand of canned fruit. Say that you are offering the brand at a very

attractive price in the expectation that retailers will make it a leader. Write to Mr. Barth (1).

9. You have made a contract with the manufacturers of the canned fruit mentioned in (8), by which you secure the exclusive sale but take the responsibility of advertising. Write to an advertising agency, saying that you are considering a three months' advertising campaign. Explain that you do not wish the expense to exceed five thousand dollars.

10. The advertising agency replies that, as five thousand dollars is a comparatively small sum for a campaign, it would suggest that the advertising be confined to one class: street car, billboard, newspaper, or magazine. Write the letter.

11. Notify the agency of your choice, giving your reasons.

12. Write a series of three letters to send to housewives, advertising the canned fruit, with the purpose of having them ask for this brand at their grocers': (1) Telling the name of the canned fruit, its excellence, its price, and where it may be bought; (2) Asking if the housewife has as yet bought any, and if she has not, telling her she can get a sample at her grocer's on presentation of this letter; (3) Asking how she liked the fruit and quoting a letter of recommendation received from Mrs. A., who lives in the neighborhood. Urge her to buy, but not too abruptly. A letter to a woman should be fairly long. (See page 265.)

Exercise 265

1. For two months you have been without a credit man. You wish to be very careful in your choice because of the importance of the position. J. B. Wright of 439 Russell Ave., Indianapolis, is a personal friend of yours. He has heard that you need a credit man and he recommends Joseph Haddon, who worked for him three years in that capacity until a year ago when he went to Colorado because of the ill-health of his wife. Meanwhile, Mr. Wright's son has been acting as his credit man. Mrs. Haddon has now recovered, and her husband is anxious to get another position. Reproduce Mr. Wright's letter.

2. Write the letter Mr. Wright sends Mr. Haddon in Colorado, suggesting that the latter apply for the position.

3. At the same time Joseph Haddon writes, applying for the position. Write the letter of application.

4. Write Mr. Haddon's letter thanking Mr. Wright for his interest. Remember that the two men know each other.

5. Joseph Haddon, whom you have engaged, is proving to be a very alert credit man. He has made a study of your credit files and has discovered that you have a great many accounts of long standing that ought to be collected. He prepares a courteous letter to send to the debtors, telling them that he has just been made credit man and that he personally would like to get into closer touch with their particular situation to find out how soon he might expect a remittance from them, so that he could plan the future of his department. Write the letter. (See page 254.)

6. A number of retailers remit the amount that they owe. Some explain their situation in detail, but a great many do not respond to (5). Write another letter, still courteous, but more emphatic than (5), to those who did not respond. (See page 255.)

7. Still a number do not respond. Write a third letter, saying that you will place the matter in the hands of your attorney unless you receive a remittance within ten days.

8. Mr. Haddon discovers that there are about a hundred retailers who used to be customers, but who have bought nothing for about two years. He reports this to the sales manager, Mr. James Woodworth, who writes a letter to the retailers to induce them to send another order, using the canned fruit spoken of in (8) of Exercise 264 as a means of interesting them.

9. Nathaniel Sears, a dealer in general merchandise at Joplin, Mo., writes to you asking for an open account. He says that he did a $10,000 business last year and that, apparently, sales this year will be larger. He gives no references. You refer the matter to Mr. Haddon, who looks up Mr. Sears in Bradstreet and then writes to one of your salesmen at St. Louis, asking him to investigate the financial standing of Mr. Sears. Write to the salesman.

10. After three days the salesman reports that Mr. Sears seems to be doing a good business, but he thinks the dealer is living beyond his means. He owes two wholesale houses $500 and $850 respectively; his property in Joplin is heavily mortgaged, and yet he is making extensive improvements on his residence; his son and his daughter are at expensive boarding schools. Write the letter. Be exact in your information.

11. As Mr. Woodworth, write Mr. Sears a courteous letter, refusing him credit but attempting to secure his cash business.

12. Charles Freeman, 141 Park Place, Newark, Ohio, writes in answer to (5) saying that he is unable to pay his account of $500. After the harvest his outstanding bills will be paid by the farmers, and then he can remit. He says he is willing to give his 90 day note for the amount he owes.

13. Mr. Haddon writes, accepting the note.

III.—The Mail Order Merchant

Exercise 266

Oral

1. Suppose you were starting a mail order business. Would it make any difference in possible profits if your center of operations were in a large or a small city? Give your reasons.

2. Would you try to be near good transportation?

3. What kind of stock would you advertise principally: bulky articles or those easily handled? expensive goods or those of more moderate price?

4. Your catalogue is your salesman. What would this statement suggest about the cost of running your business as compared with that of Peabody, Harper & Co., who employ five salesmen?

5. How would you bring special attention to your leaders in your catalogue?

6. Why is it advisable not to give your catalogue away free, but to charge a nominal sum for it?

7. Would you sell as cheaply as you could or would you try to sell for as high a price as possible even if you sold less?

8. Is it profitable for a mail order merchant to sell one spool of thread or one pocket-knife? Consider the handling and the packing.

9. Why can the mail order merchant sell more cheaply than the country dealer?

10. *a.* How is the parcel post favorable to the mail order dealer? *b.* Why did the country merchant object so strenuously to the passage of the parcel post law?

11. Some distributors who handle only one kind of article sometimes pay the freight. Would this plan be advisable for a mail order house to adopt?

12. Since the purchaser pays the freight, is it advisable for him to buy a large or a small order at one time?

Exercise 267

Written

1. A customer who wishes to buy some furniture complains that he can purchase what he wishes from another firm that will pay the freight. Write a letter meeting his objection.

2. You have just added a new clothing department and have published a special clothing catalogue, which you will be glad to send to your customers free of charge. Write a letter telling of the new department and drawing special attention to your three-piece serge suit for $15. Enclose a sample of the cloth.

3. Write, especially to farmers, saying that with the facilities now offered by the parcel post you are able to supply their wants quickly; as, for example, for a broken part of a piece of farm machinery. Write a fairly long letter in a friendly tone.

4. In the fall write a letter, addressing the farmers' wives, saying that, as winter is at hand, it would be well for them to put in a supply of groceries when prices are reasonable. Enclose a folder giving some attractive bargains. Write the folder.

5. Write a letter, saying that you have just put up a new building. Invite your customer to come to see it. Explain that every afternoon from 2 to 4 o'clock there will be a band concert in your large visitors' hall.

Exercise 268

1. Let one pupil be chosen to dictate to the class each of the letters outlined below. He is to use no notes. The class will represent stenographers.

2. Discuss and improve the letters that have been dictated.

1. Borroughs & Brown, a mail order firm at N. 11th and Callowhill Streets, Philadelphia, send you their catalogue and an advertising letter. Write the letter.

2. Write, stating that in their catalogue No. 6, page 673, Borroughs & Brown list a washing machine such as you wish, called the "Pride Swing" washing machine, No. 4-A-459. The measurements as listed are: depth 13 inches, diameter 21 inches. The price is $5.25. This is too small for your purpose. Ask if they can supply you with the same style 30 inches in diameter. Ask the price.

3. Borroughs & Brown write that they have no such machine in stock, but, since there have been many requests lately for a larger machine, they

have decided to consult the factory, and if it is advisable, they will reproduce the "Pride Swing" machine in larger size. (Letter head.)

4. Borroughs & Brown, Dept. 18, House Furnishings, write to the W. F. Wiggins Mfg. Co., Saginaw, Mich., stating that they have had several orders for a larger "Pride Swing" washing machine which the Wiggins Company manufacture. Burroughs & Brown ask concerning a 30-inch machine. Write the letter.

5. The W. F. Wiggins Mfg. Co. telegraph Borroughs & Brown that before they can state a price on a 30-inch "Pride Swing" machine, they must make samples, calculating cost of materials and workmanship. Write the telegram. Confirm by letter. Write the letter.

6. Borroughs & Brown write you, giving the information contained in (5) above.

7. The W. F. Wiggins Mfg. Co. write Borroughs & Brown, stating that after several experiments they find that the coil springs by which the "Pride Swing" machine is operated are too weak for the larger sized tub. The manufacture of suitable springs will cause some delay in their final report.

8. Ten days later. Telegram. The W. F. Wiggins Mfg. Co. to Borroughs & Brown, stating that they have now perfected a "Pride Swing Special" machine; width 30 inches, depth 18 inches; price $8, with a discount of 50%.

9. Borroughs & Brown write you that they have perfected a "Pride Swing Special" washing machine, No. 4-B-459, 30 inches in diameter, 18 inches in depth, price $7. Add a courteous close.

10. Order five machines. Give full shipping directions. Say that you will pay according to the offer made on page 25, catalogue No. 6; viz., $20 upon receipt of the goods and $5 per month until they are paid for. Give two references.

11. Borroughs & Brown telegraph the W. F. Wiggins Mfg. Co. ordering 100 machines, five of which are to be sent directly to you. Write, confirming the telegram.

12. Two weeks later than letter (10) write again, explaining that you have not received the machines you ordered. Ask the reason for the delay.

13. Two weeks later than (11) write a telegram from Borroughs & Brown to the W. F. Wiggins Mfg. Co., asking why the machines have not been sent.

14. Send a telegram from the W. F. Wiggins Mfg. Co. to Borroughs & Brown, saying that, owing to a teamsters' and shipping clerks' strike, they have not been able to fill any of their orders for the last two weeks. The

machines have been sent. (State how and when.) Write a letter, confirming the telegram.

15. Borroughs & Brown write to inform you that the strike was the cause of the delay in the shipment of the machines you ordered ——. The machines were shipped ——. Add a courteous close.

Exercise 269

Conduct a transaction of your own, using the above as a model, except in the method of payment.

IV.—THE SALESMAN

Salesmanship is a branch of distribution about which many volumes have been written. We cannot consider it minutely from the personal view of the salesman, but can only touch upon it from the point of view of distribution. The salesman is merely a force in distribution like correspondence, circulars, and advertising. But the salesman has the advantage over these in that he is able to bring his personality to bear in the problem of getting business. It is by means of his personality that the salesman gets the attention and confidence of the customer,—a thing which is extremely hard to do in a letter, a circular, or an advertisement. Securing a buyer's confidence is very important, because no suspicious customer has ever yet bought anything.

In addition to a pleasing personality a good salesman must have a wide and thorough knowledge of his wares. If he does not know his goods, the sale drags; whereas, if he knows everything good there is to be known about them, his enthusiasm instills enthusiasm into the customer.

After bringing his knowledge and his enthusiasm into play, he must next call on his perseverance and his tact; perseverance to keep at the customer until he gets the order, and tact to know in each case just how to go about getting the order and just when to stop. Many salesmen talk too much; many more do not talk enough.

Exercise 270

Oral

In talking on any of the following subjects be sure you know just what you are going to say before you begin, and then say it clearly and convincingly. Don't say too much and don't say too little. Just exactly how much you should say no one can tell you. You must watch your audience. If they look puzzled, give more details; if they look bored, try shorter, more concise sentences, or bring your talk to a close. After you have explained all your points, sum them up briefly at the end. Remember that your talk must, first, attract attention; second, hold the interest; and third, create enthusiasm and desire to buy.

To supplement what facts you get from observation, study advertisements and catalogues to get material for (9) to (20) below:

1. Get up a talk to persuade a freshman or a group of freshmen to subscribe to the school paper.

2. To persuade girls to contribute to a fund to be used to buy suits for the football team.

3. To induce particularly uninterested freshmen to buy tickets for a school activity; for example, a debate.

4. As a real estate agent induce a classmate to establish a home in your neighborhood.

5. Try to sell the manager of the baseball team a new line of athletic goods.

6. Try to sell a set of Dickens' (or any other author's) works to a boy who is not fond of reading. You must enjoy the books that you recommend.

7. Try to sell the class or the teacher a new kind of loose leaf note book for science or English work.

8. As an agent for the publishers try to sell this text book to your English class or to your English teacher.

9. You are trying to sell an automobile to a farmer. By means of concrete examples develop the following items into a talk:
a. The business opportunities to be gained.
b. The social opportunities to be gained.

10. Get up a talk to sell a runabout to a physician who has a small practice. Suppose that he owns a horse and a buggy. Be tactful.

11. You are a salesman for an automobile house and are trying to sell a gasoline car to a man who is partial to an electric car. Meet the objections to the gasoline car and put forward its advantages.

12. You are trying to sell an electric runabout to a woman. Develop the following into a talk:
a. Ease of operation.
b. Noiselessness and comfort.
c. Elegant appearance.

13. You are trying to sell the manager of a local express company a motor truck. Gather all the data you can and present it in a talk on why he should replace his horses and wagons with motor trucks. Be as specific as possible.

14. Get up a talk showing why a man with considerable means should trade his two year old car as part payment for the latest model.

15. Get up a talk to sell a phonograph.

16. To sell an electric washing machine.

17. To sell a piano.

18. To sell a vacuum cleaner.

19. To sell a subscription to a magazine.

20. To obtain an order for groceries or teas and coffees. The offer of premiums might add to the effectiveness of your talk.

Exercise 271

The following paragraph was adapted from William C. Freeman's *Advertising Talks*.

George Washington's Cherry Tree Story has served a good purpose through all of these years. "I cannot tell a lie" is a phrase that has been used in every schoolroom in America to impress upon young minds the importance of truth telling. The phrase is also serving its purpose outside the schoolroom. In all professions and in all kinds of business, men know that in order to make good they must tell the truth. There never was, in all the history of the country, a greater movement than now toward universal truth telling. There is not even that winking at "white" lies that used to prevail. The man who does not make a direct statement, who does not earn a reputation for being honest, has no chance of succeeding. Time was when the trickster was regarded as shrewd and was accepted in the community as being right both socially and commercially. To-day the man who has money without a reputation for integrity is a bankrupt, as far as real friends and public opinion are concerned. The expression "I cannot tell a lie" has been changed to-day to "I will not tell a lie even if the lie seems more expedient than the blunt truth." So George Washington's Cherry Tree Story is as good to-day as it ever was.

Prepare paragraphs on the following suggestions, expanding each by examples:

1. As a salesman, be honest with your customers.
2. Cultivate tact.

3. Cultivate a conscience.
4. Learn to avoid friction.
5. Acknowledge your mistakes.
6. Don't criticise.
7. Don't procrastinate.
8. Don't boast.
9. Don't buy your clothes on time.
10. Don't borrow from fellow clerks.
11. Don't think your employer can't see whether you are working.
12. Don't sell a merchant a larger order than he can move.
13. Study the duties of the man ahead of you.
14. New ideas count with your employer.
15. He can who thinks he can.

Exercise 272

Written

1. A request has come in from your territory for your automobile catalogue. Write a letter to accompany the catalogue, inviting the inspection of your cars. Make it as personal as possible.

2. You have just been talking with a prospective buyer. Drive home some of the strong points of your car in a letter exploiting strength, reliability, and speed. Use the following as a basis of your letter: The Up-to-the-minute car breaks the record from New York to San Francisco, making the trip in ten days, fifteen hours, and thirteen seconds.

3. You have just shown your motor truck to a business man. Strengthen the impression you made on him by writing him a letter summing up the important advantages of the motor truck. Use the following extract from a letter:

"It has not missed a single trip since I have had it, and it takes the place of three wagons and twelve horses. My route from Waltham is so long that a pair of horses going over it one day has to be laid off the next."

"This truck makes three trips each day. I have had it on the road nearly four months and have covered over four thousand (4,000) miles with no expense for repairs."

4. A prospective customer has lost interest. Try to arouse him once more by telling him of a particularly good sale recently made, or of a new model just received, or of a new device lately perfected. Your object is to get him to inspect your cars again.

5. Write a letter to a wealthy man who bought one of your cars two years ago, offering him half of what he paid for the car in exchange for a new model. Make him see that it would be to his advantage to accept the offer.

6. Write an advertisement to appear in a local newspaper asking for an automobile salesman.

7. Answer the advertisement, telling why you think you could sell cars, although you have had no experience.

8. Write a letter to a friend telling him you have been offered the agency for the Up-to-the-minute car. Ask him to be your partner, and try to show him why you will succeed. He will be expected to bear half the office expenses, and he will get half the commissions.

Exercise 273—Suggestions for Debates

1. The mail order house ruins the trade of the country merchant.

2. The giving of free samples does not attract desirable purchasers.

3. The use of trading stamps should be abolished.

4. The motor wagon is more advantageous for the average grocer than the horse and wagon.

5. All manufactured food products should be sold in sanitary, sealed packages.

Exercise 274

Oral or Written

Prepare paragraphs on the following:

1. A merchant must know his neighborhood before he buys his stock.

2. Selling by weight rather than by measure benefits dealer and consumer.

3. Giving short weights does not prove profitable.

4. The price of a certain kind of goods, or of an article, that is going out of style should be reduced to move it quickly.

5. If merchants did not deliver purchases, goods would be cheaper.

6. Hard work and patience spell the merchant's success.

7. The middle man gets the bulk of the profit.

8. The telegraph is a great aid to the business man.

9. There is a difference between day and night telegraphic rates.

10. Money may be sent by telegraph.

11. The night letter is very useful to the merchant.

12. The parcel post is a great help to the farmer.

13. The parcel post tends to increase the business of the mail order firms.

14. The object of an automobile exhibit is to sell cars.

15. The five-and-ten-cent stores have succeeded because ——.

Exercise 275

Prepare paragraphs on the following:

1. The importance of transportation facilities to the farmer.

2. The importance of transportation facilities to the manufacturer.

3. The steamship in international trade.

4. Transportation before the days of the railroad.

5. The influence of the railroad in the advance of civilization.

6. Electrifying the railroads.

7. Speed, the cause of railroad accidents.

8. The observation car.

9. The care of food in the refrigerator car.

10. The work of the railroad repair-shop.

11. The advantage of railroad transportation over water transportation.

12. The advantage of water transportation over railroad transportation.

13. Why the larger railroads in our country run east and west.

14. The advantages of the pay-as-you-enter car.

15. The importance of the interurban electric railroads in country trade.

16. The disadvantages of the elevated system in large cities.

17. Congestion in the business district of a large city.

18. The underground system as a solution for congested traffic.

19. The work of a transfer company.

20. The motor truck decreases the business of the express companies.

21. The automobile decreases railroad suburban business.

Exercise 276

Topics for Investigation and Discussion

1. The work of the Interstate Commerce Commission.

2. How railroads control other railroads.

3. Railroad earnings.

4. Different kinds of railroad traffic.

5. The relation between the express companies and the railroads.

6. Railroad rates and rebates.

7. Government ownership of railroads.

8. The influence of the Panama canal in the growth of business in the southern states.

9. The influence of the canal in the growth of business in the central West.

10. The influence of the canal in the growth of business in South America.

11. The deep water way.

12. The parcel post zones.

Exercise 277

Books that will Suggest Topics for Talks

BOLTON, S. K., Successful Women.

CHAMBERLAIN, J. F., How We Travel.

DRYSDALE, W., Helps for Ambitious Boys; Helps for Ambitious Girls.

FOWLER, N. C., Practical Salesmanship; Starting in Life.

HALE, E. E., What Career?

HIGINBOTHAM, H. N., The Making of a Merchant.

LASELLE, M. A. and WILEY, K. E., Vocations for Girls.

LUNDGREN, CHARLES, The New Salesmanship.

LYDE, L. W., Man and his Markets.

MALLON, I. A. S., The Business Girl.

MANSON, G. J., Ready for Business.

MARSDEN, O. S., The Secret of Achievement; The Young Man Entering Business.

MITTEN, G. E., The Book of the Railway.

MOODY, W. D., Men Who Sell Things.

REED, *et al.*, Careers for the Coming Men.

ROCHELEAU, W. F., Transportation.

ROLLINS, F. W., What can a Young Man do?

STOCKWELL, H. G., Essential Elements of Business Character.

STODDARD, W. O., Men of Business.

THE VOCATION BUREAU, Boston, Vocations for Boys. (Pamphlets on *The Grocer, The Machinist, The Architect, etc.*)

WHITE, S. J., Business Openings for Girls.

Exercise 278

Write the following from dictation:

1

Transportation is a great business as well as manufacturing or farming. History tells us that very early people did not have a settled home, but, when the grass began to give out in one part of the country, several members of the community, perhaps whole tribes, took their belongings on their backs and sought for a new place to settle. It is reasonable to suppose that they wished to keep up some sort of intercourse with their friends. At once difficulties arose, since hostile tribes lived between them and their old home. It was a brave man, indeed, who ventured to encounter the dangers of the trip between the settlements. Such a set of men arose in the peddlers, who set out alone or in caravans with articles of produce or manufacture and braved the dangers even of a desert to exchange what they carried for the produce of the old home. This is the earliest form of transportation. Compare this simple form with the modern railroad, steamship, and express service.

2

CAPTURING THE LATIN AMERICAN TRADE

No empty iteration of the Monroe doctrine, no reservation of canal privileges, will capture the trade of Latin America. This will be accomplished only by efforts to produce and to sell those countries the kind of goods that they want; measured, labeled, and packed their way; offered in the language that they understand; and, moreover, sold at attractive prices. Our consuls abroad report that in all these essentials American dealers are deficient and that British, French, and German manufacturers fill the South American markets.

To these rivals must be added another, for, in spite of old South American prejudices against Spain and Spanish goods, the Spaniards are quietly regaining their footing in those republics of whose trade a century ago the home country enjoyed the monopoly. Her advantages, we know, are a common language and familiarity with the ways of life and the tastes of the buyers. Spain produces just the kind of wine, olive oil, and canned goods that South America wants; she turns out the kind of paper, the patterns of cotton goods, the styles of tools and implements, the clothing, shoes, and weapons used in Latin America; and the result is that she gets the trade. One-sixth, at least, of her entire exports goes to her former possessions.

3

South Africa has been successfully operating an agricultural parcel post. By its instrumentality gold, diamonds, minerals, wool, feathers, saddlery, boots and shoes, confectionery, fruit, plants, seed, butter and eggs suitably packed, and other farm products are transported, and the producer and consumer have been brought together. From the report of the Department of Posts and Telegraphs we learn that the scheme has worked well, is a recognized and popular feature of the postal system, and is entirely feasible. The sparse settlements and widely scattered population have not operated to bar its success, as was feared at the time of its introduction.

4

The duty of applying the remedy for wrecks rests, primarily, with the railroad managers. And what is the remedy, and how is it to be applied? It would seem that there can be but one answer: there must be stern discipline for taking risks. There must be thorough instruction as to what risks are and how to avoid them, just such instruction as the "safety first" movement is leading up to, but extended to every man in every department of every road.

In addition, the promise that no engineman will be censured for losing or not making up time or for not running fast when it is not considered safe to do so must be changed to the positive, unequivocal statement that there will be a substantial penalty for every case of running fast when it is not safe to do so.—*Railway Age Gazette.*

5

More and more attention, each year, is being given by the railroad managers to the locating of new kinds of industry along their lines. The roads in the West and the South nearly all have efficient industrial departments, land departments, or immigration departments. Their men seek out new industries, meet the steamers to tempt immigrants into their region, arrange for the purchase or rental of lands, and get together reports of the soil, the products, and the advantages of any desired location. Perhaps the greatest effort, however, is bent upon the location of new factories along the route. In one year one southern railroad induced more than seven hundred men to establish industries along its lines, after the railroads had made complete and painstaking investigation of all the conditions that would confront the prospective manufacturers.

CHAPTER XVIII

ADVERTISING

ADVERTISING is one of the most vital forces in the problem of distribution. Every advertisement is a salesman and is written and sent out with the idea of doing the work of one. It may bring in actual orders or it may merely do "missionary work"; that is, it may introduce a certain article or product and educate the people to see its advantages so that when next they desire that particular sort of article, they will order the one that they have seen advertised.

Many an article that has had practically no sale has by means of an effective advertising campaign been brought to a point of wide distribution and ready sale. How many safety razors would the manufacturers sell if they had never advertised their product? Very few. But when day after day, everywhere a man looks—in street cars, newspapers, magazines, and on billboards—he sees staring at him a reason why he should use a safety razor, he soon comes to feel that he needs one. It is just the same as though the country were covered with salesmen who were constantly after every one to get him to see the advantage of the safety razor. The advertised articles may in themselves be no better than the unadvertised brands, but advertising has created a demand for the one over the other. The secret of selling success is creating a demand.

The importance of advertising is demonstrated by an experience which the city of Chicago had on Wednesday, March 2, 1911. On the afternoon before, a dispute arose between two newspapers and their printers, ending in a temporary strike of the printers. As a result, all papers published on March 2 contained only four pages each, in contrast to the usual twenty-four, because they contained not a single advertisement. Fortunately, the strike lasted only one day, as the local printers were at once reprimanded by the International Typographical Union. But the losses that newspapers and retail business men suffered on this one day convinced them of the power of advertising. Street cars, downtown streets, and department stores were almost empty. To be sure, billboards still proclaimed their wares, but, as soon as newspaper advertising ceased, the great mass of shopping stopped.

Exercise 279

Oral

1. What are some of the advertising methods used in a retail business?

2. What are some of the advertising methods used in a wholesale business? Where are the advertisements published?

3. What is the principal advertising medium of the mail order house? Explain why it is effective.

4. What is classified advertising? Why are newspapers anxious to increase it? Name several reasons.

5. What is "display" advertising as distinguished from classified? What is the principal medium of this kind of advertising?

6. Give several instances of advertising by means of the distribution of "novelties," such as calendars. Is such advertising effective?

7. Is the distribution of samples good advertising? Be specific in your answer.

8. Is it a good thing to have a trade-mark? Name some trade-marks that you think are good advertising.

9. Is a bargain table good advertising? What is its advantage in a retail store?

10. What class of advertising is done in the classified columns of a newspaper?

11. What class of articles and products is advertised in the street cars and trains? Expensive or inexpensive? Things you use every day or not?

12. Are articles advertised by billboards usually widely advertised articles or not?

13. What kind of articles would you advertise in:

1. The newspaper rather than the magazine?
2. The magazine rather than the newspaper?
3. The street car rather than on the billboard?
4. The trade papers rather than the newspapers?

14. Suppose you were bringing out a new soap and you could use only one of the following mediums: (1) newspapers; (2) local and trade magazines; (3) street cars; (4) billboards and posters. Which would you choose and why? Would your answer be the same if you had real estate to sell? A new machine? If you were producing a new play?

15. NEWS ITEM.—The University of Wisconsin has issued a bulletin, stating that of all the money spent for food, shelter, and clothing 90% is spent by women. Would the following be good advertising for a magazine: "The women of the country read this paper"? Give reasons for your answer.

16. Do handbills suggest cheapness to you?

Exercise 280

Oral

Discuss the value of each of the following as forms of advertising:

1. Location.
2. Furnishings of the office or the store.
3. Letter headings.
4. Window displays.
5. Electric (or other) signs.
6. Moving electric signs.
7. Colors (especially reds, greens, and yellows) as against black and white.
8. White lettering on a black background.

Exercise 281

Fundamentally, the same principles apply to the advertisement as apply to the sales letter (See page 230). First of all, you must look at your goods from the standpoint of the user; see his gain in buying rather than your profit in selling. Your products, then, will probably fall into one of the following general classes:

1. Something entirely new for which you must create a demand by showing its advantage to the buyer, arousing his sense of need and, consequently, his desire to possess.

2. Something new but filling a long-felt need—"Just what you've been looking for"—the value of which will appeal to the buyer almost as soon as the product is explained. Comparison with the article that now imperfectly fills the want suggests itself.

3. A new brand of an old staple, like crackers, of which the superiority must be dwelt upon to induce buyers to ask for it. Even after the article is selling well, continuous advertising is necessary to keep the name before the public.

A paying advertisement appeals to a large class of people or, better still, to several classes. For a moment let us analyze a few of the appeals to which almost every one responds; let us consider the reasons back of our purchases. Why do we buy one article and not another? We buy it first, perhaps, because we need it or think we need it; second, because we think it will taste good or be comfortable or good-looking or because it will afford us amusement; third, because we think it is better, though possibly more expensive, than any other brand on the market, and our pride or our desire to emulate responds to it; fourth, because we think it is good for our health or our safety; and, fifth, because we shall save money or make money thereby. Summing up, we may say that the motives to which appeals may safely be made are:

1. Need, conscious or unconscious (usefulness, quality, or durability).
2. Comfort, amusement, or appetite.
3. Pride, desire to emulate, or vanity.
4. Safety (of health or personal possessions).
5. Economy or gain.

Clip from magazines and bring to class good advertisements that appeal to the motives named above. Try to find those advertisements that make an appeal to only one motive in one advertisement.

Exercise 282

The following catch phrases have been taken from advertisements in various places. Tell (1) whether their appeal is general; (2) whether they induce one to buy; and (3) if they do, which of the motives given above have been used by the advertiser. Frequently more than one motive is used in one advertisement.

1. For a delicatessen store: Good things to eat.

2. For a chewing gum: The taste lasts.

3. For a motor washer: Two cents a week pays your washing bill.

4. For a refrigerator: Are you poisoning your family?

5. For a summer drink: It's wet.

6. For stockings: Wear like 60, look like 50, cost but 25.

7. For a shaving soap: Comfort for your face, economy for your purse.

8. For a liniment: Don't rub—it penetrates.

9. For a hair tonic: What does your mirror say?

10. For a clothing store: Exclusive styles for exclusive women.

11. For an inexpensive scouring powder: Why pour money down the sink?

12. For canned goods: When company comes.

13. For a varnish: Water won't hurt it.

14. For bread: The human hand never touches it.

15. For a fountain pen: It can't leak.

Exercise 283

Bring to class two advertisements containing catch phrases that you think are good. To which of the motives given above does each appeal?

Exercise 284

Bring in two advertisements of articles that have suggestive names. What is the value of a suggestive name?

Exercise 285—Good and Bad Headlines

A good headline has the following qualities:

First, it should be short. Professor Walter Dill Scott determined by experiments that the average person can ordinarily attend to only about four visual objects at the same time—four letters, four words, four simple pictures, or four geometrical figures. As the headline of an advertisement is intended to be taken in at one glance, it should, therefore, be not longer than four words—preferably less, provided the interest of the phrase is the same. Short words, too, can be taken in more readily than long words.

Second, the best headline is a command. People instinctively obey a command, unless it is so worded that they rebel against the manner of expression.

Third, a good headline is suggestive. It touches upon the things that the reader is thinking about. It shows that the article that is offered for sale has a close connection with the interests that absorb the reader's mind. It is a direct answer to his thoughts, feelings, hopes, or worries.

The following headlines were taken from the advertisements in one issue of a magazine. Judge of their effectiveness, using the three principles given above as a basis for your decision:

1. Get That Job!
2. Foot Comfort.
3. Ventilate, but Don't Catch Cold!
4. A New Filing Cabinet.
5. Are You Open to Conviction?
6. Low Priced Envelope Sealer.
7. Shave for 1c Without Stropping.

8. What a Wonderful Trip!
9. Save 30% on Your Furniture.
10. You Have a Right to Independence.
11. Just Out!
12. Get the Dust Out of Your Home—It's Dangerous.
13. The Easiest Riding Car in the World.
14. Our Seeds Grow.
15. That Raise! (Sub-heading in smaller type: What Would a Raise in Salary Mean to You?)

Exercise 286

Some advertisers choose headlines merely for the purpose of attracting attention, forgetting that the headline should suggest what the following illustration and text explain. A few years ago a well-known automobile company ran an advertisement with the headline *$1000 Worth of Folly*. The headline was followed by a picture of the automobile. The advertisement was intended to convey the idea that, as this car might be bought for $3000, any one paying $4000 for an automobile was foolishly squandering $1000. As a matter of fact, the only suggestion that the reader got from the advertisement was that any one who paid $1000 for the illustrated car would be a fool.

1. Bring to class an advertisement in which the headline has no connection with the rest of the advertisement, being used merely to catch the attention.

2. Find an advertisement in which the headline suggests the opposite of what the advertisement is intended to convey.

3. How might either advertisement be improved?

Exercise 287

Still-life advertisements are not interesting. The picture of a furnace, or a typewriter, or a house attracts less attention than the same objects with human beings represented moving in the picture.

Bring to class two advertisements of the same kind of article, in one of which a still-life illustration is used and in the other of which human beings are used to center the attention upon the article that is offered for sale.

Exercise 288

Bring to class (1) an advertisement that is not good because it contains too much—lacks a center upon which the attention naturally focuses; and

(2) an advertisement that is good because it has a definitely defined center of attraction.

Exercise 289

Bring to class an advertisement in which the principle of balance is used to advantage, two illustrations, one on each side of the text, being used to convey one impression.

Exercise 290

In writing the following, try to embody the principles that have been brought out in previous exercises:

1. An entertainment is to be given in the school hall. Write an advertisement to appear in the school paper.

2. Write an announcement of the same entertainment—to be posted on the bulletin board.

3. Write an advertisement for a debate.

4. For a football, baseball, or basket-ball game.

5. For an inter-class contest.

6. You have permission to secure advertisements to be printed in the program of the entertainment spoken of above. Suppose that you are to write the copy for the different advertisements. Use one-eighth, one-quarter, one-half, or one page, as you wish.

Advertise a grocery.

7. A meat market.

8. A dry goods store.

9. A candy store.

10. A bakery.

11. A bank.

12. A tailor's shop.

13. A photographer's studio.

14. A barber shop.

15. A drug store.

Exercise 291

1. Write a handbill announcing a 20% discount sale to run three days in your dry goods store.

2. Describe a chair, table, or other article of furniture in your own home. The description is to form part of an advertisement to appear in a mail order catalogue.

3. You are advertising a new brand of coffee in the street car. Write the card. Would you use an illustration? If so, of what kind?

4. As in (3) advertise a new brand of pork and beans.

5. As in (3) advertise a shoe sale.

6. Advertise a well-known brand of soap in a magazine. Use your own idea. Would you use an illustration?

7. How would you advertise an automobile which has proved its merits? Remember, your object is to keep the name before the public. How would you advertise a new make of automobile? How much space would you use in either case? Write both advertisements.

8. A half-page advertisement by the Hudson Cereal Company, 110 Hudson St., New York, of their Nervo-Cereal Coffee contains the item: "Can you thread a needle, holding the thread one inch from the end? If you cannot, you are nervous. Is coffee to blame?" Exploit the aroma and flavor of the cereal coffee.

9. The Central Packing Company is running a series of advertisements of their Premium Extract of Beef. This one is to appear just before Thanksgiving. Entitle it "Four Delicious Dishes for the Thanksgiving Dinner," and then in as attractive a form as possible give four recipes, making a point of the necessity of using Premium Extract for the right flavor. At the end sum up the merits of Premium Extract and mention the silver premiums given with the certificates under the metal caps.

10. The Bay City Mill Co., Bay City, Mich., sells fine finished lumber suitable for making furniture at home. Prepare an advertisement to show how simple it is to make tables and chairs at home with their plans and their specially cut lumber. Illustrate by giving the plans and working directions for making a useful table, showing how easy it is with their specially cut lumber. Set an attractive price on the lumber necessary to make this table. Sum up by exploiting a book of plans, which may be had for the asking.

Exercise 292

The following paragraph is taken from Professor Scott's *Theory of Advertising*. What is the subject of the paragraph? Is there a topic sentence? By what plan is the paragraph developed?

Many of those who use illustrations for their advertisements follow the philosophy of the Irish boy who said that he liked to stub his toe because it felt so good when it stopped hurting. Many of us are unable to see how the boy had made any gain after it was all over, but he was satisfied, and that was sufficient. The philosophic disciples of the Irish boy are found in advertisers who have certain things to dispose of which will not do certain harmful things. First they choose an illustration which will make you believe that what they have to sell is just what you do not want, and then in the text they try to overcome this false impression and to show you that what they have to offer is not so bad after all. Most of us are unable to see how the advertiser has gained, even if he has succeeded in giving us logical proof that his goods are not so bad as we were at first led to think. We are not logically inclined, and we take the illustration and the text, and we combine the two. The best that the text can do is to destroy the evil effect of the illustration. Of course, when we read in the text that the illustration does not correctly represent the goods, we ought to discard the illustration entirely and think only of the text, but, unfortunately, we are not constructed in that way. The impression made by the illustration and that made by the text fuse and form a whole which is the result formed by these two elements.

Write paragraphs on each of the following:

1. Advertising is essential in modern business.

2. Advertising helps the housewife economize.

3. The study of advertisements saves the shopper's time and strength.

4. Advertised goods cost more than the unadvertised brands. (Give the reasons.)

5. Trade-marked and advertised goods have increased the cost of living.

6. Increased advertising causes the styles to change quickly.

7. Every advertisement must catch and hold the attention. Some accomplish this object by causing a laugh. (Describe one such.)

8. Some advertisements hold the attention because they appeal to our love of the mysterious. One such is —— (describe it).

9. Some advertisements succeed because of their clever color scheme. One such is ——.

10. Every successful advertisement contains a convincing argument.

11. Mouth to mouth advertising is the best and the cheapest.

12. Advertised goods are better because they have to be.

13. The consumer pays for all the advertising.

14. The cost of advertising is paid by the competitors who do not advertise.

15. Advertising tends to create uniform prices.

16. The advertising expert is a student of men.

Exercise 293

Give your opinion as to the effectiveness of the following advertisements:

1

A department store that was anxious to increase its trade on Mondays and Wednesdays included the following coupons in its circular advertisement one week:

THIS COUPON AND
19c
Monday only
good for
6 Spools J. & P. Coats' Best 6 Cord Machine Thread
Regular 30c value

THIS COUPON AND 50cWednesday only
good for
Misses' or Children's White Canvas Pumps
2 strap model, heavy or light soles, trimmed with dainty bow on vamp. All sizes up to 2.
$1.50 value

2

$10,000 IN CASH TO CHARITY

We ask our customers to decide by their votes the 250 institutions that shall receive this amount. Each ten cents' worth purchased entitles the purchaser to one vote.

3

The following appeared in the center of a page otherwise blank. On the opposite page appeared the advertisement of a well-known article.

The announcement on the following page is so important that we have decided to leave this page blank.

4

The following was part of a circular:

Following our annual custom we will again this year give away absolutely free a beautiful silk flag to every customer making a purchase of $1 or over, Tuesday and Wednesday, July 2 and 3.

5

The following appeared in a newspaper:

A Word of Appreciation

We have now been in our new location somewhat over a month. Our business has been all that we expected; in some departments, indeed, there is an increase, notably in the neckwear, ready-to-wear clothes, hats, and tailoring departments.

Naturally, we had an abundance of faith in our new location; nevertheless, we must confess that there were times when we had anxious moments. We discovered, however, that our moving was at the "psychological moment"; we soon learned that in the minds of the people there was but one thought—success for Michigan Avenue.

We have always felt that there was a closer bond of sympathy between our customers and us than is usually the case between buyer and seller. The unusual interest taken in our new store and in our success has more than confirmed us in this impression. Our experience during the last forty days has really made life worth living.

The minds of hundreds of our customers have reverted to the beginning of our business in our old Dearborn Street store, twenty years ago, and they have made comparisons between that and the wonderful establishment we now possess; they have done it in a way that would almost suggest that it was their business that they were talking of rather than ours. It made us feel that, although we have made our mistakes, nevertheless we must have served the public well, and we insert this article in the hope that a few of our well-wishers may read it and understand that we appreciate and are grateful.

Exercise 294

Books that will Suggest Topics for Talks

BALMER, EDWIN, The Science of Advertising.
BELLAMY, FRANCIS (ed), Effective Magazine Advertising.
BRIDGEWATER, HOWARD, Advertising, or The Art of Making Known.
CALKINS, E. E. and HOLDEN, R., Modern Advertising.
CHERINGTON, PAUL T., Advertising as a Business Force.
DELAND, L. F., Imagination in Business.
DE WEESE, TRUMAN A., Advertising (The Business Man's Library, Vol. vii).
EDGAR, ALBERT E., How to Advertise a Retail Store.
FOWLER, N. C., Building Business.
SCOTT, W. D., The Theory of Advertising.

CHAPTER XIX

REAL ESTATE AND INSURANCE

Lands, buildings, and houses are called real property or real estate, and the business pertaining to them, the real estate business. Every one of us has more or less to do with this business. If we do not own property, we pay *rent.* Rent is the money paid for the use of a piece of land, or a building, or part of a building, and is usually paid at certain stated intervals of time—monthly, for example. The owner of the building is called the *landlord;* the one who rents, the *tenant.* Sometimes there is no condition as to how long a tenant shall remain in one place and pay rent, but, as a rule, the landlord requires the tenant to sign a *lease.* This is a contract between the landlord and the tenant, stating that in consideration of the landlord's furnishing the tenant a place in which to live with certain conveniences—such as heat, hot water, and other services—the tenant agrees to pay rent for a certain length of time, usually a year or more. If the tenant moves out before his lease expires and refuses to pay the rent, he breaks the contract and, as is usually the case when a contract is broken, a lawsuit may follow. In large cities where land is in some places very valuable, owners may not care to sell the property on which others wish to build, but lease it to the builders for a certain term of years, usually ninety-nine years.

Suppose you no longer wish to pay rent, but to own the house in which you live. If you buy a piece of property from John Smith and pay him your money for it, you wish to be assured that after a few months John Smith will not come to you and claim the property as his. To protect you John Smith gives you a *deed* to the property. A deed is a contract between the buyer and the seller of the property. It states that, in consideration of the buyer's paying a certain stipulated sum of money, the seller releases and conveys the property to the buyer. This deed shows that you now own the property. At the same time you should receive a *clear title* to the property; that is, you wish to be sure that no one else has a claim on the property. If John Smith guarantees that the title is clear, he gives you a *warranty deed* for the property, in which he will "warrant and defend the same against all lawful claims whatsoever." If, however, he simply turns over the property to you as it stands, he gives you a *quitclaim deed,* in which he relinquishes or quits all his interest in it. If you have no debts on the property, you own it in *fee simple.*

Very often in buying property, the purchaser pays only a part of the purchase price himself, paying for the balance by borrowing the necessary amount from a third party. For example, if the house you bought from John Smith cost $6,000 and you had only $4,000, you would be forced to borrow the other $2,000 to pay John Smith. You would then go to your bank or to some person who had money to invest and would borrow the required amount, and to guarantee that you would pay the money back, you would give a *mortgage* on the property. A mortgage is a contract which states that, in consideration of one party's giving the second party a certain sum of money, the second party agrees to pay interest on that money at a stipulated rate, and at the end of a certain length of time agrees to pay the money back; and that, in case the second party does not pay back the amount at the end of the time, the first party is empowered to take possession of the property, to sell it, and to get the amount due him. This last procedure is called *foreclosing the mortgage.* It is a common practice to mortgage property; almost all the property in a city is mortgaged.

Some men and firms make a special business of transferring property, buying and selling it for others, making leases, and collecting rents. They are called real estate agents, and for their services get a *commission*, which is a certain percentage of the purchase or the selling price and a certain percentage of the amount of rent collected. This percentage varies according to whether the amount of money involved is large or small, the percentage being larger when small sums of money are involved than when large sums are involved.

Exercise 295

Oral

1. What is a lease?

2. Explain why owners of valuable property lease it.

3. What is a deed? Explain the two kinds.

4. What is meant by a clear title?

5. What is meant by fee simple?

6. Why is it important to be careful about the title?

7. What is a mortgage?

8. Explain why property is often mortgaged. Does the mortgage benefit the owner? Explain.

9. What is meant by foreclosing?

10. What is an agent? How is he usually paid?

11. Why do people employ real estate agents to take care of renting? To sell their property?

12. Why is property near a railroad valuable? For what?

13. Why is a corner lot worth more than an inside lot?

14. Why is property on a car line more valuable than on a side street?

15. What effect would the building of a new street car line have on the value of adjacent property? Why?

Exercise 296

Oral

1. Suppose that you are a landlord and that in your lease no mention is made of giving your tenants janitor service, but you yourself take care of the furnace. Other landlords in the block supply janitor service. After one of your tenants has moved in, he demands that the back porch be scrubbed once a week and the garbage emptied daily. What would you do? Consider the points for and against.

2. Suppose some boys playing ball on the street break a plate glass window in the store you own. Would you expect your tenant to pay for repairs?

Written

3. Write to Francis L. Russell, a real estate agent, asking his terms for collecting the rent of —— (tell the location of the house, the number of the tenants, and the rent you receive).

4. As if you were Francis L. Russell write a reply, saying that you will undertake the collection for a commission of 5%.

5. Imagine you are a tenant in the same building. The kitchen sink cannot be used in your flat because of a stoppage in the plumbing. You have told the agent once. Write him (see 3) again, stating that unless he sends a plumber you will not pay your next month's rent. (Is there any reason for writing this, rather than telephoning it?)

6. The plumber has submitted a bill of $5.98 for the repairs suggested in (5). The agent writes to the landlord, enclosing a check for the rent that he has collected, less the amount of the plumber's bill and his commission.

7. You are a lawyer. Write to the landlord, informing him that the mortgage which your client holds against the landlord's property expires in thirty days. Ask the landlord whether he expects to pay the money or whether he wishes a renewal of the loan for three years. Your client is willing to give such a renewal.

8. The landlord replies that he is enclosing $100 to pay the interest due on the mortgage and that he desires a renewal of the loan. If the lawyer will prepare the papers, he will come to sign them at the specified time. Write the letter.

9. You are an insurance agent. Write to the landlord that the fire insurance on his property expires in sixty days. Ask him to allow you to write a new policy. Inform him that the rate now will be 3¾% instead of if 1¾% as it was formerly, because a garage has been erected one door north of his property. (Why should the rate be higher?)

10. One of the tenants has paid no rent for two months. You decide that he never will be able to pay. As landlord you make out and deliver to him a *Five days' notice of removal.* At the same time, you write a letter to your lawyer, explaining the state of affairs and asking him to take charge of enforcing the notice. (This means that if the tenant does not move, the case must come up in court. If it is decided in the landlord's favor, the tenant must move. If he refuses, the lawyer engages a constable to eject him.) Write the letter.

11. Francis L. Russell writes three short advertisements, offering for sale (1) a large 12 room residence, mortgage $6,000, price $15,000; (2) a 3 apartment building, clear, price $16,000; (3) a large 12 apartment building, mortgage $25,000, price $41,000, terms to suit. Where would you advertise? Write the advertisements.

12. You get inquiries about all of the above. Write answers describing the buildings more fully, and make appointments with the writers to inspect the property.

13. A man is interested in the 12 flat building, but he has only $10,000. Offer him the property for $40,000 on these terms: $10,000 down, a first mortgage for $20,000 to run 10 years at 5%, and a second mortgage for $10,000 to run 5 years at 5½%, $2,000 to be paid each year with interest. Make it as attractive as possible. Tell him you will arrange for the mortgages.

14. (*a*) Write to your bank, the First National, and explain that, although the first mortgage on the 12 flat building for $25,000 still has 3 years to run, you would like to arrange for a 10 year mortgage for $20,000, if your prospective buyer takes the property. (*b*) Write to George R. Scott, who owns the building, offering him the second mortgage. Explain that although it is a second mortgage the fact that $2,000 of the principal is paid each year makes it attractive. (How would the owner benefit if the buyer failed to make his payments after 2 years?) Sign yourself Francis L. Russell.

15. You have put through the deal. Write to the new owner, offering to take care of the renting for a commission equal to 2½% of the amount collected.

Exercise 297—Farm Lands

1. You own a large tract of land in the South, West, or Southwest. Choose your own locality. Prepare a pamphlet setting forth the advantages of this particular spot in a series of paragraphs: (1) scenery, (2) climate and healthfulness, (3) crops, (4) profits from the crops, (5) price of labor, (6) chances for pleasure, e.g., hunting, fishing, etc., (7) transportation facilities, (8) price of the land. Use a firm name and address.

2. Arrange and punctuate:

Nov. 1, 19— [For the introduction supply the same firm name used in (1)]. Gentlemen I have just returned from an extended trip through (the district spoken of above) with reference to the forty acres I purchased from you I desire to say that I am convinced that it will prove a paying investment I am so pleased that I shall certainly try to induce several of my friends to purchase near my site while on the property I carefully inspected the farm worked by Mr S R Jackson I must say what he is accomplishing the immense crop of vegetables and fruit he is marketing amazed me no doubt what he is doing I may do for I made sure by careful examination that the soil on my land is exactly like his you may depend upon it that within the next two months I shall move my family upon the land for I am eager to develop it sincerely yours F W Farrell

What advantage would there be in including such a letter as (2) in the booklet spoken of in (1)?

3. To prove the possibilities of the land spoken of in (1), you intend to start a model farm. Advertise for a farmer. Your plan is to give him 60 acres to develop for himself, in return for which he shall demonstrate the possibilities of the land.

4. Write a letter applying for the position. You must have farming experience, some money, a knowledge of crops, and a good deal of enthusiasm.

5. Write an advertisement of your land for a big newspaper. Exploit its most striking features, especially the price. Study such advertisements before you write yours.

6. Reproduce a letter you received in answer to (5), asking for more information concerning the lands.

7. Write the reply to (6). Say you are enclosing the booklet spoken of in (1); tell of the model farm being established (3); and induce the inquirer to become a purchaser.

8. Prepare a series of three follow-up letters to be sent out to prospective purchasers who write as in (6) but who do not answer your letter in (7). Make each letter set forth one of the following advantages of buying a piece of your land: (1) The profits from the crops are large; (2) The conditions are ideal—mention climate, water, neighbors, transportation; (3) It is a good investment, since the land will certainly rise in value—tell of other land in the neighborhood that has risen in value within the last year. Arrange the letters in the order that you think will be most effective.

Exercise 298
Topics for Investigation and Discussion

1. The cause of changes in city real estate values.

2. The price of downtown property in your town.

3. The rise in property values in the last few years.

4. The causes of the rise.

5. Stove heated or steam heated property—which is the better income producer?

6. The Mortgage.—(*a*) Why people mortgage their property; (*b*) Why people loan money on mortgages.

7. The increase in the total value of farm lands during the last ten years.

8. The decrease in the value of farm lands in the East.

9. The reasons for the growth of the West.

10. Will the South be a new West?

11. The reclamation of swamp lands.

12. The success of irrigation.

Exercise 299—Insurance

An exposition of the subject of insurance is hardly in place here, especially as every one, to a certain extent at least, is acquainted with the fundamental reasons why insurance is purchased. The questions below should be used as a rudimentary review that will prepare for the letters that follow.

Oral

1. What is the object of insurance?

2. What is meant by a policy?

3. By the premium?

4. By the beneficiary?

5. By life insurance?

6. By fire insurance?

7. By accident insurance?

8. By marine insurance?

9. What is the difference between a straight life and a 20 year endowment policy?

10. Between the above and a 20 year pay policy?

11. Between the above and a term policy?

12. Why is it that the mortgagee, and not the owner, holds the fire insurance policy? Why must the amount of insurance equal or exceed the amount of the mortgage?

Written

1. You are an insurance agent. A man came to your office to-day to inquire about a life insurance policy. Write him a letter, repeating what you told him, advocating his taking out a straight life policy.

2. A new building has just been erected in your neighborhood. Write to the owner, soliciting him to let you write the fire insurance policy.

3. Write to a man who rides downtown on the train every day. Convince him that he needs to take out an accident insurance policy. Point out that the premium is only $25 a year. If the man is injured he will receive $25 weekly; if he is killed by accident, his beneficiary will receive $5,000; if he is killed on a train or in an elevator, $10,000.

4. Write to one of your clients, informing him that the premium on his life insurance policy falls due in ten days.

5. Write to another of your clients, informing him that the insurance on his property runs out in ten days. Inform him that, if he wishes the policy renewed, he should let you know at once and remit the premium.

6. From the client mentioned in (5) you receive a letter in which he explains that the paint store which formerly adjoined his property has been replaced by a grocery. He would like a new policy at a lower rate. Reproduce the letter. A paint store is insured at the highest, or hazard, rate. The rate on property adjoining a paint store would also be very high.

7. You investigate the matter and find that the facts are as stated in (6). Write your client, offering him a rate of 1½% and enclosing a bill for $45.

8. He replies that, since the risk of fire is now so much less, he wishes to take only $2,000 worth of insurance. He asks you to write such a policy, and he encloses his check for $30. Write the letter.

9. A man writes to you, saying that he wishes to take out an endowment policy for his fifteen year old daughter, who has already been examined. He wishes to give the insurance to her as a birthday present. He encloses a check for the premium and asks you to send the contract to her on her birthday (Name the date). Write the father's letter.

10. Write a letter to accompany the birthday present. Remember you do not know the daughter.

Exercise 300

Write the following from dictation:

1

MUST REFORM OUR FARMING

The average yield of wheat in the United States for the five years ending in 1910 was eight-tenths of a bushel per acre more than in the five years ending in 1905, but it was less than four-tenths of a bushel more than for the ten ending in 1900. The average corn product for the ten years ending in 1910 was a little less than for the ten years ending in 1875. Thirty-five years had not advanced us a step. European countries—Great Britain, France, Germany—with inferior soils and less favorable climate produce crops practically double our own. In our studies of conservation we find no waste comparable, either in magnitude or importance, to this. The farm will fail, and the foundations of our prosperity be undermined, unless agriculture is reformed. The percentage of our people actively engaged in farming had fallen from 47.36 in 1870 to an estimated 32 in 1910. Every man on the farm to-day must produce food for two mouths against one forty years ago.

—*J. J. Hill.*

2

THE FARMING SPECIALS

One of the latest and most successful activities of the railroads is the practice of carrying knowledge of the best farming methods to the farmers by means of special trains equipped like agricultural colleges. These trains, bearing experts and all the equipment for exhibiting the new methods of agriculture, bring the knowledge to the farmers free, and the railroads are glad to give it, for every bit of knowledge comes back to them in a hundred fold profit in freight. In the summer eager audiences all over the country listen to the preaching of better methods and larger crops. Dozens of special trains travel through the agricultural regions disseminating information. The "Breakfast Bacon Special" has been run to encourage Iowa farmers to raise more hogs to take advantage of the high price of bacon. The Cotton Belt Route southwest of St. Louis runs the "Squealer Special" to prove to the Arkansas and Panhandle farmers the money-making advantages of blooded hogs over the razor-back variety. Down the Mississippi Valley the Illinois Central sends the "Boll Weevil Special" to conduct a campaign against that pest. The Harriman lines have six trains operating in California every year. In one year they visited more than seventy-five thousand people. Better farming specials run in practically every state south of the Ohio and Potomac and west of the Mississippi. The New York Central also has two trains in operation in New York.—*The Business Almanac.*

3

A large proportion of farmers give little or no attention to the selection of seed; yet it has been demonstrated that a careful selection would add hundreds of millions of dollars to the total value of the crops. If, for example, a variety of wheat were developed capable of producing one more kernel to the head, it would mean an addition, so Burbank says, of 15,000,000 bushels to our average wheat crop. It is possible, however, to do even more than this. At the Minnesota station a variety, selected for ten years according to a definite principle, yielded twenty-five per cent more than the parent variety. Applied to our average crop, that increase would amount to 185,000,000 bushels, worth about $140,000,000. As for corn, it has been officially stated that our average yield could easily be doubled. After exhaustive experiments the Department of Agriculture says that by merely testing individual ears of seed corn and rejecting those of low vitality an average yield of nearly fourteen per cent could be secured, adding about $200,000,000 to the value of the crop. Does scientific seed selection seem worth while?—*The Wall Street Journal.*

CHAPTER XX

BANKING

IMAGINE that you are a druggist in a small town. Suppose that a woman comes in to buy two ounces of camphor and in exchange gives you three eggs. In a few moments, perhaps, a man enters to buy a safety razor and brings with him wheat enough to pay the bill. Another, again, wishes to trade a turkey for a fountain pen. You can readily see the inconvenience to which you would be put in such exchange of actual commodities; yet this was the method used in primitive times, a method called *barter*.

To overcome the inconvenience of barter, as civilization advanced, it became necessary to establish a common medium of exchange, which could be accepted for anything one had to sell and with which one could buy anything he wished. This is what we call *money*. To meet the requirements, money must not be bulky, must be durable, and must not readily change in value. In civilized countries gold and silver are the bases of exchange.

But gold and silver are heavy and inconvenient to carry about in large, or for that matter in small, quantities, and for convenience the following kinds of paper money have been established:

1. *Gold Certificates* are issued with the government's guarantee that there is gold deposited in the Treasury equal to the amount of the face of the bill. At any time the one holding such a bill may demand of the Treasury that he receive gold for it.

2. *Silver Certificates* are similar to gold certificates, except that silver is deposited in the Treasury instead of gold.

3. *United States Treasury Notes* are promissory notes of the government to pay the sum indicated. They are not payable on demand.

4. *National Bank Notes* are promissory notes issued by the national banks and are payable on demand of the bearer. Before a national bank may issue such notes, it must own United States government bonds of at least the amount for which it issues notes. These bonds are held by the Treasurer of the United States as security that the bank will pay its notes. According to the Owen Glass Bill, passed in December of 1913, national bank notes may at the option of the banks be gradually withdrawn from circulation.

Credit

Credit is a promise to pay at some future time for a thing which you receive now. Its use is probably as old as the practice of exchange and quite as important. The simplest and most extensive form of credit is "book" credit, such as you get at the grocer's or butcher's or at the department store. To explain a little more complex kind of credit: Suppose you owe Smith one hundred dollars. At the same time Smith owes Jones one hundred dollars. Because you owe Smith, he may give Jones an order to collect the money from you. With this order Jones may pay his lawyer, let us say. Perhaps the lawyer has bought a bill of goods from you. He pays you with the same order. You destroy the "note," and thus four actual transactions have been taken care of without the use of any money. The business institution which deals especially with credits is the bank.

Banks

A bank which fulfills every banking function must have these three departments: (1) the commercial department, (2) the savings department, (3) the trust department. Some institutions specialize in one department more than in either of the others, and thus, taking the name from their principal function, banks are known as follows: (i) commercial banks or banks of deposit, (2) savings banks, (3) trust companies.

Banks of Deposit

DEPOSIT SLIP

MARINE NATIONAL BANK

OF BUFFALO

Deposited to Credit of

Gerald W. Porter

Buffalo, N.Y. *Apr. 23* **1918**

	DOLLARS	CTS.
CURRENCY	125	
GOLD		
SILVER	18	75
CHECKS		
Bank of Buff.	38	70
Cleveland	183	40
AMOUNT	365	85

Banks of deposit or commercial banks are business men's banks. Their two principal functions are (1) receiving money for safe-keeping on deposit, and (2) loaning money to business men at interest. The deposit function is based on confidence and credit. The business man takes his money to the bank not only because it is convenient for him to do so, but also because he has confidence that the money will be more carefully protected than if he kept it in his own possession. In depositing his money in the bank, the business man uses a *deposit slip* such as the one illustrated here. The teller puts down the amount in the *bank book* of the depositor, who is credited with that amount on the bank's books. He is entitled to draw just that much actual cash or that much credit in the form of *checks*. (See page 339.) Most firms do not deposit a sum of money and then promptly draw it out again in the form of checks to pay current liabilities, but maintain a fairly steady balance in the bank. On large average monthly balances most banks allow interest, varying from one per cent on balances of one thousand dollars to three per cent on balances of ten thousand dollars or more.

Discount

Because a large bank has many depositors, the aggregate of all the balances makes a considerable sum of money. Bankers have learned by experience just what proportion of their deposits they can depend on to remain steadily on deposit as a balance, and thus they know what proportion of their deposits it is safe to use for the purpose of *discount*. The simplest case of the discount function is the discount of a promissory note. In the note shown in the illustration after ninety days John H. Blodgett will receive from Lucius Thomas five hundred dollars with interest. But perhaps Blodgett cannot wait ninety days for his money. In this case, he takes the note to his banker, who will pay him the five hundred dollars less a certain percentage or discount, which is the bank's profit on the transaction. The bank then collects the note when it becomes due.

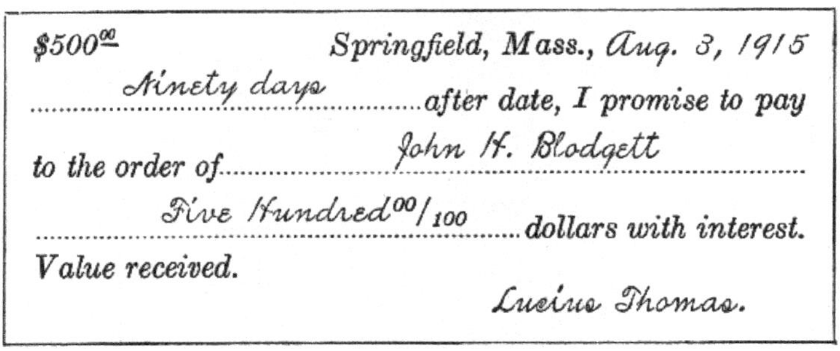
$500.00 Springfield, Mass., Aug. 3, 1915
Ninety days after date, I promise to pay
to the order of John H. Blodgett
Five Hundred 00/100 dollars with interest.
Value received.
Lucius Thomas.

PROMISSARY NOTE

Collateral

Instead of cashing a note held by one of its customers, the bank may itself loan money at interest for a short period of thirty, sixty, or ninety days, taking the note of the business man to whom the money is loaned. In most cases, however, unless the bank knows the business man well, a certain amount of *collateral* is demanded as an assurance that the borrower will pay the loan when it becomes due. The amount of collateral deposited with the bank is usually 10% to 25% in excess of the amount loaned, and it may take the form of stocks or bonds; mortgages on real estate; liens on stock, fixtures, or personal property; or warehouse receipts. When the amount borrowed is paid, the collateral is returned; if it is not paid within a reasonable time, the collateral is sold, and the amount loaned, with interest to date, is taken from the proceeds.

There are, of course, other functions of banks of deposit practised quite generally by all banks, and these will be explained later. The functions just described, however, distinguish banks of deposit in a general way from the other two classes.

Savings Banks

A savings bank accepts from its depositors small amounts of money which are not subject to withdrawal by check, but on which it pays a low rate of interest. As a general rule, an account may be opened with one dollar; and when the initial deposit is made, the depositor is furnished with a pass book, similar to the bank book, in which further deposits, interest credits, and withdrawals are recorded. Interest is compounded every four or six months, and money must, as a general rule, remain on deposit until an interest payment date before the depositor receives any interest on it. The usual rate of interest is three per cent, although four is often paid. Frequently, before banks allow deposits to be withdrawn, they demand a certain number of days' notice, usually thirty. It is well to investigate the conditions under which the depositor places his money in the safe-keeping of the bank, because the withdrawal requirements are often stringent. Because of the stability of this class of deposit, banks are always anxious to increase their savings accounts, as a large proportion of the funds may be used for loans.

A form of the savings bank established in the United States in 1911 is the postal savings bank, in which the post-office is made the depository for savings. The post-office in the town deposits its funds in the local national or state bank, which, as security for safe-keeping, must deposit with the Treasurer of the United States bonds at least equal in value to the amount of savings deposited in the bank. Postal savings banks are practically absolutely safe, because, if the bank which takes care of the funds should fail, the bonds may be sold, so that the savers will receive their money. From deposits made in the postal savings bank, the return to the depositor is only two per cent, whereas the return from deposits made in the bank's own savings department is three, three and a half, and sometimes four per cent.

Trust Companies

The Richards' Baby Stocking Fund

A miner named Richards was killed in an accident in an Alaska mine. Among his possessions were found a number of letters and a baby stocking containing a little gold dust. The letters told that Richards had a little six-year-old daughter, who was now left destitute. The rough miners made up a fund of $2,500 in gold dust, depositing it with the United States Commissioner of the Territory of Alaska, to be held by him until the proper disposition of it could be made. A committee was appointed, who agreed that one hundred dollars a year for ten years should be used to give the child a common school education, and then five hundred dollars each year to give her a college education. A legal guardian was appointed, and the Kansas City Trust Company asked to act as co-guardian to invest the money and make the required remittances. The funds were first deposited by the commissioner in a bank in Portland, which sent them to the Kansas City Trust Company. Correspondence was of course carried on at the same time, the Kansas City Trust Company agreeing to accept the trust without remuneration. They have invested the money in five per cent bonds, thus increasing the fund yearly.

This is called a *trust* because the money is entrusted for safe-keeping and investment to the bank, which is called the *trustee.* A bank may also become the trustee for property left at the death of a person, both when there is a will and when there is none. When there is no will and the bank takes charge of the affairs of the deceased, the bank is called the *administrator;* when there is a will, the *executor.* Another important function of the trust company is acting as *receiver* for a company which has failed; that is, adjusting the company's affairs in the way fairest both to the stockholders and to the company's creditors. The trust company often acts, also, as *agent* for its clients' property, performing the same duties as a real estate agent.

Form of Remittance

Banks as a class are distinguished one from the other according as they specialize in one or more of the functions described above. However, there are certain services that all banks perform and certain facilities that they all offer in connection with the payment of money from one person to another. These concern the forms of remittance.

If you have studied business arithmetic or bookkeeping, you very likely know the definite forms that are used. At all events, you know that currency should never go through the mails. The following is a brief review of the more important forms that may be used. Study the illustrations carefully, noticing particularly the similarity of form in all. Uniformity in such matters is desirable because it saves time as well as misunderstandings. The forms we shall consider are:

1. The check
a. Personal
b. Certified

2. The money order

a. Express

b. Postal

3. The bank draft

4. The time draft

5. The sight draft

Check.—A check is a written order on a bank, signed by a depositor, directing the bank to pay a certain person a certain sum of money. When the bank pays the order, it deducts the amount from the depositor's account. The one who signs the check is called the *drawer* or maker; the person to whom or to whose order a check is made payable is called the *payee;* the bank on which a check is drawn is called the *drawee.*

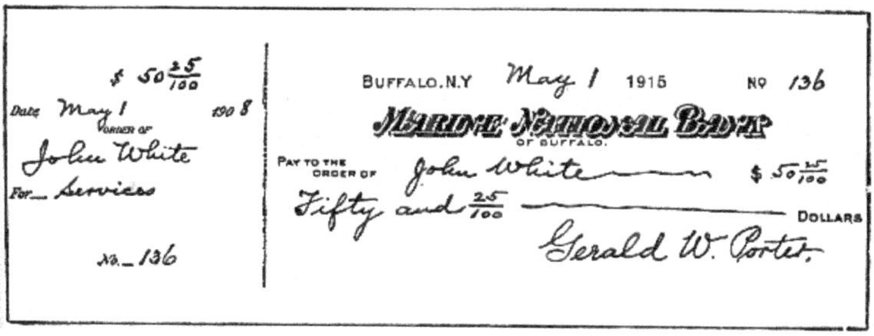

CHECK AND STUB

Of course, before you could write a check for one hundred dollars, you must have deposited at least one hundred dollars in the bank on which the check is drawn. The bank supplies you with a check book, consisting of blank checks, each attached to a stub. When you write a check, you put the same information on the stub to be kept for reference. Then you tear off the check through the perforated line, using it to pay for whatever you may have purchased.

Certified Check.—Suppose, however, that you are writing this check to pay a debt to a stranger who lives in another city. He may hesitate to accept it as money. That he may have no cause to doubt your ability to pay the check, you take it to your bank to have the cashier investigate your account. If he finds that you have sufficient funds, he writes or stamps *Accepted* or *Certified* on the check and signs his name. At the same time the amount of the check is deducted from your account. Such a check is accepted without question when the holder is properly identified.

Endorsement.—If A gives you his check for twenty-five dollars, you could not receive the money until you had endorsed the check; that is, put your name on the back, which is, in effect, giving a receipt for the money. You may do this in various ways. You may endorse:

1. In blank; that is, merely write your name across the back.

2. In full, by saying, "Pay to the order of ——" and signing your name.

3. By restricting the payment to a particular person; as, "Pay to ——" This check cannot now be cashed by anyone except the one named in the endorsement.

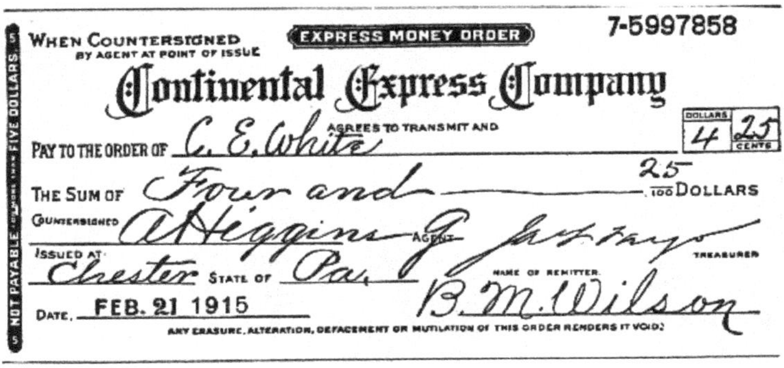

WHEN COUNTERSIGNED BY AGENT AT POINT OF ISSUE
EXPRESS MONEY ORDER
7-5997858
Continental Express Company
AGREES TO TRANSMIT AND
PAY TO THE ORDER OF C. E. White
DOLLARS 4 25 CENTS
THE SUM OF Four and 25/100 DOLLARS
COUNTERSIGNED A Higgins AGENT
TREASURER
ISSUED AT Chester STATE OF Pa.
NAME OF REMITTER B. M. Wilson
DATE FEB. 21 1915
ANY ERASURE, ALTERATION, DEFACEMENT OR MUTILATION OF THIS ORDER RENDERS IT VOID
NOT PAYABLE ... FIVE DOLLARS

EXPRESS MONEY ORDER

Express Money Order.—An express money order is much like a check, except that it is drawn on an express company instead of on a bank and reads, for example: Continental Express Company agrees to transmit and pay to the order of —— (the one to whom you are sending the money) —— (the amount). The order is signed by the treasurer of the company and countersigned by the agent who sells it. You can buy such an order at any express office. It may be endorsed like a check.

[Name of office issuing the order] NO.
DATE
THE POSTMASTER AT [Name of office on which order is drawn]
WILL PAY THE SUM OF DOLLARS | CTS.
DOLLARS CENTS
words for dollars figures for cents
TO THE ORDER OF [Name of person to whom order is payable]
[Signature of] POSTMASTER
NAME OF REMITTER

POSTAL MONEY ORDER

Postal Money Order.—The other form of money order, the postal, is an agreement signed by the postmaster of one city that the postmaster of another city will pay the amount of money named in the order to the person named in the order.

Bank Draft.—A bank draft is very much like a check, except that instead of two individuals dealing with each other two banks conduct the transaction, their places of business being in different cities or villages. A bank draft is sometimes called a bank check, because in the case of both a draft and a check one party draws upon another with whom the first has funds deposited. As a general rule, banks and business houses require that remittances be sent to them by drafts drawn on New York or Chicago banks, as there is a charge called *exchange* made in the collection of checks drawn on local banks.

In the draft that follows, the State Bank of Utah, of which Henry T. McEwan is Assistant Cashier, makes out the draft. The bank which is ordered to pay the money is the National Park Bank of New York. The money is to be paid to Henry L. Fowler. The State Bank of Utah is called the drawer; the National Park Bank of New York, on whom the draft is drawn, is the drawee; Henry L. Fowler is the payee.

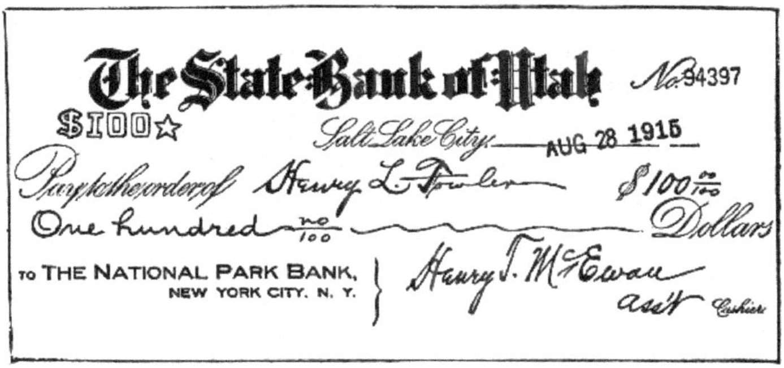

The State Bank of Utah No. 94397

$100☆ Salt Lake City AUG 28 1915

Pay to the order of Henry L. Fowler $100 no/100

One hundred no/100 Dollars

to THE NATIONAL PARK BANK,
NEW YORK CITY, N. Y.

Henry T. McEwan
Ass't Cashier

BANK DRAFT

ENDORSEMENT

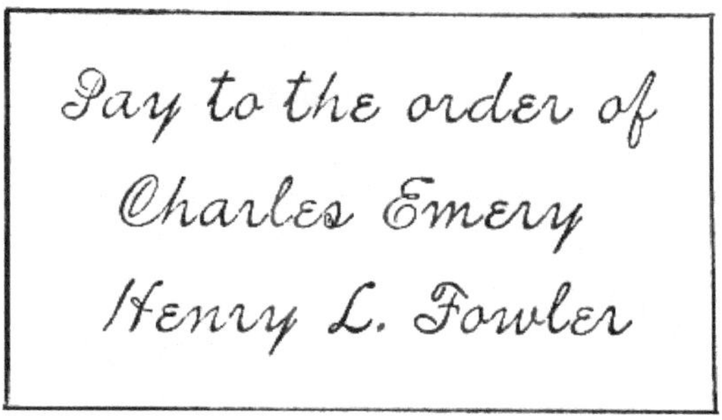

Pay to the order of
Charles Emery
Henry L. Fowler

The payment indicated above was probably made without actually sending the money from Salt Lake City to New York. It was done in this way:

Henry L. Fowler of Salt Lake City owes one hundred dollars to a man living in an Eastern city, let us say Charles Emery of Rochester, N. Y. Mr. Fowler goes to the State Bank of Utah in Salt Lake City and "buys a draft on New York," made payable to himself. The bank makes out the above, charging Mr. Fowler one hundred dollars plus a fraction of one per cent for its trouble. Mr. Fowler endorses it in full to Mr. Emery of Rochester and sends the draft to the latter. He has the draft made payable to himself so that the endorsement will constitute a full record of the transaction. Mr. Emery takes the draft to his own bank in Rochester, endorses it in blank, and receives the one hundred dollars. Thus Mr. Fowler has paid out the money and Mr. Emery has received it.

The way the banks conduct the transaction is as follows: There are certain big money centers in the country; e.g., New York, Chicago, St. Louis, San Francisco. Important banks in other places have money on deposit in at least one bank in each of these centers. The banks which thus deal with one another are called *correspondents.* The National Park Bank is the correspondent of the State Bank of Utah. When Mr. Emery cashes the draft at his Rochester bank, the latter sends it to its New York correspondent, and at the same time charges the correspondent one hundred dollars. The correspondent presents the draft to the National Park Bank, which pays the money and charges the same amount to the State Bank of Utah. Explain how this settles the transaction.

Time Draft.—A time draft is much like a bank draft, in that two banks conduct the principal part of the transaction for two individuals, but no money is actually paid at the time the draft is drawn. The details of a transaction of this kind are explained on the following page.

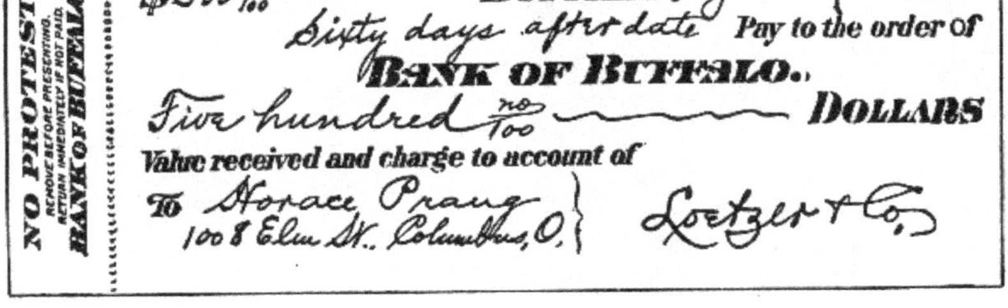
NO PROTEST.
REMOVE BEFORE PRESENTING.
RETURN IMMEDIATELY IF NOT PAID.
BANK OF BUFFALO.

$500 00/100 BUFFALO, June 27 1915

Sixty days after date Pay to the order of

BANK OF BUFFALO.

Five hundred no/100 DOLLARS

Value received and charge to account of

To Horace Prang
1008 Elm St., Columbus, O. Loetzer & Co.

TIME DRAFT

Horace Prang of 1008 Elm Street, Columbus, Ohio, owes Loetzer & Co. five hundred dollars, due August 27, 1915. Loetzer & Co. make out the draft above and deposit it in the Bank of Buffalo. The latter sends the draft to its correspondent in Columbus, which presents the draft to Horace Prang. If he is willing to pay the note when it falls due, he writes across the face of it, "*Accepted*" adds the date, and signs his name. It is now returned to the Bank of Buffalo. The Bank of Buffalo will then discount the draft for Loetzer & Co.

Sight Draft.—A sight draft is much like a time draft, except that the amount is paid by the person on whom it is drawn as soon as it is presented, instead of after a stipulated length of time.

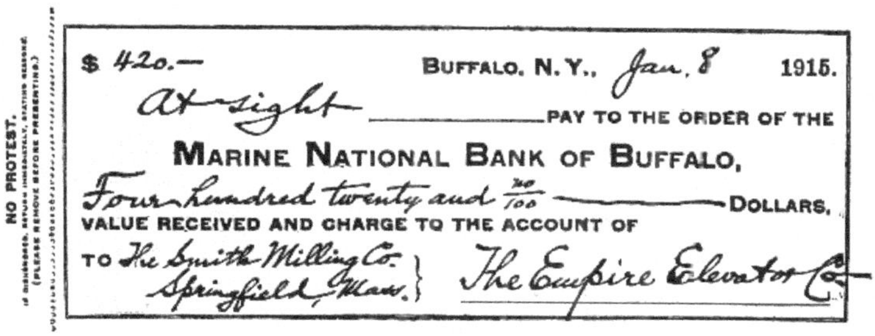

NO PROTEST.

$ 420.— BUFFALO, N.Y., Jan. 8 1915.

At sight ______ PAY TO THE ORDER OF THE

MARINE NATIONAL BANK OF BUFFALO,

Four hundred twenty and 00/100 ——— DOLLARS.

VALUE RECEIVED AND CHARGE TO THE ACCOUNT OF

TO The Smith Milling Co.
Springfield, Mass. } The Empire Elevator Co.

SIGHT DRAFT

Suppose the Empire Elevator Co. of Buffalo has sold $420 worth of grain to the Smith Milling Co. of Springfield, Mass. When the grain is loaded on the cars, the railroad company gives the Empire Elevator Co. a bill of lading. Now, the Smith Milling Co. must possess this bill of lading before it can take the grain from the cars at Springfield. The Empire Elevator Co. deposits the bill of lading with the above draft in the Marine National Bank of Buffalo. This bank sends both to its correspondent in Springfield. The Springfield bank presents the draft to the Smith Milling Co., who may take the grain from the cars on payment of the draft. In case of non-payment, both draft and bill of lading are returned to the Marine National Bank of Buffalo, and the Empire Elevator Co. must make arrangements for the return or the disposal of the grain.

Exercise 301

1. F. R. Thompson, sales manager of the New York Trust and Savings Bank, sends a circular letter to a number of banks, saying that he is enclosing a booklet that describes a number of bonds suitable for the security of postal savings deposits, the legality of which has been carefully investigated. In his letter he mentions especially Omaha, Nebraska, School $4\frac{1}{2}$% bonds, price to net 4.40%; Seattle, Washington, Harbor 5% bonds, price to net $4\frac{1}{2}$%; and

Hoquiam, Washington, Bridge 5½% bonds, price to net 5%. Reproduce the letter, addressing it to W. W. Fallows, Cashier of the Mercantile National Bank of Pueblo, Colorado.

2. Mr. Fallows answers, saying that his knowledge of the postal savings law is vague and that he would be glad if Mr. Thompson would give him definite information on the subject.

3. Mr. Thompson replies that he is enclosing a copy of the postal savings law. He assures Mr. Fallows that he can serve the latter both in buying the proper securities and in depositing them with the Treasurer of the United States. Application for such deposits must be made by the bank itself. Mr. Thompson will gladly inform him if Mr. Fallows does not know the steps to be taken or the report to be submitted.

4. Punctuate, using a letterhead:

Mercantile Trust Company New York City Dec 2 19— manager the bank of Scotland 3c bishop E C London England dear sir we are sending you herewith advice of the issuance of our circular letter of credit No. 262 in favor of Miss Helen Jackson for 300 pounds sterling Miss Jackson is at present in Paris France and the letter of credit has been forwarded to Messrs Thomas Cooke and Son 1 Place de l'Opera Paris we have requested Messrs Thomas Cooke and Son to forward to you two specimens of Miss Jacksons signature which we have signed and forwarded to Messrs Thomas Cooke and Son for that purpose so that you may have these signatures before any drafts against the letter of credit are presented to you yours very truly James R Hudson treasurer.

What is a letter of credit? How did Miss Jackson get it?

The Bank of Scotland is the correspondent of the Mercantile Trust Company. Explain.

Why should the New York bank forward Miss Jackson's signature?

5. Write the letter that the Mercantile Trust Company sends to Messrs. Thomas Cooke and Son.

6. Write the letter that Messrs. Thomas Cooke and Son send to the Bank of Scotland.

7. W. T. Randall, cashier of the Milwaukee Trust and Savings Bank, Milwaukee, Wis., writes a letter, the purpose of which is to secure savings accounts. A club of 500 members is to be formed. Each member is to buy a share by paying one dollar and to pay one dollar per week per share, the amount to draw interest at 3%. After forty-eight weeks he gets credit for fifty

dollars per share, thus securing over 5% interest on his money. Make the offer attractive.

8. Some time ago a bank in your city discounted a note held by George Carpenter, signed by Martin Kugerman. The note falls due in ten days. As cashier write to Mr. Kugerman, telling him that you hold the note and that you hope he will be able to remit on the day of maturity.

9. Your bank loaned Clarence Wentworth $500 for ninety days, taking as security $700 worth of collateral. The note falls due in a week. Write to Mr. Wentworth, reminding him that the note falls due and asking him whether he wishes to pay it off or whether he wishes it extended.

10. John Elsworth, who has an account with you, writes, saying that by registered mail he is sending you certificates of 20 shares Union Pacific common stock, 50 shares National Biscuit Co. preferred stock, 5 (bonds) American Telephone and Telegraph convertible 4½'s, 3 (bonds) New York and East River Gas Co. first mortgage 5's. He asks you to take care of them and collect dividends and interest when they are due, crediting them to his account.

11. Your correspondent, the First National Bank of Janesville, Wis., writes, asking you to forward by registered mail $5,000 in currency.

Exercise 302

1. Mr. Henry Carroll of Wausau, Wis., writes to Mr. Randall (Exercise 301, 7), asking him to buy 10 shares of C. & N. W. R. R. preferred stock at 134 or better. When they are bought, he adds, they can be sent through any bank in Wausau.

2. Mr. Randall replies by sending the 10 shares of stock to the bank's correspondent in Wausau, the First National Bank, telling the latter to deliver them to Mr. Henry Carroll on payment of the enclosed draft for $1340 with exchange. Write the letter.

3. A dressmaker in South Bend, Ind., has applied to Marshall Field & Co., Retail, State and Washington Streets, Chicago, for a charge account. The department store makes inquiries concerning her at her bank, the Commercial and Savings Bank of South Bend. Write the letter.

4. The bank replies that she has maintained a small but steady balance, that she has never overdrawn her account, and that in their opinion her credit would be good up to $100 monthly. Write the letter.

5. Theodore Buchanan of St. Louis sends Philip Newborg of your city a check for $100 with which he pays a debt to Charles Springer of Minneapolis.

Springer endorses it and deposits it in the Security National Bank. The check is returned marked N.S.F., and the Security National Bank notifies Springer of the situation and of the fact that his account has been charged with $104, the amount of the draft plus expenses.

6. One of the depositors of the Milwaukee Trust and Savings Bank brings to the Cashier a note which is about due, and asks the bank to collect it. The maker of the note is William T. Adams of Seattle. The Cashier writes to the bank's correspondent in Seattle, the Scandinavian American Bank, asking the latter to collect. Write the letter. (See Exercise 301, 7.)

7. The Scandinavian American bank writes to William T. Adams, telling him that it holds a note signed by him, due ——, and asking him to make prompt payment. Write the letter.

8. Mr. Adams pays the note. The Seattle Bank notifies the Milwaukee Bank, enclosing a draft for the amount. Write the letter.

9. See Exercise 301, 10. As John Elsworth's banker send the coupons for the American Telephone and Telegraph bonds to your correspondent in New York, the National City Bank, because the interest is payable in New York. Ask the bank to make the collection. Write the letter.

10. The National City Bank makes the collection and informs you by means of a printed form that it has credited you with the amount, $112.50. The form is just like a letter except that it is already printed with blanks left for the name and the address and for itemizing the coupons collected. Write such a form.

11. One of your depositors has overdrawn his account. Notify him of the fact. Do this courteously so that the depositor may have no reason to withdraw his account.

12. In your city there is a real estate dealer who often has large sums of money idle for a short time because, when he sells one piece of property, he does not always have another immediately in view. He is not a depositor in your bank. Write to him, inducing him to take out a Certificate of Deposit at such times and telling him that the advantages of such a certificate are that he will get 3% interest on the money deposited and that he may draw out the money at any time.

13. One of your depositors has written to you, asking for a loan of $5,000 for nine months. Write to him, saying that it is not your practice to make time loans for definite periods longer than six months, as it is not a good plan thus to tie up your deposits. Explain that as most of a bank's deposits are payable on demand, you would suggest his taking out a demand loan for

$5,000, payable on the demand of the bank. Under ordinary business conditions such a loan might easily run for nine months.

14. R. F. Marsden, President of the Truesdale Cotton Mill, Birmingham, Ala., has written to you, asking whether he can secure a loan next fall on the cotton in the mill as collateral. Reply that you feel certain that satisfactory arrangements could be made if the cotton were stored in an accredited warehouse, so that you could accept the warehouse receipt as collateral.

Exercise 303

Punctuate and paragraph the following letter, which explains one function of a trust company:

Dear sir as you are one of our clients you are familiar with the reputation of this bank for sound banking and conservative investments you may not however be aware that we have a fully equipped trust department prepared to act in any of the numerous capacities in which the services of trust companies have proved of special value at this time we wish to call your particular attention to the service which this department is prepared to render as trustee under agreement it is natural that one who has accumulated property should desire to superintend or direct its disposition formerly this was done by will now however as the complex laws of the various states frequently necessitate the payment of double or triple inheritance taxes it is becoming a more and more common practice for a man during his lifetime to administer his own estate so to speak this may be accomplished through the establishment of a trust with respect to either a part or all of one's property it can be accomplished not only with absolute safety to the donor but with entire secrecy as well the terms of the trust being regarded as absolutely confidential furthermore the donor has the satisfaction of disposing of his property during his lifetime in accordance with his desires the life of a trust company unlike that of any individual is of perpetual duration death does not interfere with its management of the trust estate its financial responsibility and the safeguards thrown around trust estates by the state laws insure the safety of a trust fund if you are interested in this subject let us discuss it with you either in person or by correspondence when this bank is named in a trust capacity no charge is made for service or advice in connection with the drafting of the trust instruments yours truly

Before writing the following, re-read The Richards' Baby Stocking Fund, page 337.

1. Suppose that you were a newspaper correspondent in Alaska at the time Richards was killed. For your home paper write an account of the

finding of the baby stocking. In what ways would this account differ from a magazine article on the same subject?

2. As if you were the United States Commissioner of the Territory of Alaska, write to a Portland bank saying that you are sending the $2,500 to them, and asking them to put the funds in the care of a reliable trust company.

3. The Portland bank writes to the Kansas City Trust Company, asking if the latter will accept the trust. Write the letter.

4. The Kansas City Trust Company replies that it will accept the trust without remuneration. Write the letter.

5. The Portland bank informs the United States Commissioner of the Territory of Alaska of the disposition of the funds. Write the letter.

Exercise 304

Topics for Investigation and Discussion

1. The panic of 1907 and some of its lessons.
2. Future banking reform.
3. Government supervision of banks.
4. Unscrupulous banking companies.
5. Clearing house certificates.
6. Postal savings banks.
7. The work of the clearing house.
8. The need of banks in a community.
9. The development of real estate firms into banks.
10. The Owen Glass Currency Bill.

Exercise 305

Books that will Suggest Topics for Talks

CROCKER, U. H., The Cause of Hard Times.
FONDA, ARTHUR J., Honest Money.
GIBBS, H. C., A Bimetallic Primer.
MCADAMS, GRAHAM, An Alphabet in Finance.
NEWCOMB, SIMON, The A B C of Finance.
NORTON, S. F., Ten Men of Money Island, or The Primer of Finance.

REEVES, JOHN, The Rothschilds: The Financial Rulers of Nations.
WHITE, HORACE, Money and Banking.

Exercise 306

Write the following from dictation:

1

THE DAILY ROUTINE OF THE CLEARING HOUSE

Each bank sends two clerks to the Clearing House: a delivering clerk and a settling clerk. There are three rows of seats running through the clearing room lengthwise, one in the center and one on each side parallel with it. The settling clerks occupy these seats and each one has a sufficient amount of desk room in front of him to do his work on, his space being separated from his neighbors' by a wire screen. The delivery clerks, with their packages of checks in separate envelopes, stand in the open space in front of the settling clerks. At two minutes before 10 o'clock the manager, whose station is an elevated open space at the extreme end of the room, strikes a bell.

The movement has all the precision of a military drill. When the second bell sounds, at exactly 10 o'clock, each delivery clerk takes one step forward, hands the proper package to the settling clerk of the bank next to him, drops the accompanying ticket showing the amount into an aperture like a letter box, and places before the settling clerk his schedule, on which the latter places his initials. Thus the procession moves uninterruptedly until each delivery clerk has presented to each settling clerk the proper package and ticket. Usually this part of the operation is completed in ten minutes. Meanwhile the proof clerk, who occupies a desk near the manager, has entered the claims of each bank under the head "Bank Cr." on a broad sheet of paper.

Inasmuch as the amount of each bank's claim against the Clearing House (entered under the head "Banks Cr.") is the sum of all the tickets which its delivery clerk has pushed into the letter boxes of the other banks, it follows that all the tickets of all the banks should equal all the entries under that head. The next step in the operation is for each settling clerk to arrange the amounts of all the tickets in his letter box in a column, add it up, and send the amount to the proof clerk, who transcribes and arranges it according to the bank's number under the head "Banks Dr.," so that the debit of Bank A shall be on the same line with its credit.

Then the difference between the two will show how much the bank owes the Clearing House or how much the Clearing House owes the bank. The time occupied by the settling clerks in arranging their tickets and adding up the columns is about half an hour. As fast as these footings are completed, they are sent to the proof clerk, who puts them in the debit column opposite the credits of the banks, respectively. When all are completed, if no error has been made, the footings of the credit and debit columns must be exactly equal and the footings of the two other columns, which show the differences, must be exactly equal. Then these differences are read off slowly and in a distinct tone by the manager, so that each settling clerk can write down the sum that his bank has to pay or to receive. As time is money at the Clearing House, a fine is exacted for every error and every delay in making footings, for every disobedience of the orders of the manager, or for every instance of disorderly conduct.—Horace White: *Money and Banking.*

2

The Treasury, in connection with its money washing, has asked national banks to exercise more care in sending in money for redemption. Banks frequently put into the same bundle, good notes, bad notes, and notes of different denominations. When they are mixed in this way, it requires a good deal of work to separate the money. The Treasury thinks that the banks could do this work, so that, when the money reaches Washington, it could easily be separated by packages instead of each package having to be separated first. The Assistant Secretary says he believes that, when he gets the subject worked out in detail, new washed money will be returned to the bank in any denomination desired on the same day that it is received; that money unfit for laundering will be destroyed and new money issued. This expeditious handling of money sent in for redemption cannot, however, be attained, he admits, without the co-operation of the banks. In a short time, he believes, all banks will see that it is to their benefit to do this.

CHAPTER XXI

THE CORPORATION

THE study that we have thus far made of the various kinds of businesses would be incomplete did we not briefly outline the different types of organization by which modern business is conducted. This will naturally lead us to a discussion of stocks and bonds, which are of great importance in every big business and of interest to individuals as means of investment. However, as the subjects are probably outside the experience of most students, we shall treat them as simply as possible, letting the chapter stand rather for the information it contains than for its application to the study of English expression.

Business to-day is carried on in three different ways; viz., by individuals, by partnerships, and by corporations. The grocer, the butcher, the baker, or any one man who carries on a business is an example of the first. If, however, the grocer and the butcher, or the grocer and the baker, combine their businesses for the good of both, they form a partnership. When the amount of capital necessary for carrying on the business becomes so large that the money of many people is needed, a *corporation* is formed. The amount of money which any one individual invests in the company is represented by a certain number of shares of the *capital stock* of the company, entitling him to his portion of the dividends, or interest on the money he has invested. These shares of the capital stock are transferable and can be bought and sold like an automobile or a house. Since there is no time limit as to how long a corporation may do business, a change in the ownership of part of the stock, or the death of a stockholder, is not accompanied by the same result as in a partnership, where the death of one of the partners sometimes breaks up the business. Furthermore, in a partnership each one of the partners is personally liable for any debts made by any of the partners in behalf of the business, whereas the personal possessions of a stockholder in a corporation cannot be held as security for any debts incurred by the corporation. These are two of the more important advantages of corporate organization over partnership.

The Finances of a Corporation

It has been estimated that if one were to count money, dollar by dollar, one dollar every second for eight hours six days a week, it would take him six weeks to count one million dollars, and over one hundred years to count a billion dollars. This may help us to appreciate the sums of money spoken of in the following: In 1914 the market value of the Commonwealth Edison Company of Chicago was over $83,000,000. The valuation placed on the properties of the Chicago Railways Company in 1914 exceeded $79,000,000. The Union Pacific Railroad Company had invested in its properties in 1914 approximately $500,000,000. The capital obligations of the United States Steel Corporation in 1914 were over $1,500,000,000. There are hundreds of such organizations in our country, the investments in which run to and beyond $50,000,000 each. It must be plain that, except in a very few cases, these vast amounts of money do not represent the investment of one, or of a few, but of many persons. In uniting their capital, these persons decrease the cost of making or distributing the product and so increase their profits.

Stocks

When a large company of this kind is organized, a certain amount of money is agreed upon to be the capital of the company, and it is divided into small portions, ordinarily $100 each, called *shares*. The total of the shares is called the *authorized capital stock*. These shares are sold, the purchasers of the shares being called *shareholders*, or *stockholders*, of the company. The number of shares a person holds determines what part of the profits he is entitled to. For example, if a company is organized for 1000 shares of $100 each, or a capital stock of $100,000, and you owned 100 shares, you would be entitled to one-tenth of the divided profits of the company. Such profits of the company, divided proportionately among the stockholders, constitute the *dividends*.

Often the capital stock is of two kinds, *preferred* and *common*, as in the case of the Union Pacific R. R., which has $200,000,000 of authorized preferred stock and $296,178,700 of authorized common stock. As the names signify, preferred stock is ordinarily better than common stock, the dividends on preferred stock being paid before any dividends are paid on common stock and usually at a stated rate of interest; as, 4, 5, or 6 per cent. In the case of the Union Pacific, this rate is 4 per cent. If the company earns only enough profits to pay the dividends on the preferred stock, the common gets no dividends. On the other hand, if the profits are enormous, the common occasionally gets more than the preferred.

Par and Market Value

The *par value* of a stock is the face value of one share of stock, indicated on the face of the certificate. This may be $10 or $50 or $100, whatever the amount agreed upon for one share when the company is organized. The amount most commonly used as par is $100. The *market value* of the stock, however, need not be this amount, but may be greater or less, dependent on how successful the company is and what rate of dividends it pays. If a company's standing is very good and the dividends are high (over 6 per cent), the stock will probably sell on the market above par. If the company's finances are in a doubtful condition and there are evidences that the company will pay small dividends, if any at all, the market price of the stock will fall below par. For example, in January, 1914, Union Pacific R. R. common stock sold for about $158 per share, because the finances of the company were in good condition and the company had paid 10 per cent dividends steadily each year since July 1, 1907. If, however, any occasion should arise to make the public doubt the payment of future dividends at the same rate, the stock would probably decline. To go to the other extreme, in the same month Wabash R. R. common stock sold as low as $8½ per share, although the par is $100. This was because for some years the company had paid no dividends and was then in the hands of receivers. To take a middle case in the same month and year, Erie R. R. first preferred stock sold at about $45 per share, notwithstanding the fact that since 1907 no dividends had been paid. The reason for this seemingly high price was that the company had for some time been reconstructing its property, had gradually increased its business, had earned a $9,000,000 surplus in 1913, and had a good outlook to a dividend in the near future.

These are not the only influences that affect the price of stocks. The old factor of supply and demand has a great influence on price. If, for example, a financier decides to buy a large "block" of some stock, the market will almost immediately be affected, and that stock will go up. One example will suffice. In 1901 E. H. Harriman set out to buy $155,000,000 worth of Northern Pacific stock in the open market to gain control of the Northern Pacific railroad. Of course, the market felt the demand, and the price of the stock rose from a little above par until it touched $1,000 a share before it started back to normal. When Mr. Harriman unloaded that same stock in 1906, because he failed to gain control, the market went down so considerably that he lost $10,000,000 and almost caused a panic.

Often the stocks of a company sell below par because the stock is watered; that is, the company has issued more stock than there is value invested in the property. Many of our railroads, for example, were built on borrowed money—that is, from the proceeds of the sale of bonds—and, to make the bonds sell more readily, stocks were given away with them. This, of course, increased the capitalization greatly without increasing the value. The temptation in forming new companies, especially in mining schemes and wildcat ventures, is to water the stock heavily by voting a large block of stock gratis to the organizers. Before one invests in any of these companies, he should thoroughly investigate them. Sometimes companies water their stocks when their dividends have become very large and they wish to bring the rate down to that commonly paid. The Wells Fargo Express Company did this in 1910, presenting their stockholders with $16,000,000 worth of new stock without any new investment in the property.

Bonds

Suppose that A owns a house with a store in it, and in the store he carries on a grocery business. Suppose that by enlarging his store and putting in a bigger stock of goods he can make more money. The improvements will cost $1,000, but he hasn't the money. He goes to B to ask B to lend him $1,000 for five years, offering B the house as security. B gives A the $1,000 and in return gets a certain amount of interest each year and A's mortgage note against the property. This means that, if at the end of five years A cannot pay the $1,000, B has the right to sell A's house and collect the money due him.

When a corporation borrows money to extend its properties, plants, or rights, the transaction is really the same, although the form is somewhat different. Just as all the capital stock of a corporation is divided into shares owned by a number of people, so, when the corporation borrows money, the amount borrowed is divided into smaller parts of $500 or $1,000 each, called *bonds*, which the corporation sells through its bankers to people who have idle money to invest. Twice each year, as stated in the bond, the corporation pays interest on the borrowed money at the rate, probably, of 4, 4½, 5, or 6 per cent. After a definite number of years, as stated in the bond, the corporation is obliged to pay back the amount of money that it borrowed. This is called *redeeming* the bonds. To show that it intends to pay back the amount borrowed at the end of the time stated, or redeem the bonds when they become due, the corporation puts a mortgage on its real estate, buildings, machinery, and equipment. When the bonds become due—or *mature*, as it is called—if the corporation does not pay back the amount borrowed, the holders of the bonds may take possession of the company's real estate, buildings, machinery, and equipment on which the company has placed the mortgage and may sell them to recover the money they have loaned. Thus, while the stockholders of a corporation have no assurance that they will ever get their money back or will ever get any interest on it, the holders of carefully selected bonds are reasonably sure of getting a certain amount of interest each year and of getting their money back when the bonds mature. Shares of stock represent the investment made by the stockholders who own the company, whereas bonds represent the investment of those who loan money to the company. We can readily see, then, that the stockholders take the greater risk. For this reason it is expected that stocks should yield a higher profit than bonds, and this is usually the case.

The greater portion of the bonds that are issued by corporations run for long periods—twenty, forty, fifty, and even one hundred years. At times when money rates are high, corporations that need funds are reluctant to pay a high rate for so many years, and so they issue *short time bonds* to run from two to five years, in the hope that at the end of the time money rates will be lower and more favorable to their issuing long time bonds. Many companies, especially industrial corporations and railroads, have issued obligations to pay, *notes* running from six months to five years. They are not usually secured by a mortgage on the property but are merely the company's promise to pay, the interest and the principal taking precedence over the dividends on the preferred and the common stocks.

Corporate Organization

Before a corporation can carry on its business, it must obtain a charter from one of the states of the United States, whose laws it must obey. The laws of some states are more lenient than those of others, allowing the corporations more privileges. New Jersey is thus lenient; consequently we find many large corporations—such as the United States Steel Corporation, the American Sugar Refining Company, and others—organized under the laws of New Jersey. After the charter is granted and the stock bought by the stockholders, the latter have a meeting, at which they elect a small number of men to be *directors*, who, as the name signifies, conduct the business of the company for the stockholders. They choose a president, one or more vice-presidents, a treasurer, a secretary, and any other officers necessary to carry on the business under the control of the directors. The term of office of the directors is usually so fixed that the term of a part of them expires each year, so that each year the stockholders have an annual meeting at which they elect new directors or re-elect the old ones whose term has expired.

The Railroad

Corporations divide themselves into three large groups; viz., railroad companies, public utility corporations, and industrial corporations. Of these, the group composed of the largest and most powerful corporations is the railroad group.

Railroads have two general sources of income, the larger being the revenue received from operating trains, both freight and passenger; and the smaller being the return from investments in other companies, from real estate, and from the rental of lines, terminals, stations, and cars to other railroads. To carry on the second or smaller part of its business, the company needs an organization much like any other business, but to conduct the first part it requires a special organization. This divides itself into four departments, usually with a vice-president at the head of each: (1) the traffic department, (2) the operating department, (3) the finance and accounting department, and (4) the legal department.

It is the duty of the traffic department to get the business for the company and adjust all traffic claims. In short, it does everything to increase the business and the earnings. This department naturally divides into the freight traffic and passenger traffic departments, with a superintendent or manager at the head of each.

After the traffic department has solicited the business for the company, it is the duty of the operating department to render the services required by the traffic department. The work is done by four large divisions: (1) the engineering or construction department, whose duty it is to build the roads over which the company may operate; (2) the maintenance-of-way department, whose duty it is to see that the roadbed and rails are kept in good order and repair; (3) the equipment department, whose duty it is to see that the company is supplied with proper locomotives and cars and to see that such equipment is kept in repair; and (4) the transportation department, which has to do with the operating of the trains.

The financial policy of a railroad is usually in charge of one of the vice-presidents, who must be a man of experience in financial matters and who acts with the approval of the directors. The accounting department is more important than may appear at first sight. Railroads are now under the supervision and regulation of the government, and one of the rights that the government has is to examine the books of the company at any time and to require all companies to submit a monthly report to the government.

The legal department of a railroad is especially important for two reasons: (1) In performing its services, the company has business dealings with a large number of persons, and in the adjustment of claims against the railroad, expert legal advice is constantly necessary. (2) The railroad, as stated above, is under the regulation and control of the state and the national governments, and the enforcement of this regulation makes the railroad a party to numerous proceedings in the courts and before the Interstate Commerce Commission. The large railroads operate in from ten to twenty states. It can thus easily be seen that the legal department has a great deal more to do than if the railroad operated under but one political power.

Public Utility Corporations

Public utility corporations supply services without which the people of to-day could not very well live. They are those supplying water, light, heat, power, telephones, local transportation, gas, etc. They may properly be called public necessity corporations. The nature of these businesses practically gives them a monopoly in their locality; this is the reason that they have grown so enormously during the last thirty years. The Commonwealth Edison Company, which supplies a large part of Chicago with light and power, began in 1887 with a capital of $500,000 and in 1914 its capital obligations had a market value of over $83,000,000. The American Telephone and Telegraph Company began in 1885 with $12,000,000 of capital stock and in 1914 had practically $340,000,000. The other public service corporations have kept pace, according to the growth of the locality they serve. In the depression of 1907 this class of corporation kept steadily increasing the volume of its business when all others went back a step. Since these corporations are dependent on the local community for their business, if the community grows the company must grow, and usually faster than the community. For this reason the stocks and bonds of these companies are usually a good investment.

It is a common practice for municipalities to demand a share of the profits of the company, by way of a fixed sum, a certain percentage of the gross profits, or a share of the net profits. For example the city of Chicago receives, from the Commonwealth Edison Company each year 3 per cent of its gross receipts from the sale of current and 10 per cent of its gross receipts from the rental of conduit space, amounting in 1913 to more than $300,000, quite a considerable sum. The Chicago Railways Company and the Chicago City Railway Company, the two large street car companies of Chicago, after deductions for expenses and charges and 5 per cent on the amount invested are made from the gross income, pay to the city 55 per cent of the surplus earnings, keeping for themselves 45 per cent. Whenever these companies pay part of their earnings to the municipality, they are really under municipal supervision, and their books and accounts are open to examination by the city at any time. These companies are called quasi-municipal corporations.

Industrial Corporations

As the name indicates, industrial corporations are those that carry on our industries. They are by far the largest class of corporations and have among their number some very powerful companies, whose assets run up toward the billions. This class of corporations has not had the gradual, steady growth of the public utility corporations, but in the case of the most successful, the growth has been amazing. The Standard Oil Company for many years prior to its dissolution had paid dividends on its capital stock of about $100,000,000 at the rate of 40 per cent a year. The Steel Corporation is said to have produced a thousand millionaires and is still producing them. This class of corporations has not been so closely under the supervision of the federal and municipal authorities as the railroads and public utility corporations, and their financing has been carried on in a looser fashion than that of the other two classes. For this reason the securities of these corporations are not generally regarded as highly as those of the other two. However, the federal government has taken and is taking steps to regulate these corporations, and this will tend to bring them eventually to the standards of the railroad and public utility corporations.

Exercise 307

Oral

Explain carefully:

1. What is a corporation?

2. What is a share of stock?

3. What is a bond? a security?

4. Explain the difference between par and market values.

5. Why do stocks and bonds vary in value?

6. What is the difference between preferred and common stock?

7. What are dividends?

8. What is meant by watered stock?

9. What are the advantages of a corporation over a partnership?

10. The following was copied from a morning paper. Explain it.

"The Canadian Westinghouse Company, Ltd., declared its regular quarterly dividend of 1½% and an extra dividend of 1% on its stock, both payable Jan. 10."

11. Explain the following bond quotations:

MUNICIPAL BONDS

Security	*Maturity*	*Yield per cent about*
Albany, Ga., 5's	Nov. 1, 1941	4.75
King Co., Wash., 4½'s	Nov. 1, 1931	4.50

RAILROAD BONDS

Atchison, Topeka, & Santa Fé, general mortgage, 4's	Oct. 1, 1995	4.20
Louisville and Nashville, unified mortgage, 4's	Feb. 1, 1946	4.35

PUBLIC SERVICE CORPORATION BONDS

New York Telephone Co., 4's	Nov. 1, 1939	4.75
Chicago Railways, first mortgage, 5's	Feb. 1, 1927	4.99

12. Why are the bonds of successful public utility corporations a good investment?

13. Which company do you think would grow faster, a light and power company or a gas company? What effect would the growth or the failure to grow have on the price of the stocks of each?

14. Should a street car company pay part of its earnings to the city?

15. If the population of a city doubled, what effect would there be on the price of public utility stocks?

Exercise 308
Topics for Investigation and Discussion

1. Harnessing our streams to secure electric power.

2. The growth of the Interurban.

3. In your own town:

a. Have gas rates increased or decreased? Can you explain the change?

b. Have electric light rates increased or decreased? Can you explain the change?

4. Street railway, electric light, and gas company franchises.

5. The earnings of the street car company in your city.

6. Municipal ownership of public utility corporations.

7. The effect of mergers and consolidations of big corporations.

8. The effect of a trust on competition.

9. Trusts and prices.

10. Government suits against trusts.

11. The tariff and the steel industry, the wool industry, and the sugar industry.

12. Railroad rate increases.

Exercise 309

Write the following from dictation:

1

In New London, Connecticut, stands the oldest grist mill in the country. It is a picturesque building, having a water wheel like the one that it originally used when New London was first settled. The town was in the center of an agricultural community, and a mill to grind corn was a need that soon manifested itself to the settlers. Accordingly, in 1650 at a town meeting, six men were chosen to build a mill. John Winthrop and his heirs were granted the right to carry on the grist mill as long as they maintained the building placed in their charge. This is one of the first monopolies recorded in New England history.

2

The same standards by which a farming or a manufacturing investment may be judged are not applicable to a mining investment. A farmer may earn eight per cent on his capital, and with care his investment may increase in value. A manufacturer may earn eight per cent on his investment, and, if he keeps up his machinery, his business may be as valuable ten years, or even twenty years, hence; but a mine, after each dividend is paid, is that much nearer its end. Now, it is well known among mining men that the average life of a gold or silver mine is under, rather than over, ten years. There are exceptions to this rule, of course, but, granting that the life of a certain gold or silver mine is to be ten years, then, in order to pay back both principal and interest, dividends of at least sixteen per cent should be distributed. Copper mining, of which the statistics have been most accurately kept in New York and Boston, offers many inducements to the investor; but too much care cannot be taken in the matter of selection, for copper stocks, in not a few instances, have been boosted out of all reason. As with gold and silver mines, so it is with copper mines. They have so much ore to begin with, and after each dividend are that much nearer to the day when they will close down. For such mines, provided they have a good lease of life, eight per cent or even ten per cent may be regarded as only moderate returns. These are merely samples of some general principles to be followed.—*Roger W. Babson.*

3

Dear Sir:

At the close of a year which has presented many perplexing problems, not only to investors and dealers in bonds, but also to borrowing municipalities and corporations, there are several factors in the situation which in our opinion offer strong encouragement to every one in any way interested in bond investments.

Of special significance is the marked change in sentiment which has recently taken place. There is every indication that this country enters the new year with an unusually substantial feeling of confidence. While a notable increase in the demand for bonds would undoubtedly bring out a large amount of new financing, on the other hand, there has been an accumulation of funds during the period of depressed markets, and it is generally understood that investment dealers are carrying comparatively small amounts of bonds.

January has an almost unbroken record of higher average bond prices than the average prices in December. It is not our intention to predict an advance this January, although there are unquestionably many reasons for anticipating at least a moderate improvement; but, viewing the question in its broader aspects, we find many convincing arguments in favor of the purchase of bonds at this time. It is recognized that the decline in prices has been due to a variety of causes, which, except in a few individual cases, are not the result of any depreciation in real values. Basic conditions are admittedly sound. We, accordingly, not only recommend the judicious purchase of bonds for the investment of surplus funds, but also suggest consideration of the advisability in some cases of converting short time securities into long time bonds.

What conditions could be more favorable from the standpoint of the purchaser of bonds than an extremely low level of prices; a wide-spread belief that fundamental conditions are sound; a general feeling of confidence that the problems which have tended to disturb business during the past year have been, or are being, solved; and a conviction that we are entering upon a period of probable ease in money rates?

Very truly yours,

FOOTNOTES:

[1] If one of the words so joined is plural, the verb should be plural.

[2] See note on page 115

[3] *Loan* for *lend*, though common in the United States, is not in approved use except sometimes in financial language.—*Webster's New International Dictionary*.

[4] Supply heading and introduction (see page 232).

CPSIA information can be obtained
at www.ICGtesting.com
Printed in the USA
LVHW042147040522
717863LV00005B/246